PENGUIN BOOKS

A FOOL AND HIS MONEY

A former editor of *The Washington Monthly* and the author of five previous books, John Rothchild now writes frequently for *Harper's*, *Rolling Stone*, *Esquire*, and other magazines. He lives in Miami Beach, Florida, with his wife and three children.

THE ODYSSEY OF AN AVERAGE INVESTOR

A Fool AND His Money

BY John Rothchild

PENGUIN BOOKS

PENGUIN BOOKS
Published by the Penguin Group
Viking Penguin Inc., 40 West 23rd Street,
New York, New York 10010, U.S.A.
Penguin Books Ltd, 27 Wrights Lane,
London W8 5TZ, England
Penguin Books Australia Ltd, Ringwood,
Victoria, Australia
Penguin Books Canada Ltd, 2801 John Street,
Markham, Ontario, Canada L3R 1B4
Penguin Books (N.Z.) Ltd, 182–190 Wairau Road,
Auckland 10, New Zealand

Penguin Books Ltd, Registered Offices:
Harmondsworth, Middlesex, England

First published in the United States of America by
Viking Penguin Inc. 1988
Published in Penguin Books 1989

1   3   5   7   9   10   8   6   4   2

LIBRARY OF CONGRESS CATALOGING IN PUBLICATION DATA
Rothchild, John.
A fool and his money.
1. Investments. I. Title.
HG4521.R777   1989   332.6   88–28919
ISBN 0 14 01.1989 2 (pbk.)

Printed in the United States of America
Set in Times Roman

To CHAUNCEY, BERNS, AND SASCHA

ACKNOWLEDGMENTS

Many people were such a help along my journey that a mention here in no way satisfies my indebtedness. Thanks to Susan Rothchild, who wondered what I'd done with the money; the children, who discovered that my daily moods depended on the Dow Jones Industrial Average; my brother-in-law Steve Solomon, who still calls with stock tips; Chris Harte, who shares his stock market newsletters; and Dan Okrent, who shares my attraction for ill-fated investments.

Several others provided material assistance, especially lodging, that gave me extra working capital that otherwise would have gone to hotel bills: Pat Jaffe, David Oppenheim, Howard Senzel and Norina Reif; Taylor and Christy Branch; plus Beth Dunlop and the offices of Florida International Realty for computer and duplicating services.

For introductions to various market experts I thank John Lahr, Alfie Dancona, the late Jon Bradshaw, Sam Schulman, Scott Armstrong, Tom Herman of the *Wall Street Journal,* Jim Adams of *Forbes,* and Robert Prechter, Jr. Among investment professionals who took extra time and effort to show me what they do all day, I thank Richard Bermont, Linda Garrett, Dick Davis, Chuck Epstein, Dan Gressel and Claudia Rosett, Martin Zweig, Steve Schulman, the staffs of the training centers at Merrill Lynch and at Prudential Bache, plus all others whose mention in the text itself carries with it my sincere thanks.

And for crucial intellectual and emotional support: Elizabeth Darhansoff; Abigail Thomas; my editor, Amanda Vaill; and her able associate, Lisa Kaufman.

CONTENTS

	ACKNOWLEDGMENTS	vii
1	AN INTRODUCTION	1
2	MY EXPERT CREDENTIALS	7
3	WANTING TO BE RICH	11
4	MONEY IN THE BANK	15
5	THE FINANCIAL CHECKUP	21
6	THE LESSONS OF HISTORY	29
7	SOME PRACTICAL ADVICE	35
8	SHOPPING FOR THE BROKER	43
9	BUYER'S REMORSE AND OTHER SIDE EFFECTS	55
10	HOW THE EXPERTS PICK THEIR STOCKS	61
11	A FOOL AT THE STOCK EXCHANGE	79
12	ON THE FLOOR	87
13	MY SECOND INVESTMENT	93
14	WHAT THE FED WAS GOING TO DO	105
15	GOING OVER-THE-COUNTER	113
16	SEEING THE ANALYST	119
17	A WALK ON THE BUY SIDE	131
18	AMONG THE BILLION-DOLLAR BRAINS	135
19	ON BECOMING A STOCKBROKER	145
20	SELLING MYSELF SHORT	157
21	REFLECTIONS ON MY PROGRESS TO DATE	161
22	ON TO CHICAGO	167
23	OPENING A COMMODITIES ACCOUNT	173
24	MY KILLING IN COMMODITIES	187
25	MY DOUBTS ABOUT FUTURES	195
26	MY ETHICAL DILEMMA	205
27	A BOUT WITH LOEWS	211

CONTENTS

28 A Household Correction   217

29 In Search of a Forecast   221

30 My Inside Information   233

31 A Street Gone Mad   239

    Postscript   243

    A Fool's Glossary   249

A FOOL
AND HIS
MONEY

ONE

AN INTRODUCTION

THIS BOOK IS THE RECORD OF A BUSINESS TRIP. I TOOK IT IN THE name of all regular people who feel they know next to nothing about the financial world, and yet have some money and wonder how to invest it. How often have you muttered to yourself: *If only I had enough spare time to study the stock market, I could make a fortune.* How often have you heard your friends say: "It's silly to go to work for a living when there's so much profit on Wall Street." With half a chance, a common-sense person could make the money do work, just as the Wall Street professionals claim to do.

In the late summer of 1985, during an extraordinary bull market, I decided to drop everything and devote an entire year to learning how to invest, especially in stocks. I resolved to begin at the beginning, finding out as much as I could about the business and how it really operates, meanwhile putting my own funds into whatever would make the biggest profit. After adopting the winning strategy, increasing my net worth, and achieving financial independence, I'd return to tell you how I did it.

At this point, an actual accounting of gains and losses would ruin the suspense, but let me assure you that writing this book has nothing to do with my needing the money. I know there's widespread suspicion that people write investment books because they need the royalties to make up for their own unprofitable investments, or else they'd be sunning themselves on some Caribbean island instead of staring at a word processor, but in my case, the suspicion is unfounded. I've recently discovered that sitting in front of a word processor is a great delight and preferable to any Caribbean vacation. Plus I have a philanthropic interest in helping my fellow average investor by passing along all the knowledge I've gained. I hope you'll applaud my selfless efforts on your behalf.

You may also be wondering what sort of expertise qualifies me to speak out on financial matters, an issue I'll address more fully in a moment. I hope this doesn't sound like bragging, but being a stranger to Wall Street turned out to have been a terrific advantage. Unburdened by important connections and free of the weight of any previous knowledge, I could ask such apparently stupid questions as: "What is a Treasury bill?" or "Why do stocks go up and down?" and inquire about the basic facts that average investors often pretend to know already, since we're too embarrassed to admit our ignorance.

Just as many experts sprinkle tips and rules of investing throughout their books and articles, I offer my own tips and rules as often as possible. Since mine are based on actual experience, hard evidence, and/or irrefutable logic, you can have complete confidence in every one of them.

In preparing for this wealth-building journey, I realized how much I'd been thinking about money in recent years. Thinking about money is a well-known consequence of middle age. As the waist expands and the arteries contract, sex seems to take a merciful back seat in the libido, supplanted by an obsession with where to eat and how to increase one's net worth. The frequency of thought has no apparent correlation to practical success in either instance.

When you get right down to it, thinking about money has become the national pastime. Regardless of how much or how little you may have, you are almost forced to contemplate assets from daybreak to midnight. If I'm any example, the average person is being flooded with opportunities in stocks, bonds, mutual funds, options, commodities, certificates of deposit, Ginnie Maes, or the additional equity that can be squeezed from the house.

You can't browse at a magazine counter without glimpsing some investment headline in the current *Money*, *Fortune*, *Forbes*, *Institutional Investor*, *Business Week*, *Inc.*, *Barron's*, *Nation's Business*, *Future*, *Venture*, or *Personal Investing*, not to mention the *Wall Street Journal* and *Investor's Daily*. There are endless special sections on family finance and how to build a nest egg published in the daily press and the human-interest magazines.

You can't turn the dial on the radio without passing through a roundtable discussion of tax-free municipal bonds. You can't open the mailbox without being invited to convert to Eurodollars, to switch from shorter to longer bond maturities, or to cash out of local certificates of deposit and invest in Australian government debt. You can't answer the telephone without hearing from the occasional penny-stock broker, regular stockbroker, or money manager who wants to introduce himself and chat about your economic objectives.

If you watch television, you're a cinch to get caught up in the financial news that abounds. They had to cancel "Dollars and Sense," hosted by a former football player—but "Money Line," "Money Talk," "Your Money," the "Nightly Business Report," and "Your Money Matters" more than make up for the loss. Louis Rukeyser of "Wall Street Week" has become the average person's Virgil on the subject. The Financial News Network runs an all-day business report above the stock quotes that pass across the screen, and this video ticker tape mesmerizes thousands if not millions of spectators as the voices of TV guests convince them to buy or sell shares.

The financial opportunities have multiplied and become so complicated that even the simplest wage earner is forced to strategize. Every routine household economic decision requires as much conniving as old John D. Rockefeller employed to control world oil production and the U.S. railroads.

You can't buy a car without wondering if you should accept the lower sticker price or take the reduced rate of interest, opt for deferred interest, lease the car with a buy-back provision, or go for the cash rebate, which then must be reinvested. The same applies to buying appliances and furniture. You can't walk through a shopping center without worrying whether you've got a competitive mortgage, since current yields are posted on every other storefront. You can't loiter in an airport without considering whether to leave your retirement account with the bank or transfer it to a brokerage firm. You can't frolic with your children without wondering if they would benefit from a separate trust, or if you should take out a loan for their further education or buy more life insurance.

Perhaps because of these constant daily reminders of financial opportunity, everything in and around the house has become an investment, including the occupants. This I discovered as I took a complete personal inventory before embarking on my journey.

What used to be known as acquaintances, relatives, children, husbands, and wives have all become investments. A few years ago—though I'm not certain when—we began calling children "our investments in the future." Soon we found ourselves investing in their education, which used to be called putting them through school. Some people invest in relationships, as opposed to just having friends over for dinner. My wife, of course, is a perpetual investment, as I am to her. It's also possible to invest in pets and sell the offspring, though I doubt we could pay anybody to take our cats.

Lately, I've begun to think of the hereafter as the Keogh plan and life after death as the tax-deferred IRA. Once I regarded my car as simple transportation, and now it is a depreciated holding. The roof over our heads has become an inflation hedge, next-to-useless during a deflationary cycle. Every other week we're debating whether to sell out or stay, whether to refinance or hold out for lower rates, whether to rent the place and move into something with a bigger mortgage-interest deduction.

The dining room table is a fixed asset; the dishes set down upon it are collectibles. The smart money, I realize now, would have divested the dishes in the early 1980s, when collectibles were at a premium, and gone into paper plates. The last spike in silver prices destroyed all feelings of loyalty for the family flatware, which now serves only as a painful reminder of our missed opportunity to cash in at $41 an ounce. Ditto the silver backgammon cube, which I transported to the safe-deposit box but which is no longer worth protecting.

The silver samovar is corroded, but we maintain it in spite of no sign of inflation. Its ultimate purpose may depend on whether the Federal Reserve continues to lower the discount rate. Looking through our closets, I see dozens of examples of poor market timing, things that were bought too early or held too long: the $2,000 Apple computer in the former category, the art deco water pitchers in the latter. The old train set and the baseball cards thrown away long ago by mistake once had a sentimental value, but since prices of such items are now common knowledge, I now remember them as hundreds of dollars lost in the restructuring of my childhood closet.

A couch was once a place on which to sit, and a chest of drawers a place in which to put things, but these, too, have evolved into collectibles—and so the cat-claw marks, the jelly stains, the rips, the tears, the broken handles, the gouges in the record cabinet, the scratches in the marble table, the mildew spots on stuffed armchairs left outside in the rain are no longer simple repair jobs. They're threats to the bottom line, and a great deal more fuss is made over mishaps these days.

Our clothes are a continual source of fiscal disappointment, especially during the frequent catastrophes when they are soiled, ripped, or otherwise damaged. Having spaghetti dumped in one's lap is the dinner-party equivalent of a 30 percent drop in a stock or the cancellation of a dividend. The same can be said for high heels that are sheared off by a hidden sprinkler head.

Since clothes have become investments, many of the hand-me-down items that we once kept in paper bags for Halloween costumes or used as car rags are now hung in the closets. This includes old Pucci dresses and houndstooth coats too big in the shoulders, feather boas worn by relatives from café society, discarded kilts from Scottish festivals, Hawaiian shirts retained since college, scarves, trout vests, riding jodhpurs, and smocks made from Panamanian molas. Someday, we assure ourselves, there'll be a bull market in molas.

Have we just gotten greedy, or have we been forced into it: routed from our passbooks by fantastic opportunities; lured by the irresistible increases in the price of gold, silver, grandfather clocks; convinced that it is highly speculative not to speculate; millions of us and our loose cash, wandering from chance to chance, desperate for good advice yet almost always confused; our net worth vacillating with the monetary system, the fiscal system, the balance of trade; our futures papered in CATS funds and zero-coupon bonds;

our very daily moods tied to the discount rates. Is it possible not to be financially obsessed? I find time for little else.

This brings me to the first problem I encountered: how would I raise enough cash to invest in the great opportunities that would soon come my way. My plan to sell some extra furniture, old clothes, and other household effects met with strong resistance in my own family. They argued that if these things were investments already, what was the point of sacrificing them to some wild idea of running off and winning on Wall Street?

Fortunately, I was able to sell my own car, an old Renault, and also a twice-used sailing dinghy. The proceeds from these two sources, plus the first third of an advance from my publisher, added up to $16,500. That is the stake with which I set out into the world of finance.

MY EXPERT CREDENTIALS

IGHT AWAY, LET ME SHARE MY QUALIFICATIONS, TRAINING, and general suitability for this challenge—this being the place most authors of works like this lay out their credentials, such as "veteran of Wall Street" or "hottest commodities trader from Chicago" or "became a millionaire in stock options," and so on. Before this project, what I knew most about money was how to lose it. In fact, I could claim an unerring instinct for personal speculative failure, based on the following solid evidence.

Before I married into a modest portfolio, I had no capital to invest at all. Well, that's not entirely accurate. Once in the 1960s, I opted for some long-term capital growth—which I was told was a mature thing to do. Somehow I managed to spare enough cash to buy two shares of Technical Tape at $14 a share. These were worth $4 apiece twenty years later. The two shares, plus some worthless employee stock from a liberal magazine in perpetual Chapter 11, were the only investment assets for which I could take sole credit.

A decade or so ago, in the mid-1970s, I began to apply my talents to the spousal holdings, which was too bad for them. An acquaintance with a seat on the American Stock Exchange proposed an IBM option spread, where you buy the June "call" and sell the October "put" simultaneously. Until then, I would have thought a June call was a duck whistle and an October put a geranium bulb. Asking questions only made things worse. There wasn't much risk, my advisor said, as long as IBM was going up or sliding sideways.

On this reassurance, I went ahead and bought the Junes and

7

sold the Octobers, but IBM neither went up nor did it slide sideways, and I lost $6,000 in the process. Experience can be an expensive teacher, but at least I can save you some expense already with the first of my Useful Tips:

Never buy the June call nor sell the October put simultaneously, unless you know what they are

---

I tried to recoup with Ramada Inn at $15, on the advice of my brother-in-law's broker. My brother-in-law plays commodities, the stock market, and tennis in Palm Springs, California. That I was getting ideas from his broker across the country via long-distance calls tells you something about the state of my relations with my own broker, but we'll discuss that later. Anyway, his broker insisted that Ramada was first in line for the next Atlantic City casino license. This it must not have received, since the stock fell straight down and hasn't seen $15 in the 10 years since.

Prior to this Ramada deal, I got another friendly tip from a go-go dancer who'd just returned from Nassau: buy Resorts International at $3. I realized that it was unwise for the serious investor to take buy signals from go-go dancers, and therefore ignored the recommendation. After Resorts International went to $200 and something and split several times, I confided to a wealthy friend how I'd missed out on the 10,000 percent profit. He informed me it wasn't too late and said the stock was "still cheap at $47" On the belief that wealthy people don't get that way by accident, I bought a couple of hundred shares at that price. Almost immediately, Resorts International retreated to $29, where it sat for a decade, and only recently shot up to $75 on the news of the chairman's death. This postmortem surge took place long after I'd despaired of any improvement and sold out at $33.

Meanwhile, I picked up Charter at $9 and got out at $12 as the stock moved on to $100. I counteracted this rare bit of profit with Anacomp at $20 (which promptly plummeted to $2¾) and Sykes Datatronics at $11 (now bankrupt). I'm no stranger to metals either, having bought silver at $19 and on its way down, not up. With other commodities, such as coffee or feeder cattle, I claim no prior experience, but I'm sure I would have done no worse with them than I did with the silver.

On the eve of this financial journey, I reviewed my previous gains and losses overall, and concluded that I'd "broken about even." So many friends and acquaintances told me they'd also "broken about even" on their stocks, and other such investments that I'm convinced this result is not unusual. From what I'd gathered at cocktail parties, there are millions of people who are constantly breaking even all across the country. This convinced me I was fully qualified to speak for the average investor.

THREE

WANTING TO BE RICH

I WAS TOLD THAT BEFORE YOU CAN ENRICH YOURSELF, YOU HAVE to *want* to get richer. Here I have a confession to make. In the past, I've flirted with the dangerous notion that money isn't everything. This usually occurred to me after I'd made a bad investment. On those sad occasions, I'd announce that rich people were "miserable," "living empty lives," or "too greedy for their own good," or I'd repeat such mottos as "It's better to be happy than greedy," "Any dummy can make a fortune," and "At least we have our health." Prosperous couples featured on the program "Lifestyles of the Rich and Famous" never looked gloomier nor more forlorn than after I'd suffered some financial setback.

Now that I'm getting all this out in the open, I might as well make a clean breast of it. Beyond the idea that money isn't everything, I also believed that the dumb investor was morally superior to the smart one. If money makes people hate their children and lead miserable lives, then any of the numerous losses I've described could only have brought me closer to spiritual perfection and ultimate enlightenment. I felt especially virtuous as Sykes Datatronics was plunging from $11 toward zero, and nearly saintlike as Anacomp declined from $20 to $2.

I can trace this primitive attitude back to my college days, when many among us were convinced we never wanted to get richer. A majority of college students in the mid- to late-1960s was determined to avoid financial success. In those days, an A in pre-Colombian politics was more highly prized than an A in accounting fundamentals. We never bothered to learn how to account for anything, unless it was for the differences in pre-Socratic creation myths. Many of us knew more about the Norman Conquest than the basics of accelerated depreciation. We'd do almost anything to bypass the master's degree in business, a well-known first step toward making a fortune.

After graduation, those of us who didn't move to small towns or join the Peace Corps dedicated ourselves to handicrafts, obscure academic endeavors, low-paid arts jobs, or public-service careers. All along, we pitied our unfortunate acquaintances who'd wanted to get rich from the start and had proceeded directly to Wall Street. How unhappy and narrow these poor souls must have been, we thought. Those same poor souls are now the managing partners at Goldman, Sachs or Salomon Brothers, making millions of dollars a year, and no doubt just as friendly, charitable, courteous, and kind to their children as the rest of us who've just begun the struggle to get richer—having belatedly recognized the advantages of economics over the pre-Colombian politics we've already forgotten.

Convinced that motivation is the key to success, I forced myself to stay awake for several evenings in a row so I could watch the television programs on how to get rich. Most of these are shown after midnight and wasted on an audience that is half-asleep, which is too bad. Otherwise, we might be a much more prosperous country than we are today.

During these broadcasts, many nice-looking men and women step out of their Rolls Royces or hop from the cabins of their parked Lear jets to give testimonials to the advantages of wealth, after which they promise to reveal the proven ways of acquiring more of it. Most favor investing in real estate, where, to hear them tell it, you needn't put up any cash at all. One man described how he'd upgraded himself from short-order cook to millionaire in just a few months by purchasing distressed properties with his credit cards. Though of course he no longer lacked for money, he was selling a mail-order course to share his techniques as a public service.

Mr. E. J. Cossman, another TV millionaire, stood beside an American flag and told how he'd made a fortune selling metal spud guns and plastic ant farms. His idea was to get the rights to back-yard inventions and to promote them with common-sense marketing. He was convinced that with his help—which wasn't free—all of us could do the same.

If you ask me, the most inspiring of all the late-night millionaires was Dave Del Dotto. His program was broadcast from the balcony of a Hawaiian condominium, overlooking the Pacific ocean. Mr. Del Dotto explained that from boyhood he'd carried a picture of Hawaii in his pocket, and this picture inspired him to get rich and move to the island paradise, though there was some confusion as to his permanent whereabouts. In one program, he said he lived in Hawaii while in another he claimed to visit the place as much as possible. Hopefully, he'll clear this up.

In his striped leisure shirt and cotton deck trousers, with two pinky rings and a gold watch for each arm, Mr. Del Dotto looked as if he'd be just as comfortable in Reno, Nevada, as he was on the Hawaiian waterfront. Among his several money-making mottoes, the most memorable were "From My Impossible Dream to Yours," "Don't Be a Floater," and "Consider the Ends First"—the latter an alleged quotation from Leonardo Da Vinci, though I couldn't find it in any of my reference books.

To assist the general public, Mr. Del Dotto devised a comprehensive home-study course with books and tapes that more or less covered everything offered by his late-night competitors, including a cash-flow system, how to buy foreclosed real estate, how to get more credit cards, equity sharing, creative finance, tax-sale land, and the like, all in one package. As a bonus, there was a special certificate for a vacation to Hawaii, complete with sunset cruise and Polynesian cruise, plus the most favorable airline and hotel rates offered through Mr. Del Dotto's personal travel agent. The entire home-study course cost only $289, and for this low price you'd get $1,475 worth of information, not including the vacation.

Though I didn't rush to send in my $289—in fact, I carelessly forgot the 800 number and lost Mr. Del Dotto's address—I learned a great deal from watching his broadcasts. I learned that Mr. Del Dotto's having been a C student in high school, which resulted in his using words like *analization* when he meant to say *analysis*, hadn't stopped him from getting rich. Among his followers was a blind boy named Chad Hazen who'd listened to the tapes and followed the plan, and in spite of his handicap, he, too, had gotten rich. Then there was the "little black lady from Chicago"—recently destitute and unable to feed her family—who now controlled some valuable downtown real estate.

Mr. Del Dotto couldn't overemphasize the point that before you can get richer you have to *want* to get richer. In fact, that was the universal conviction of all the late-night financial advisors I'd tuned in during the week.

If I needed further convincing that my old beliefs were ill-conceived and impediments to success, Mr. Del Dotto did the job. After I watched him a few times on TV, all my "money isn't everything" notions were exorcised. Without hesitation, I was able to swear that I envied Mr. Del Dotto's position and would like to be just as rich as he is. Such an admission was necessary to any further progress, and it brought me to my Second Useful Tip:

People who think that money isn't everything will never have enough

FOUR

MONEY IN THE BANK

M Y FIRST DECISION ABOUT MY STAKE WAS TO PUT IT SOME-place where it would gain simple interest while I looked for better ways to invest it. But these days, simple interest is no longer so simple. First you have to choose the best bank, or savings-and-loan, or money-market fund, or other competing depository.

In my neighborhood in Miami Beach, Florida, there were two or three banks and/or savings-and-loans to the block. Along one side of one street where I walked, the personal computer store, the drugstore/luncheonette, a hairdresser, and an optometrist all had been replaced by various financial services. In this short stretch of shops, there was a new Savings of America, a Southeast Bank, a First Nationwide Savings, and a Glendale Federal, plus Dis-Com Securities, a discount stockbroker that offered a money-market alternative to the banks.

In the two blocks that followed, there was a Chase Federal, Safra Bank, Citicorp Savings, Carteret Savings, Lincoln Savings and Loan, American Savings and Loan, Centrust Savings and Loan, the Jefferson National Bank, as well as a Prudential-Bache, a Merrill Lynch, a Drexel Burnham Lambert, and Chicago Commodity Corporation. Down the road was a Sun Bank.

If the few remaining clothing stores, delis, beauty salons, and restaurants go out of business and this banking trend continues, soon there will be nothing to shop for except interest rates, and we'll be cashing checks and making deposits up and down both sides of the street, 24 hours a day. If the country as a whole moves any further in the same direction, we'll quickly become a nation of brokers and tellers.

I read in the *New York Times* that financial services was the fastest-growing industry in America, faster than fast food, faster than real estate, faster even than legal services, which was reproducing at two percent a year. Financial services was multiplying at 4 percent a year, or faster than the population of Mexico. It was multiplying faster than home health care, cappuccino salons, exercise clubs, croissant cafés, and alternative long-distance. The department stores—Sears, K Mart, and so forth—had begun to sell financial services right alongside the rain gear and the toaster ovens. Meanwhile, you could get toaster ovens and rain gear as prizes for putting your money into a bank. Perhaps the department stores had gone into banking in retaliation for the banks' appliance giveaways. In any event, there was a great blurring of inventory, which promised to blur more as banking was further deregulated.

By calling the federal banking officials in Washington, I learned that there are 4,000 separate S&Ls and 14,000 different banks, plus many thousands of local branches operating in our country. The biggest difference between the banks and the S&Ls seems to be that banks are allowed to make bad loans to far-off places like Peru and Mexico, while savings-and-loans are restricted to making bad loans in nearby commercial construction, especially empty office buildings. None of this should bother the depositor, as long as the assets are protected by the Federal Deposit Insurance Corporation (FDIC) in case the bank goes bankrupt—or by the Federal Savings and Loan Insurance Corporation (FSLIC) in the case of an S&L flop.

The older and better-established banks in my neighborhood tend to look like mausoleums. Apparently, it was common practice, especially during the Depression, to build banks out of granite or other long-lasting materials, and to protect the entrances with heavy steel doors and gates. These thick exteriors and impressive gates reassured patrons that the banks contained something worth protecting, during periods when the assets were depleted and solvency itself was in doubt.

Newer banks and S&Ls are often installed in storefronts and easily confused with boutiques. Many were opened during the recent national prosperity. When public confidence in the banking system is unusually high, bankers can get away with building flimsier structures and spend less money on walls. In my neighborhood, I noticed several S&Ls that resembled greenhouse nurseries, and others that could have been health clubs. Some had fountains and indoor pools.

I was surprised to see that these indoor pools are used as wishing wells by bank customers. A few years ago, when a penny saved was a penny earned, you'd never have found a wishing well in a bank, and certainly not with dimes and quarters on the bottom. That some people prefer to throw away their pocket change on a wish, as opposed to depositing the coins in their savings accounts, is the unfortunate result of inflation. After hours, these coins no doubt are scooped up by the tellers, to add to the banks' overall profits.

We might as well face the fact that small change is only valuable in large quantities, which leads me to my Third Useful Tip:

A penny saved is a penny earned, but so what?

At the old banks, the new banks, and most of the S&Ls I visited, I found long lines at the tellers' windows. The lines seem to grow in direct proportion to the amount of interest that customers received on their deposits. After an informal survey, I concluded that the more interest a person gets for his or her savings, the longer he or she has to wait to get it. Also, eight out of ten tellers' windows in each of the institutions I visited were always tellerless. These seemed to serve as fronts, giving false hope to the customers forced to stand for hours at the occupied windows.

Banks and S&Ls change owners so frequently it's hard to keep up with the names. According to sources in Washington, there have been 670 bank mergers and more than 200 savings-and-loan mergers in the last two years alone. In my own neighborhood, First Nationwide Savings was once known as Washington Savings, Carteret Savings absorbed Amerifirst, Citicorp Savings used to be Biscayne Federal, Centrust was lately called Dade Savings, and Sun Bank was spun out of Flagship, which itself was spun out of United National.

Though we may be a transient population, I'd bet that the average bank client moves less often than the average bank has been restructured. Instead of getting some benefit from their loyalty, longtime customers are forced to reintroduce themselves to a succession of new presidents, officers, or tellers and must show their driver's licenses again and again for identification, as if they—and not the institution—had just arrived in town.

Inside the doors of banks and S&Ls I found rate charts that explain all the options. These charts have gotten progressively more complicated as more features are added. At Chase Federal they offered the one-year CD, the two-year CD, the three-year CD, the four-year CD, and the five-year CD, plus the "tiered rate passbook" and a "tiered rate money market" to go along with "tiered rate checking" and the silver VISA card.

I informed Linden Barrett, a friendly young teller at Chase, that I had a large amount of money to put on deposit—enough to deserve at least one toaster. Mr. Barrett said his institution no longer gave away toasters. Keeping to its own core business, Chase Federal was giving away money. Mr. Barrett offered a $20 cash bonus for every $10,000 I'd invest in the one-year CD, $40 for every $10,000 in the two-year CD. Curiously, there was no bonus for the five-year CD.

At competing institutions, I found savings with checking, checking with savings, floating rate and capped, minimum balance and no minimum balance, service charge and no service charge, automatic transfer, among other options. There were variable-rate CDs and fixed-rate CDs with different maturity dates. I confided to an officer of one bank that I was interested in the stock market. He said the bank would be delighted to serve as my broker. "We can save you money on commissions," he insisted. "We're much lower than Merrill Lynch." Merrill Lynch, I later discovered, was not standing still for this. They'd be delighted to serve as my banker.

At Sun Bank, née Flagship, née United National, a large neon sign flashed a message to all holders of the 24-hour money card: PICK UP YOUR FREE GIFT. Beyond the lobby was a median strip of flowers, and beyond the median strip the grazing area for bank officers. Amid ten or twelve desks and a huge expanse of carpet, I saw only three people at work. As I waited in the reception area,

I read the advertisements for the Sunservice hot line, for the special discount on a family portrait, for the all-in-one account, for the credit card with no yearly fee, and for the Sunline Equity loan.

Eventually, I was assigned to an officer, Jane Gautier, who at least looked old enough to vote. Others I'd seen would have been refused a beer. Ms. Gautier said there'd be no toaster, no free money, no incentive awards, no prizes of any kind to accompany my deposit. I told her it sounded like Sun Bank really didn't want my money, and she shook her head in agreement. She expected I'd get a better deal elsewhere. It's sad to be turned down for a loan, but being discouraged from opening a savings account is an insult.

Centrust Savings, was more solicitous. Julio, a young officer in a checkered tie that was no match for his striped shirt, insisted that Centrust's superior rate of interest made up for any lack of prizes. He recommended the two-and-a-half-year Head Start savings, which returned 10 percent for three months and 6.34 percent thereafter, for a combined 7.20 percent average yield or 7.52 percent annual yield for the full term. He explained the difference between average and annual yield three times, and still I didn't understand it. I'd heard similar explanations dozens of times before, and I never understood them then or since.

(I suspect that bankers know we're baffled by such things as compound yields, and this confusion allows them to pay us whatever amount of interest they feel like paying at any given time. Since I'd have to comprehend average yield and annual yield before I could prove this, it seems futile to pursue the matter any further.)

When I asked if I could borrow any money I decided to invest in Centrust Savings, Julio's face brightened appreciably. "Of course you can," he said, "up to 90 percent." He went on to describe how a loan could be structured for interest only, with the due date set to coincide exactly with the expiration of a certificate of deposit. Then he introduced me to the Equity Credit line—no fees, no closing costs, and approval in 48 hours—through which I could borrow even more on the equity in my house. The interest rate could be fixed or variable.

In all the various banks and S&Ls, I sensed a greater enthusiasm for increasing my indebtedness than for encouraging my savings, with more brochures and TV promotions devoted to the former. In fact, our so-called thrift institutions would be better understood if they were called debt institutions, since the current level of public saving is at its lowest in modern American history, while public borrowing approaches infinity.

In the end I decided to keep my stake in an existing Centrust checking/savings account that paid a floating rate of interest above a minimum balance with no penalty for early withdrawal. That accomplished, I considered the next course of action.

FIVE

THE FINANCIAL CHECKUP

I HEARD ON THE RADIO THAT INVESTORS SHOULDN'T MAKE A MOVE without getting a full financial checkup from a reputable financial planner. It occured to me that I'd never undergone a full financial checkup and if there was ever a good time to have one it had to be now, before I engaged in any strenuous money-making.

There were as many financial planners as major household-appliance dealers in the yellow pages of my local phone book. Ten years ago, financial planning wasn't even a category in the yellow pages. Back then, financial planners were hired by rich clients who planned to avoid paying taxes. Thanks to computers, the cost of planning was drastically reduced, and planners began offering their services to the general public.

The idea of an average person having any financial future at all is quite contemporary. I spent several hours in the library browsing through old books, looking for the earliest mention of a financial future as applied to a popular audience. I found it in a 1922 pamphlet. The author, a Mr. Alquist, writes as follows:

> Only two and a half per cent of men who die between the ages of 60 and 70 leave enough money for funeral expenses. Do you realize where you're headed if you don't begin to lay plans for your financial future?

What Mr. Alquist meant by "where you're headed" I wouldn't want to guess, but this much is obvious: the idea of a financial future begins with the worry over how to pay the funeral bill. This makes sense when you realize that the funeral bill was the first household debt that had to be paid postmortem. Before there were funeral homes, people buried each other for free, so nobody had an automatic reason to fear insolvency after death.

From what I could gather, both the financial planning industry and the life insurance industry owe a big thank-you to the organized morticians. The earliest life insurance for the masses was introduced as a way of paying off funeral bills. From there, the coverage was gradually expanded to benefit the surviving members of the family. As the average person began living longer and longer, newer forms of life insurance provided benefits to policyholders even before they'd died, or in industry parlance, while they were predeceased. Thus did the notion of a financial future work its way up from the burial fee, through the maintenance of the bereaved, finally to become a goal that an average person could hope to attain while he or she was fully conscious.

Now we've got Social Security, pension plans, profit-sharing plans, annuities, Keoghs, and IRAs—all of which complicate the financial future to the point where we can hardly stand to think about it. These complications have given thousands of new planners the opportunity to offer their help.

From out of my yellow pages, I picked a reputable-sounding name: M. H. Senzel & Co. I called up and made an appointment for the free introductory consultation. M. H. Senzel occupied a seventh-floor suite in a large concrete building near a freeway in my town. The waiting room was right out of a doctor's office, except that instead of *Newsweek* or *People* on the coffee table there was a *Money* and a *Forbes*. I sat a few minutes reading the *Money* until an earnest young fellow in a sport coat and leisure slacks appeared. He introduced himself as Boyd Leffert.

Mr. Leffert led me through a hallway into a conference room and motioned me to sit in a chair midway down a long table. He set up a vinyl display board that had been leaning against a wall and picked up a felt-tipped pointer from the table. He stood by the display board and drew things on it with the pointer as we chatted.

The first thing Mr. Leffert wanted to talk about was the "universe of financial planners," which now includes more than 200,000 in this country alone. Apparently, there are twice as many of these experts as there were a decade ago, which is what Mr. Leffert was getting at. It's very easy to call yourself a financial planner. In fact, any out-of-work diesel mechanic or laid-off saxophone player can become one by putting up a shingle to that effect. The 10,000 stockbrokers at Merrill Lynch have renamed themselves financial consultants and have received new business cards, while the stockbrokers at Shearson Lehman refer to themselves as financial consultants as well.

A dilemma for the client, Mr. Leffert recognized, is finding a planner who knows what he's about. The hard part is that there's no simple measure of success and no agreement as to what good planning really entails. In other fields where it's difficult to distinguish success from failure—such as in government bureaucracy, academia, or European aristocracy—titles and certifications abound. This is also true in financial planning.

Mr. Leffert said there are certified financial planners and registered financial planners, plus several gradations of consultants. He named various organizations to which planners belong—including the International Association for Financial Planning (IAFP)—and the various tests that planners may take, including the CFP given by the College of Financial Planning and the ChFC, which is an offshoot of something called the CLU.

Mr. Leffert guessed that of all the planners only a thousand or so had an adequate foundation and less than half that number were "extremely well qualified." Though he admitted there's no agreement on this, he suggested that to be absolutely safe the client should look for a firm that covers as many bases as possible, and whose employees are connected to the CFP, have passed their ChFC, and are registered with the IAFP as well. Happily, this was the case with his own firm, M. H. Senzel. Personally, Mr. Leffert was both a certified and a registered financial planner, CFP and RFP.

(Later, I was disturbed to read in the newspapers that a dog named Boris Bo Regaard of Tampa, Florida, was accepted into the IAFP, one of the important associations that Mr. Leffert had mentioned. I phoned their headquarters in Atlanta and spoke to Dick Williams in public relations. He assured me that the application for the dog was filled out with false information and its acceptance was not indicative of the general quality of the association's other 24,179 members. Mr. Williams insisted there is little chance another dog would get into the IAFP, though he did admit that whoever sends in the $125 and fills out all the questions is given the full benefit of the doubt. He reminded me that the IAFP is a trade association, not a licensing bureau.

I also phoned the Institute of Certified Financial Planners in Denver, Colorado, affiliated with the College for Financial Planning, to find out about their CFP exam. The person I talked to, who must have been a secretary, told me the CFP exam is the culmination of a six-part course that can be studied at home. Two thousand new planners passed it in the most recent year. She also volunteered that the CFP is a lot harder than the ChFC. To check this, I called the ChFC people at the American College for chartered financial consultants of Bryn Mawr, Pennsylvania. They said their ChFC test is an offshoot of the older CLU for chartered life underwriters and, if anything, is harder than the CFP.

Finally, I contacted the National Association of Personal Financial Advisors, which represents a special category of professionals who charge a fixed yearly fee for services. The NAPFA has no exam, and can be joined for $120 a year. To its knowledge, it hadn't accepted any dogs.)

After describing the financial universe, Mr. Leffert began to explain some of the things financial planning could do for me. The most important was to "help clarify my financial objectives." I thought these were pretty clear already, especially after those nights I'd spent watching late-night television. "I want to get rich. That's my objective," I told Mr. Leffert. He laughed, as if this were a joke! When I didn't laugh back, he got a disturbed look on his face and subsequently took on a more patronizing attitude toward my case.

If you visit a financial planner, I'd advise you not to mention that getting rich is one or your objectives. They seem to have a taboo against this. Mr. Leffert, at least, seemed more interested in helping me move around what I already had than in helping me get more of it. Also, if I were you, I wouldn't mention "blowing it on a whim," "painting the town red," "a little bit of lucre buys a lot of things," "big bangs for the buck," "easy come, easy go," "let's have a big party," or "you can't take it with you." What Mr. Leffert wanted to hear instead was whether I'd prepared for reasonable long-term growth, stability, security, the mortgage payments, the children's college education, and whether I was properly annuitized, and so forth.

To explain how I might better clarify my objectives, Mr. Leffert turned to his blackboard and gave a 15-minute lecture, complete with diagrams he drew with the felt-tip pen. It had to do with putting a coordinating umbrella over the chaos of my life, which he'd divided into asset management, tax planning, estate planning, insurance planning, and retirement planning. As he talked about the retirement planning, he drew a little happy face of a grandpa with a beard.

Between you and me, I was thinking about my actual household of bounced checks, forgotten payments, untold dollars in unpaid parking tickets, the silly monthly budgets that we'd tried and then abandoned, the thousands of dollars of incidental expenses, and wondered what possible relation it all had to the pie graph that Mr. Leffert had so carefully devised. I blurted out that I had no life insurance. This was as much a shock to Mr. Leffert as if I'd admitted to wearing my wife's brassiere. I told him I didn't know our annual income, since with me being a free-lance writer and my wife a real estate agent, income is always unpredictable. Finally I confessed that my life had nothing to do with the "totally integrated whole" that he had created with his felt-tip.

He sat down, leaned over, and in a fatherly tone advised me not to worry, that all people in need of financial planning believe their situation to be hopeless. He said he suspected that however sloppy my family finances, I was a redeemable case. He handed me a brochure published by his company, opened it to an inside page, and showed me the part that said: "Very few people whom we have met have this vital total and continuing perspective on their financial life."

Mr. Leffert soon got to the hard part. Before we could even think about a plan, there would have to be a "basic data gathering of from two to twenty hours," during which his staff would pore over my family's grocery bills, receipts, and so forth and "take a picture." After that the data gatherers would come back to the office and play the "what-if game" among themselves, moving around our debits and credits, speculating what might happen if, for instance, we bought life insurance, transferred some assets to the children, or put more savings into Treasury bills. He called the what-if game "intermediation."

I volunteered to stop paying the gardener and start mowing the lawn myself, but Mr. Leffert said don't be silly, that was premature and too simplistic. It sounded as if M. H. Senzel & Co. would apply as many calculations to our household accounts as routinely go into the budgeting of major corporations. Even after our plan was completed, we'd have to come in twice a year for checkups, just like at the dentist. Mr. Leffert said that putting us on this review schedule was essential, or else the entire effort might be wasted.

So far, there'd been no mention of the cost of all this. Mr. Leffert seemed to be saving that information for last. When I asked him about the fee, he delved a bit further into the importance of the review schedule, the "totally integrated whole," and the expert perspective. He tried to smooth the path with references to "time," "effort," and "a lot of things the client doesn't see happening." Finally, he admitted that the fee for an initial plan could vary from 2 to 4 percent of our total family assets—depending on how much we had to begin with. After that, the firm would charge 1 to 2 percent per year for the follow-ups and the checkups.

His reminder that this was tax-deductible was only slightly re-assuring. Being careful not to say anything about getting rich, I wondered out loud if the plan might at least provide us with enough extra income to cover the cost of planning. Mr. Leffert was certain the plan would save us money, but how that might be invested depended on our money manager. Here was another professional that we'd need.

The firm had its own money managers who were part of the bargain, but Mr. Leffert said I'd be free to go out and choose my own. He cautioned that it's as hard to find a good money manager as it is to find a good financial planner, so I'd have to do a lot of research into performance, fees, and the like before I could make an intelligent choice. Probably I'd be better off working with the professionals in-house.

Beyond the financial planner and the money manager, I'd need a brokerage house to make the investments. Mr. Leffert said his firm worked closely with a discount broker that offered very competitive rates. As for an accountant, he said I could continue to use the one I had, or else I could employ one from M. H. Senzel.

That more or less ended our free introductory consultation. Mr. Leffert gave me a set of contracts to review and invited me to get back to him when I was ready for the data-gathering, but I never did. The prospect of having to pay the original planning fee, plus the cost of semiannual checkups—not to mention the money manager, the stockbroker, and possibly the accountant—was worrisome. I doubted there would be much money left to manage. As capable and as thoughtful as Mr. Leffert had been, I decided to move along without the benefit of his firm's considerable professionalism. Maybe I can save you the same trouble with this Fourth Useful Tip:

Financial security is too expensive for the average investor

THE LESSONS OF HISTORY

AVING GIVEN UP THE IDEA OF FINANCIAL PLANNING, BUT still looking for some sort of guidance, I headed for the local library. I hoped to learn as much as I could from the newsletters and business publications, which there, at least, were free. Several weeks into my venture, my money was sitting in the savings account, multiplying at the paltry rate of 5½ percent per annum. No doubt countless fortunes had been made while I'd been watching television, or frittering away my time at M. H. Senzel, yet I refused to succumb to impatience. The lessons of history would not be lost on me.

In the reading room, I encountered a variety of individuals with stuck zippers on their pants and grease stains on their sweatshirts. I knew we shared an interest after I saw them absorbed in the *Wall Street Journal*. One made odd chewing noises as he perused the stock tables. Another spread rusted wristwatches across his cubicle space, and sang "Way Down Upon the Swanee River" in defiance of the QUIET signs. I asked him what investment he would make, and he mumbled "Key Pharmaceutical," a stock which has gone up handsomely since.

Well-informed students of the market can be found loitering in most libraries. From what I could observe, most of them lack capital. I decided these were former average investors who had carried my previous techniques (buy high, sell low, break about even) to an ultimate conclusion: sleeping in the alley, eating from the trash bins, living out their days in the reading room.

I could have spent more time talking to them, but fearing the effects of a prolonged association, I isolated myself in the stacks. There I scanned or studied more than 200 books about investing throughout financial history. Some of these go back to the nineteenth century. Titles I remember include: *The Art of Investing* (1888); *Playing the Game*, by Zebediah Flint (1918); *Reminiscences of a Stock Operator*, by Edwin Lefevre (1923); *Test, Then Invest* author unknown, (1927); and *The Common Sense of Money and Investments* (1929), written by Merryle Rukeyser, father of the present-day celebrity.

There were several books addressed to women, most notably *What Every Woman Should Know about Investing Her Money* (1968), penned by Herta Hess Levy, "an utterly feminine but highly-professional stockbroker," according to the flap copy. There was also *How to Lay a Nest Egg* (1950), written for women by a man named Edgar Scott. "Is the stock market like a supermarket?" he asked rhetorically.

From these books and others, I learned several important things about my average-investor ancestry. The first stock market opened in Amsterdam in 1602, but there is no evidence that the masses invested in it. They were busy buying up the tulip bulbs. Tulip bulbs were the earliest-known financial opportunity for the average person, which resulted in the unfortunate tulip-bulb bust. By 1688, regular Englishmen were investing in oil from sunflower seeds and in the importing of jackasses from Spain. The South Sea Company of the 1700s had many average shareholders who together bid up that stock to a paper value five times greater than all the cash in Europe. A subsequent collapse inspired the passage of the Bubble Act of 1720, which restricted the formation of new corporations.

In 1721, the English House of Commons passed an ordinance to prohibit the selling of stocks altogether, and in 1733 there was a second attempt to "void all wagers as to the price of stocks and securities." This must have failed, because the London Stock Exchange was established in 1762. Soon the word *wager* disappeared from the vocabulary, replaced by the more reassuring term *investment* still in use today. Meanwhile, banking for the average person was invented by the Scots.

These are the European antecedents. The first American investment of any popularity was public debt, which should come as no surprise to us. Our pioneer investors bought Revolutionary War bonds in the 1700s. From there they moved into nationalbank bonds, from bank bonds to insurance bonds, from insurance bonds to utility bonds, from utility bonds to mining- and oil-company bonds, from oil-company bonds to industrial-company bonds, more or less in that order.

Stocks went on sale in the U.S. as early as the eighteenth century. The first known stock was issued on the Bank of North America, which regrettably collapsed in 1792. By 1818, there were 29 issues traded in the coffeehouses that served as a New York stock exchange. Ten of these issues were banks. By the 1830s, there were insurance stocks, and after that came railroad stocks, then oil and mining stocks.

Since the earliest days, there have been countless bull markets and bear markets, also known as swimming markets and sick markets. These can be summarized as follows. There was the bull market of 1781; the collapse of 1792; the panic of 1837 and again of 1857; the bull market of 1877 that gave way to the bear market of 1881–85; the "reckless carnivals of prodigality" in 1892 and 1906; the collapses of 1893, 1903, and 1907; the 1919 high; the recession of 1920; the 1921 low; the so-called Crash of 1929; the low of 1932; the general uptrend into 1949; the choppy 1950s; the 1962 low; the 1969 high; the early 1970s low; the late 1970s advance into the 1980s, as of this writing the greatest bull decade in history.

In reviewing these markets, I had a hard time figuring out just how many people invested in what, and when. Curiously, every couple of decades the general public is said to have "recently discovered" investing. There's been a continual string of these discoveries ever since the eighteenth century, when the public first bought the Revolutionary War bonds. Seventy years later, in 1848, a book called *Stock Jobbing on Wall Street* reported that the masses finally had begun to invest. Again in 1906, *World's Work* magazine announced that the average investor had just become the "main-stay of the investment market." Twenty years after that, the elder Rukeyser noted that "brokers are for the first time selling to the average person." Another thirty years later, in 1956, the New York Stock Exchange celebrated the birth of "people's capitalism" and Merrill Lynch bragged about having brought "Main Street to Wall Street." Again in the mid-1960s, Wall Street was reintroduced to the inexperienced multitude, now known as the Thundering Herd.

My reading convinced me the general public had been in and out of stocks and bonds from the beginning, yet nobody seemed to remember from one decade to the next. Is there an investor's amnesia? People traumatized in earthquakes, traffic accidents, and so forth often develop healthy lapses of memory that protect them until they regain the strength to face reality. Women might refuse to have babies if they didn't forget the pain of previous delivery. Similarly, do investors collectively blot out all previous losses, only to return to the markets and repeat the process again?

On the other hand, I also learned that the average investor is progressively better-informed, craftier, more capable of making prudent decisions, and more wary of sham and hyperbole than his predecessor from the previous era, who inevitably was manipulated, whipsawed, hoodwinked, or otherwise victimized by his own ignorance into losing money. After sampling any number of Wall Street books, you'd swear there's been a steady improvement in investor sophistication since the middle of the nineteenth century.

In *The Art of Investing,* written in 1888 by a New York broker named Hume, the author describes "rascally transactions," "wild speculations," "a game reserved for habitual gamblers," "disgraceful stories," and "numberless deceptions" rampant in the 1870s, but which the canny public in the 1880s could easily see through. In May 1921, the brand new *Barron's* magazine congratulated Wall Street on its respectable, aboveboard dealings, as opposed to the disgraceful old days of "Gould houses, Vanderbilt houses, Tammany houses." In the 1930s, Wall Street once again became a respectable place to invest, as the SEC reformed the industry and many reprehensible practices were abolished for the first time.

Throughout the 1950s and into the 1960s, there were continuous published references to how well informed and highly sophisticated the investing public had become. Thanks to the brokerage reports, popular magazines, and technical help available to the smallest shareholder, the Thundering Herd was deemed unlikely to fall for rumors, rank speculations, or silly stories. The same improvements were noted in the 1970s and again in 1980s, when the home computer finally put the average investor on equal footing with the professional. I took all this to be good news.

Meanwhile, there had been some remarkable changes in what makes a reputable holding—i.e., an investment instead of a gamble. This was of particular interest to me, since I'd always assumed that common stocks were reputable. I was surprised to find out that the common stocks once had the same crapshoot reputation as the penny stocks or the futures and options of today. In the 1920s, the investing public—then called "the widows and orphans"—was discouraged from buying any stock at all. *Barron's* published a "Widows and Orphans Model Portfolio" made up almost entirely of bonds. "Investing a Deceased Friend's Funds," a how-to article from the May 1917 issue of *World's Work* magazine, recommended bonds alone.

Stocks that paid dividends were slightly more respectable, but the public was warned to avoid both. In its second issue in May 1921, *Barron's* advised that "General Motors common cannot be considered an investment." Rarely did you see a responsible person defending a common stock, especially in the company of the bereaved.

Unfortunately, the year that common stocks finally gained enough respectability to be allowed in the average portfolio was 1929. (A few days before the famous debacle, *Barron's* had speculated that "probably 1929 will be the best business year the country has ever experienced," which raises some doubts about its general reliability, but I've been assured that the staff has turned over several times since then.)

Because of the poor performance of many stocks purchased in 1929, stocks in general quickly lost their newfound good reputation and became unsafe gambles, with 90 percent of the American public continuing to distrust them through the 1930s and the 1940s. Only in the 1950s did common stocks begin a slow climb toward respectability, until today they are again regarded as sober instruments, approved for widows and orphans. Futures and options are today's wild gambles, and I reminded myself not to get involved in those.

As I reviewed all this in the library, I paid special attention to the reports of the Crash. Any serious investor must come to terms with this discouraging event, so as to be better prepared in case it happens again. What a relief to be able to tell you it never really happened in the first place! Actually, the Crash of 1929 was a rather lengthy correction, which explains my references to "so-called Crash" in the paragraphs above.

Perhaps because a few unfortunates jumped out their windows and fell straight to the pavement, we've all been given the impression that the stock market fell straight to the bottom on that same day. The true story is as follows. The market had gone into a steady decline several weeks before the loss on Black Thursday that got everybody so upset. In fact, stock prices had been dropping slowly from a high on the Dow Jones industrials of 381.17 on September 3. The week of October 21 the industrials fell 28.82, a greater drop than the 24.90 that allegedly ruined Wall Street on that tragic October 28, one of several consecutive bad days.

Even after the weeks' well-known difficulties, *Barron's* was sufficiently optimistic to print headlines such as: IS ALLIS CHALMERS ATTRACTIVE AT 56, A READER ASKS? and ARE LARGER DU PONT EARN-INGS LIKELY? By November of that year, the Dow average was down to 273.51. This was a 39 percent loss over two months and undeniably a memorable decline. What we haven't remembered is the end-of-the-year rally, reported in *Barron's* as "The Sensational Rebound in Stocks." By December 30, 1929, the stock market was happily on its way to regaining a third of its losses. Enough confidence was restored that the so-called Crash was knocked off the front page of *Barron's* by a CRISIS IN SOUTH AMERICAN BONDS.

That the Dow Jones averages didn't reach a low point until 1932, three years after the supposedly disastrous date, should be very reassuring to us all. There was plenty of time for the investing public to sell its stocks and suffer a normal setback—a 50 percent loss at the most. And where people had courage to hold on, some of their investments have come back strong, being worth much more today than they were in 1929. This leads me to Useful Tip Number Five:

One man's crash is another man's correction

SEVEN

SOME PRACTICAL ADVICE

MAYBE I'D DRIFTED OFF COURSE. I HADN'T COME TO THE library to study history. I'd come to study how to make money, and the helpful how-to books on the subject took up three aisles. I flipped through these books one after another, ignoring specific suggestions to buy this or sell that, trying to concentrate on the general principles of investing. These were the basic rules, learned after decades of painful trial and error, that various experts were kind enough to pass along.

The first book I grabbed was Gerald Loeb's *Battle for Investment Survival*. It was published after the Correction of 1929 and is regularly updated. Mr. Loeb's book is known as the average investor's Bible, and all the more believable since Mr. Loeb is reputed to have made millions in the market himself.

In the late 1960s, I met Mr. Loeb in person and regret that I didn't have the sense to pick his brains back then. That was during the period when some of us didn't yet realize we wanted to get rich, and shunned the friendly help that was often available. Now, 20 years later, I was forced to seek out Mr. Loeb's counsel second-hand in the library. It was a sad situation, but I consoled myself that Mr. Loeb wouldn't have told me anything in private that he hasn't told millions of readers in public.

Mr. Loeb can't overemphasize the importance of making just one investment at a time and then living with it. "The greatest safety lies in putting all your eggs in one basket and then watching the basket," he says. He opens his book with this rule and then devotes many pages to its support, with example after example of irrefutable evidence. According to him, most average investors foolishly try to diversify their holdings and spread their money around. This results in one thing always going down while something else is going up, so the best we can ever do is break even.

Mr. Loeb argues this point so intelligently that by the end of his first chapter I was convinced that diversification was the cause of many of my earlier troubles. I decided right then to sink my entire $16,500 stake into the first profitable opportunity that came along.

That decision lasted as long as it took to put down Mr. Loeb's work and pick up *Money Angles*, written by Andrew Tobias. It is odd to find a new investment book written by a man who earlier wrote *The Only Investment Guide You'll Ever Need*, but Mr. Tobias has a keen mind and should be allowed to change it. On page 23 of *Money Angles* Mr. Tobias offers his ironclad first rule— "buy low, sell high"—which I'd always ignored in favor of the reverse. Then on page 25, he gives an ironclad second rule: "Diversify." "It's remarkable how many of us chickens manage inadvertently to have most of our eggs you know where," writes Mr. Tobias.

This was 180 degrees from Mr. Loeb's position. I might have ignored it, except that Mr. Tobias gives example after example of irrefutable evidence. He tells enough horror stories of stocks and bonds that suffered unexpected mishaps, of companies suddenly gone bankrupt, of investors who lost their life savings on a single bad investment that Mr. Loeb's one-basket theory seemed not only foolhardly, but suicidal. I promised myself then and there that I'd spread my money around in numerous baskets.

After returning *Money Angles* to its hole in the shelf I made a frantic riffle through dozens of other how-to books, searching for the guiding principles offered by other experts of stature equal to Mr. Tobias and Mr. Loeb. To save you the same trouble, I've summarized the results in the following list. It's a comprehensive review of all the time-tested rules of investing from the best minds on Wall Street. For easier reference, I've arranged these in pairs:

1. Be patient, never panic.   2. Be nervous, keep a close watch.

3. Be flexible, change courses quickly.

4. Be steadfast, keep a steady course, have faith in your ideas.

5. Never sell too soon.

6. It's never too soon to sell.

7. Let your profits run.

8. Cut your losses, and take profits as soon as you can.

9. Invest for the long term, the short term is unpredictable.

10. Invest for the short term, the long term is unpredictable. "Short term trading is the safest form of speculation that exists" says Mr. Loeb. "In the long term we'll all be dead," says Mr. Keynes. That's John Maynard Keynes, famous economist and short-term speculator, who in the long term has proven his point.

11. Never risk what you can't afford to lose.

12. A big risk is the key to a big gain. Play for meaningful stakes.

13. Buy when the experts are optimistic.

14. "Sell when the experts are optimistic." This latter from Benjamin Graham, author of *The Intelligent Investor*.

15. Buy when prices are low and there's nowhere to go but up.

16. Buy when prices are high; things will continue to go up.

17. Set specific investment goals.

18. Don't limit yourself to artificial yardsticks.

19. Study as much as you can; the ignorant investor is a sure loser.

20. Study nothing, since a little knowledge is a dangerous thing. "If you merely try to bring a little extra knowl-

edge to bear upon your investment program, you may well find that you have done worse." This from Mr. Graham.

21. "If things aren't clear, do nothing"—Mr. Loeb.

22. "Nothing is more suicidal than a rational investment policy in an irrational world." This direct from Mr. Keynes.

No doubt you've come across some or all of the above rules of investing in newspapers and business magazines, where they are frequently repeated, though not always side by side. Reading them one after another, I was struck by the unusual tolerance we have for differences of opinion on matters of money. I tried to think of another subject, art or science, where the guiding principles contradict one another so completely and yet are simultaneously held in equal esteem by the same audience. Only in diet and health-food books is there anything remotely similar. Buyers of diet books can tolerate one contradictory scientific theory after another while failing to lose weight, and perhaps the same can be said for consumers of investment advice who have yet to see a profit.

Was there not a single principle on which the Wall Street experts could agree in print? Actually, I found only one: the average investor is always wrong. It was surprising to see this so openly admitted in the very books that offer us their help! Mr. Tobias, for instance, hardly waits a single page to announce that most people are the last ones in on a stock deal, and it's the 95 percent that enrich the other five, and so on. Then in the 200 pages that follow, he advises us 95-percenters how to go out and buy stocks! In between giving his suggestions, Mr. Loeb takes time out to declare the average investor a hopeless case. He even recommends his favorite book—*Extraordinary Popular Delusions and the Madness of Crowds*, written by MacKay in 1841—as proof that the masses are eternally misguided. In the introduction to an investment system he is trying to popularize, Benjamin Graham blurts out: "The advent of popularity marks the exact moment when a system ceases to work well."

There are numerous other examples, but it's no use wasting more space on them. I was struck by the inevitable futility of reading further, since all investment advisers want to write best-sellers, yet popularity, by definition, dooms their advice. If I'd realized this earlier, I wouldn't have camped out in the stacks.

Who, then, was an average investor to believe? As I was beginning to despair of finding an answer, I saw a newsletter called *Street Smart Investing,* in which the publisher, a Mr. Kiril Socoloff, suggests a sure way to make money from best-selling investment books: take the advice and do the opposite! He tested his theory back through the entire twentieth century and came up with the following, which is all according to him:

In the early 1920s, Edgar Lawrence Smith wrote a book called *Common Stocks as Long-Term Investments.* This book was ignored during the entire period when it would have been a good idea to buy stocks. Suddenly it became a best-seller in 1929. That's the same year the experts advanced the popular Blue Chip Theory, which said that the stock-market advance would be limitless, and that there was no such thing as a downside.

During the entire period from 1932 to 1967, which was generally a terrific time to buy stocks, not a single investment book became a best-seller. There wasn't a stock-market best-seller until Adam Smith's *Money Game* was published in 1968, after which the stock market promptly topped out and collapsed. In 1974, Harry Browne's *You Can Profit from a Monetary Crisis* turned half the reading public into gold hoarders, and was followed by a severe decline in the price of gold. Gold didn't rise again until there were no gold books on the best-seller list and the public was bored with the subject. Then it hit $800 a ounce.

In the early 1980s, several national bestsellers (most notably Howard Ruff's *How to Prosper During the Coming Bad Years*) predicted high inflation forever and offered the readership some intelligent countermeasures to protect their wealth. This, according to Mr. Socoloff, was a sure sign that inflation had abated, and the countermeasures (buying gold, silver, natural resources) would be highly unprofitable. Later in the decade, Jerome Smith's wildly popular book *The Coming Currency Collapse*, a terrifying rationale for the total collapse of the U.S. dollar, sold out several editions just as the dollar began its remarkable three-year bull market.

Megatrends, a summer favorite in 1983, predicted the triumph of high technology and pronounced the smokestack industries dead. Along with its extraordinary popular acceptance came a genuine depression in the microchip and computer industries and a huge drop in the value of technology stocks, while smokestack industries revived.

Now I was onto a tactic that seemed foolproof. Since I counted myself as an average investor, I'd simply do the opposite of anything that struck me as profitable. This idea was so exciting that I thanked Mr. Socolow under my breath, and then jotted down Useful Tip Number Six:

If you think it's right, then it's wrong—and vice versa

As quickly as possible, I quit the library for my own bedroom, where I spent several days watching the Financial News Network on television. With great concentration, I waited to be persuaded of something so I could do just the opposite. With the continuous ticker tape running across the bottom of this channel, the flow of symbols put me into the usual semihypnotic state and heightened my susceptibility to suggestion. Soon, a man from a Colorado investment service said we were going back into a deflationary period. Since I was absolutely convinced he was right, I leapt up and went looking for my wife, to tell her that the country was going into an inflationary period and we should invest in gold, natural resources, and other hard assets.

I returned to the television, where a half hour later an MIT economist said we really were going into an inflationary period, that we'd soon be in a credit crunch and the government would have to inflate its way out of debt. To me this could only mean one thing: deflation. I cornered my wife again, to inform her I'd changed my mind. Since hard assets were losing propositions, I'd decided to put my money into paper assets such as bonds. I also suggested that we sell our house and rent instead.

In these intense few days, I was convinced to buy gold because I heard it was going down, to sell gold because it was going up, to invest in a stock market poised for a 10 percent decline, to get out of a stock market poised for a 10 percent advance, to resist junk bonds due to their exceeding popularity, to buy Federal Express shares due to their recent unpopularity, to switch into European currencies because Europe was losing credibility, and especially to buy sugar, since I'd learned the price was collapsing.

Doing the opposite of what you really think is not easy. About a week after I'd congratulated myself on having stumbled onto the Contrarian approach to investing, I heard on the same FNN channel that Contrarianism was getting very popular. In fact, Contrarianism had become a preferred strategy with the general public. An advisor named Treadway came on the screen to announce that Contrarianism was so rampant that the true Contrarian was no longer a Contrarian. Mr. Treadway said he'd stopped being contrary himself just to avoid the Contrarianism of the crowd.

That meant that to be truly contrary, I'd have to contradict my Contrarianism—in other words, buy gold if I thought gold was going up or avoid bonds if I thought bonds were going down. By now, I was completely confused, and I hadn't bought a thing. Here I'd rejected financial planning in favor of my own research, and my own research had left me logically paralyzed. Meanwhile, the money was still sitting in the savings-and-loan, gathering its paltry interest. I decided that I needed help, and I could get it from a familiar source: the local stockbroker.

EIGHT

SHOPPING FOR THE BROKER

I'VE HAD SEVERAL PREVIOUS BROKERS. IN FACT, THE GENERAL turnover rate between me and the brokers is at least as high as the turnover rate in the presidential palaces of Latin American countries. In both the Latin American countries and in investing, the feeling that things could improve has been kept alive by the constant comings and goings of authorities who promise better times, only to fail and get ousted—to be replaced by new authorities.

My next-to-last broker, whose name I would like to forget, came highly recommended by a friend of mine. At first, I liked this broker much better than the preceding one, my brother-in-law's broker, who was likable herself until the failure of Ramada Inns to get the casino license. My next-to-last broker continued to be likable until the fall of Sykes Datatronics and Anacomp. During the incredible bull market in the summer of 1982, he stayed on vacation in the Vermont woods and returned to work just in time to get us in at the top. From there, the spousal assets drifted down for many months.

Toward the end of 1983 this broker said 1984 would be a good year for the first half but the second half would be very risky. Halfway through 1984 nothing good had happened and remembering his words I asked him what was going wrong. "I got it backwards," he said. "The first half was the bad part and the second half will be terrific." At the end of the year neither half had been terrific, at least not for us. Again under questioning, the broker explained it was hard to figure the market with so many investors using telephone services to switch their money in and out of mutual funds.

I always had trouble expressing my displeasure to any of my brokers. I could yell at a clerk who shortchanged me a quarter or a repairman who padded the bill for a few extra dollars, but the broker who'd lost me hundreds I was reluctant to confront, as if it were my fault the stocks went down. This next-to-last broker I dreaded even calling. The more stocks faltered, the more I'd get clammy hands and a lump in my throat, and tremble at the thought of facing him on the telephone. Facing him in person was almost unthinkable. No love affair can have more neurotic complications than the relationship between a client and his broker, and this should be explored by psychologists. It took months before I had the courage to break up.

That was in 1985. What I thought I needed, of course, was a new broker. By then there were 70,000 of them at work in the nation, or double the number from the last time I'd been forced to look. In my neighborhood, whatever failed computer stores and hair salons hadn't been replaced by banks were replaced by Paine Webbers or Merrill Lynches. It had become easier to get advice on a stock at any hour of the day or night than it was to get a pizza.

The increase in brokers, which far exceeded any increase in the population as a whole, meant one of two things. Either there were millions of new investors, or else a lot of old investors were looking around for better advice. From my own experience, I suspected the latter.

In the past, my wife and I had chosen our various brokers as follows. At a party, we'd run into friends who'd be bragging about the money they'd made in the stock market, and we'd get the name of their broker. The next business day, we'd drive to the Dean Witter or whatever firm their broker represented, to tell him or her the sad stories of our previous brokers and how we deserved better. The new broker would nod sympathetically. After a 15-minute chat, we'd hand over all our money.

That's the truth, and I doubt it's unusual. Friends of ours who wouldn't risk two dollars at a racetrack hand over their inheritance to strangers at Smith Barney. People who spend a week choosing a furniture refinisher will sign up with the first E. F. Hutton broker who calls. People who circle junkyards looking for a matching hubcap will buy mutual funds without opening the prospectus. People who check the expiration date on cottage cheese wouldn't think of investigating the background of their broker. They know next to nothing about whether the broker has made or lost money for clients, whether he's been reprimanded or sued, or how long he's been in the investment business.

People who save the little warranties on their toaster ovens throw away the annual reports of companies in which they've entrusted their life savings. People who would never reveal their net worth to friends, relatives, or psychiatrists routinely tell all to any stockbroker, even during the introductory chat.

The way these brokers are generally chosen has nothing to do with stupidity. It has to do with the numbing effect of assets on the brain. The very thought of investing money often works like an anesthetic, and all critical faculties automatically shut down.

Our latest family broker was Richard Bermont of Drexel Burnham Lambert. As usual, Mr. Bermont was highly recommended by an acquaintance who'd done very well in the stock market. My wife and I visited him in his office on the top floor of a modern high-rise—above several layers of corporate lawyers where the long-term view was excellent. We noticed that Mr. Bermont was short, balding, and partial to monogrammed shirts. He sat enraptured, pecking at his electronic rune stone, looking out across a harbor and speaking between long pauses for oracular effect.

After a short exchange of pleasantries, we decided to hand over all our money, or whatever was left of the spousal assets. The reasons were twofold: (1) we'd never had a Drexel account— though we'd been through Paine Webber, Spear Leeds, Shearson Lehman, and Prescott, Ball and Turben; and (2) Mr. Bermont seemed nice.

Before we'd memorized Mr. Bermont's name, he had the list of all our holdings, plus a signed authority to transfer them from our previous broker's account. That night, we worried that Mr. Bermont would run off to Bimini with these funds. I'd had similar worries before, so I recognized the syndrome. After every change of broker, we'd lie awake wondering if the new one would reinvest the money or abscond with it. This proves how little we knew about any of them.

Though we'd been with Mr. Bermont only a few months before I began preparing for this journey, he'd done a fairly good job investing for my wife. In fact, he'd made her some money. Perhaps I should explain why I didn't mention this earlier. To me, it was an extraordinary aberration, and so I dismissed it as freak behavior. By now, I had little to do with the remains of her portfolio.

It would have been simple—and perhaps wise—to have transferred my own capital, plus accrued interest, into a new account at Drexel and to have worked with Mr. Bermont on this project for the rest of the way. But that seemed too easy. Besides, I was determined to make a careful and well-informed choice of my personal broker—which is not the way we'd engaged him.

I never mentioned any of this to Mr. Bermont, and I hoped the news of my searching around for yet another broker would never get back to him. As quietly as possible, I made the local rounds.

My first stop was the local Thomson McKinnon, where the front door opened into a small amphitheater. An audience of senior citizens stared skyward, moving their heads in unison as if following a slow-moving skeet. Instead, they were watching a ticker tape with huge electronic letters. As various stock symbols passed by, I heard one man mutter, "Look at that IBM. I used to own it, but then my wife said, 'Let's get rid of it, it isn't going nowhere,' so I get rid of it and it splits and splits and goes to $150." Then I heard another say: "Schlumberger? Down to $40? I fell in love with that stock back in the '70s, when I should have kicked it out." This was an average investor's *This Is Your Life,* which continues day after day. I wished I'd had more time to sit down and watch the old-timers review their existence, as each SB, KO, or XON seemed to bring back memories.

At the side of the theater sat a secretary. I asked her if I could see someone in charge. "That would be our broker of the day," she said. She explained that the broker of the day is the person who gets all the walk-in business.

I was ushered back through carpeted hives where 30 or more brokers were separated by the semiprivacy of half-walls. A cirrus of cigar smoke rose above them. The secretary deposited me at the edge of the rearmost cubicle, and a young man motioned me into an empty swivel chair. He was swiveling himself while talking on the phone. Something was off five-eighths, which apparently was all right, because I heard him say, "People took some profits, so she jumped down, but there's support there, you're still in the right direction."

As I swiveled in rhythm with his swivels, waiting for him to hang up, my eyes wandered to a telephone Rolodex opened to a little reminder that said, CONFIDENTIAL. SPEAK SLOWLY, CLEARLY AND BE COURTEOUS. CONFIDENCE IS 50 PERCENT OF THE SALE." Suddenly he wheeled around, winked, put his hand on my knee, and introduced himself as Bryan Nemerov all in a continuous swoop. He looked 25, a little bowling ball of a man with a mustache. In a breathless staccato, he explained he'd been a stockbroker for several months, having drifted over from men's wear and before that women's wear. A certificate from his broker's course, the Thomson Mc-Kinnon Total Money Management Program, was visible on his half-wall.

We were interrupted by several other phone calls from clients, including two from his aunt, who was worried about Twistee Treat. "Don't worry," he said, "a good long-term hold. Did you read the paper this morning? Dick Davis mentioned TT in his column." Another snippet I heard was, "Six and a quarter already? That's moving! I'm glad you're in there."

When I finally got to ask Mr. Nemerov what he'd done to recommend himself, he said nothing about stocks, bonds, or any clients who'd made money on his advice. Instead he opened his desk drawer to show me a commendation he'd received for attracting the most new IRA accounts to his firm. I probed further for his investment ideas. He said he got most of them from *Forbes* and a couple of other business magazines. The search for new clients, he lamented, left him little time to think about investments.

Exaggerating a bit to enhance my importance, I told him I had about $50,000 to invest. He wondered if I was "growth oriented." I assured him I definitely was "growth-oriented," if by "growth" he meant "profit." He said he did. Then he asked if I was "short-term" or "long-term." Perhaps because I gave no clue as to which I might prefer, Mr. Nemerov said he was both.

"You're growth-oriented," he continued. "I like that. I'd probably put $10,000 of your funds in government securities, a solid foundation if all hell breaks loose. Don't get me wrong. If you say 'hell with safety,' we'll do something else. I'd also buy you some common stocks, growth mutual funds, real estate limited partnerships DEFINITELY. That's the best of both worlds."

I asked what he meant by both worlds. "Income and appreciation," he said. "Look at your house. If I said I'd buy it, would you sell it to me now for what it was worth four years ago?" I told him I would be happy to do that right away, since real estate values had gone down in my neighborhood. Mr. Nemerov was momentarily flustered but quickly recovered. "Just my point," he retorted. "With a real estate partnership you get income and so forth while the investment has more time to appreciate. A growth-oriented person like you would appreciate the appreciation."

During most of our talk, Mr. Nemerov gave me about a third of his attention. Another third was absorbed by the phone, and the final third directed at the computer screen suspended on a gooseneck halfway between two cubicles. Every few seconds, he'd spin the screen around to peer at a list of stock prices, and the adjacent broker would spin it back in the other direction.

After one of their tugs-of-war, the man in the next cubicle leaned over and introduced himself as Rick. Mr. Nemerov said Rick was very short-term and the two of them could go partners with me if I decided to work in that direction. "Two for the price of one," he said. I smiled, which must have made Mr. Nemerov think he was on the right track, because then he pronounced, "Out of your $50,000, we should definitely hold back a few thousand so we're ready to jump in if Rick comes up with something."

Rick, who'd gone into a new frenzy of goosenecking, announced over the half-wall that he'd come up with something already. How would I like to buy some Texaco, then selling for $30 a share, for $27 a share instead? I said I doubted that was possible, and suspected some kind of trick. Rick said it wasn't a trick. All I had to do was buy the stock and sell some put options at the same time. I told Rick I'd already had experience with options, especially the IBM October put and the June call.

"Options!" gushed Mr. Nemerov. "I'd like to see you in some covered calls. That's not so risky. We can negotiate the commissions, too. Twenty percent off. Not on everything but on some things. On the options, definitely."

Seeing no point in continuing this conversation, since I'd vowed never again to play with options, I got up from my swivel chair and prepared to leave. That two other people were waiting to see the broker of the day made it easier to get away. I could tell that Mr. Nemerov saw the couple out of the corner of his eye. "Come back anytime," he said, escorting me toward the door. "Feel free to call back and ask questions." With that, we shook hands and I left.

From Thomson McKinnon, I headed out to Sears. Halfway between the perfumes and the vacuum cleaners was the Dean Witter counter. Here I found a broker named Ralph. He, too, looked 25, and I think he wore a suit that came from the store. Like Mr. Nemerov, Ralph mentioned he'd been in the business a few weeks, but the big difference was his humility. He said he didn't feel qualified to recommend individual stocks, and would only go so far as to suggest the Ginnie Mae Fund for income and the Dean Witter Dividend Growth mutual fund for capital appreciation, with lower sales charges the longer you hold on to it.

I asked Ralph to check on the current price of Texaco on the Quotron machine behind the counter. After struggling with the keyboard for several minutes, he admitted he hadn't gotten the hang of the Quotron. Then he described the migratory patterns of Dean Witter brokers, which I found fascinating. The newest and greenest among them start out at the airports, selling financial services between flights. If they do well at the airports, they're sent to the Sears stores to learn a bit more, and only after they've succeeded at Sears are they finally assigned to regular Dean Witter offices. Ralph gets the credit for my Seventh Useful Tip:

Never buy anything from a broker at an airport

Although I admired Ralph for his humility and for his caution, I could see that neither would get him very far in this business, and I crossed him off my list immediately. Meanwhile, Ralph must have sensed what I'd been thinking because he underwent a remarkable transformation. By 8:00 P.M. that same night, he called me at home with a stock he suddenly felt qualified to recommend. "Special situation," he said. "Zayre's at $27." As of this writing, Zayre's had split twice and had risen to the equivalent of $44 a share. I'm sorry I didn't listen to him.

From Sears I spread out across town, visiting as many other brokers as I could in two days. At one Merrill Lynch, I was threaded through the cubicles and introduced to Jim Clayton, a middle-aged athletic type who'd been in the market for 20 years. He advised against buying most stocks, since he doubted the prices could go much higher. For a client like me, he said he'd recommend a Nuveen bond fund, some overseas funds, or a few utilities that paid good dividends.

I'd begun to think it's a rare stockbroker who recommends a stock these days. On my visits, most preferred to sell what they called "products"—either mutual funds, limited partnerships, or real estate trusts. Several times, I was handed expensive, full-color brochures that explained these complex investments. These brochures were as thick as college catalogs, and in some cases must have cost more to print than an average share in the product was worth.

Among the products brought to my attention was a "leveraged real estate rental-property partnership"; an energy income partnership; a partnership in the Lorimar film company introduced at the screening of a new Lorimar film, *Power;* an Australian bond fund; and a "preferred futures fund." A common element in these diverse opportunities was the substantial sales charge, often as high as 7 percent. I didn't do a national survey, but my own experience gives me confidence in Useful Tip Number Eight:

The first thing the broker recommends will make him the highest commission

From Merrill Lynch I wandered into the nearest Paine Webber and visited their broker of the day, Bob Klein. He wore an expensive-looking shirt and tasteful but expensive-looking jewelry, and could have been mistaken for a high-class lawyer.

Mr. Klein was so serious about the responsibilities of investing that I began to think he was a recruiter for the Peace Corps. Right away, he discouraged me from buying individual stocks and handed me two or three thick brochures that described his favorite products. One was a real estate limited partnership in which I'd be part owner of the Carlyle, a famous New York hotel whose rooms I could never afford. Mr. Klein read aloud from the list of the general partners, and it sounded like I'd be involved with some impressive co-owners. As flattered as I was, I wondered why these people would want to cut me in on their great deal.

There seemed to be a style of broker to suit every kind of client—lawyerly brokers for lawyers, snobbish brokers for snobs, bon-vivant brokers for bon vivants, gambler brokers for gamblers. There are brokers who talk like cab drivers and brokers who talk like college deans, brokers who dress like Mafiosi and brokers who dress like fashion models, brokers to mimic the appearance, speech, or personality of any conceivable customer, the mirror image of every station in life.

I began to wonder if it was better to choose a broker whose clothing matched mine, or one with whom I clashed. I would have preferred to choose a broker on more serious grounds, such as investment philosophy, but that seemed impossible. All the brokers I'd met were able to change attitudes, and even to switch basic investment philosophies, during the short space of an interview. I'd first seen this in Mr. Nemerov, who'd gone from the solid foundation of Treasury bills to selling me options in less than a half hour. A similar turnabout occured at a second Merrill Lynch office, where I'd headed after leaving Mr. Klein.

This Merrill Lynch office was surrounded by angry stewardesses, protesting some sort of banking arrangement between Merrill Lynch and Eastern Airlines. I snuck my way past the picket signs, thinking that this was a good example of the trouble that results when brokerage firms get into banking.

Once safely inside the building, I approached the front desk and asked for the broker of the day. A man loitering at the entrance overheard me, handed me his card, and volunteered his services. His name was Michael Todd, but he said to call him "Mickey."

As we headed toward Mickey's cubicle, I told him I was a very conservative investor, which is actually how I felt after having just visited Mr. Klein. Mickey applauded my conservatism and said something like, "There's no reason to throw away what you've worked so hard to earn."

After he sat me in the guest chair next to his desk, I expressed a sudden interest in options, just to see how Mickey would respond. Soon he was telling me about his new red Porsche and his decision to take more chances and live for today. Then he told me about a client of his who'd made a fortune in options, most recently in the Warner-Lambert July calls. He punched in the symbols for Warner-Lambert and the up-to-date call-option prices appeared on the screen above our heads. "Options can be amazingly profitable if you know what you are doing," he said. "You have to be disciplined and not greedy. Plus you have to follow good research. At Merrill Lynch, we've got the best."

Though Mickey drew the line at commodities—"only fools would play commodities"—he sensed I'd do very well in options and that I had just the right personality for the job. I returned the compliment by guessing he'd do very well investing in options himself. "Me?" he laughed. "A broker? In this office, all the brokers have been killed playing options. Brokers don't make money on options. Brokers don't make money on any investments. Here, we even lose money on stocks."

Thanks to Mr. Todd's candor, I can pass along Useful Tip Number Nine:

Never invest in anything owned by your broker

After several days of walking in and out of offices and being no closer to finding the perfect broker than I'd been at the start, I pretty much decided to return to Richard Bermont, the Drexel Burnham man who'd been working with my wife. Certainly, I'd never even considered Linda Garrett of Prudential-Bache. The only reason I visited Ms. Garrett at her office was to ask her how she liked her new job. She'd been a secretary to an earlier broker of ours and had answered many of my frantic phone calls. Recently, she'd graduated from broker's school and had become a full-fledged stockbroker herself.

Most of her colleagues were stuck out in the middle of a big open room, but they'd given Ms. Garrett a private office along the wall. That impressed me. Also, she didn't used to dress this well. As a secretary, she looked like she worked for the Clamshell Alliance, but now she would have fit in at the Republican National Committee.

I'm mentioning these factors because I don't know which may have contributed to the surprising decision that followed. As the two of us sat in Ms. Garrett's private office, I could see the stocks displayed on her Quotron, rising in value by the second. These were her own picks, she said. One called Genentech went up two points as I shifted my weight in the chair. Ms. Garrett mentioned she'd been buying Genentech for several clients. A happy phone call from one of the clients interrupted our conversation.

There was a second, longer phone call from Philadelphia. I heard only Ms. Garrett's side of it, which I remember as: "over-the-counter," "chemical field," "maybe in line for government contracts," "likely to double by Christmas," and "if this works out, I'll buy you an ice cream."

"What works out?" I demanded to know, after she'd hung up. Ms. Garrett explained it was just some little stock she was buying for herself and close friends, wouldn't be suitable for regular clients, too speculative. She said she didn't really want to sell it to me. After all I'd been through, that alone was enough to insure my interest.

"How much is it?" I asked.

"About $1.50 per share last time I looked."

"What's this about it doubling by Christmas?" (It was December 12 at the time, and I'd been studying, researching, and investigating for nearly two months.)

"I don't know. He thinks it might."

"Who thinks so?"

"The person I was talking to."

She'd only tell me that her source was a knowledgeable investor, the one who'd get the ice cream if this recommendation worked out. How fortunate I felt to have intercepted this private gossip between two people in the know, the kind of chance an average investor rarely gets.

"Did you buy some for yourself?"

"Yes," said Ms. Garrett. "So did everybody else in the office."

Was this the opportunity I'd been looking for? A voice from within me that I couldn't control blurted out: "I'll take 5,000 shares." Within minutes, my new Prudential-Bache account was opened, the 5,000-share order was sent in, and I was standing outside in the parking lot. Only then did I realize that: (1) I'd just chosen my new broker by default, (2) I'd ignored my own Tip Number Seven, and (3) 5,000 shares times $1.50 added up to nearly two-thirds of my investment stake. This putting most of my eggs in one basket made me think of Mr. Loeb.

Down the highway I stopped in a phone booth to call my wife and explain what I'd bought. As I was dialing, I realized I'd forgotten the name of the company, so I hung up before she could answer.

NINE

BUYER'S REMORSE
AND OTHER SIDE EFFECTS

I HAD SEVERAL CURIOUS REACTIONS TO BUYING MY STOCK, AND these I feel obligated to mention, on the off chance they are commonplace and should be brought out into the open. The first, as I've said, is this business of forgetting what I'd just bought. After any large purchase, such as a car or house, there's a customary period of remorse when the purchaser says to himself, *Oh, my God, what have I just bought?* What makes this case different is that the question was literal. While still in the phone booth on the side of the highway, I had to call back Ms. Garrett and ask her the name of the company so I could tell my wife at home.

This embarrassment could have been avoided if I'd written down the name in the first place. That I advise everyone to do. Luckily, Ms. Garrett was very nice about it, laughed, and said I'd bought Angstrom Technologies, symbol ATSI, a small scientific company in Kentucky. She also mentioned that my order already had been executed, and the price "we paid for it" was a bit higher than she'd anticipated—$1^{15}/_{16}$, or nearly two dollars a share. My total outlay was more than $10,000, or $10,143.15 to be exact. She asked me to put a check for that amount in the mail.

For several days after I'd sent the check, I continued to forget the name of the stock every time I tried to think of it. Since I'm known to have a good memory and since "angstrom" is a common symbol in science, I must have suffered a minor attack of the average investor's amnesia discussed earlier, brought on by the trauma of spending $10,000 on the stock.

The afternoon I returned home, expecting to inform my wife of my $10,000 interest in a small Kentucky company, I had a second curious reaction. Instead of recounting the event factually, I found myself substituting the word *promising* for *small,* and *$8,000* for the actual $10,143.15. That I couldn't face the full amount is understandable in hindsight. After all those weeks of careful research, the plunking down of $10,143.15 for an unknown company with an unknown product as recommended by a unknown advisor from Philadelphia was more than this sensible person could bear. For some reason, the plunking down of $8,000 was acceptable to my subconscious, and dropping $2,143.15 from the story enabled me to tell it.

When I received the confirmation of my purchase in the mail, I was shocked that $453.80 had gone for the commission. That this $453.80 disturbed me even more than the $10,143.15 purchase itself was a third curious reaction. Then again, I'd watched Ms. Garrett put through the order, which took five seconds or so at her end and amounted to her writing down the letters *ATSI* on a piece of paper and walking the paper to the order desk. Perhaps it's a mistake to let customers witness this process and then send them the bill for it so soon.

After learning of the $453.80, I called up Ms. Garrett again and brought up the subject of commissions as tactfully as possible. "This couldn't be right, could it?" I asked her. She patiently explained that: (1) she personally gets only a percentage of the percentage, (2) brokerage firms charge higher commissions for over-the-counter-stocks, such as Angstrom, than for stocks listed on the New York Stock Exchange, and (3) she'd gotten me the Prudential-Bache preferential rate even though I was a new customer and technically wasn't entitled to it.

This speech shut me up immediately. Her point 3 made me feel guilty that I'd mentioned anything at all, and I tried to repair the damage to our relationship by voluntarily declaring, "if a person has to worry about commissions, then he shouldn't be buying stocks in the first place." She seemed to agree with this.

If I'd learned anything from this experience, it is my Useful Tip Number Ten:

Never buy a stock whose name you forget without considering the commission

---

The next thing I realized was that Angstrom Technologies couldn't be followed in the newspaper. That my company was too tenuous an enterprise for its stock price to appear in those long columns in the local business pages was deeply disturbing, and something I didn't want my wife to know. This inspired another phone call to Ms. Garrett. She said Angstrom might be found in the *Wall Street Journal* on certain days, and she was sure it was covered in the weekly *Barron's*.

After making a huge outlay for the stock, I refused to pay the $1.75 a copy for the *Barron's* on the grounds that $1.75 was an extravagance. One Sunday, I told my wife I was going out to pick up some orange juice. This was only an excuse to drive to a local grocery/newsstand and to thumb through the latest *Barron's* there. After thumbing for 20 minutes, I finally located Angstrom in a so-called Supplemental List of over-the-counter stocks. Two Sundays in a row, I went out for orange juice, and came back knowing the weekly closing price of my stock.

These were happy trips, since Angstrom was on a remarkable upward flight. I bought the stock on December 12, and three weeks later, just past Christmas, it had risen beyond 2½ a share, making my $10,143 into $12,965. This $2,500 was the easiest profit I'd ever made. The gain had been so quick that if the trend continued, I figured I'd be rich in six months. I even bought my family some nice Christmas presents, beyond my normal miserly offerings.

By now my family knew of my wonderful run of luck, and I got us all a subscription to *Barron's*, so we could enjoy looking up Angstrom at home together.

Did I say *luck*? At first I felt lucky, but only momentarily. Mostly, I felt skillful. My confidence in my investing ability soared with each uptick. That Angstrom was a winner, I told myself, had never been in doubt. Wasn't this a tangible proof that my cautious approach, all those hours of study in the library, had paid off? Surely it took a talented investor to cull through the duller opportunities, to sense the potential in this stock, and to jump courageously into full commitment—$10,000 worth of eggs in one basket—at just the right moment. I also congratulated myself on holding out for Linda Garrett, who among dozens of potential stockbrokers had proven superior in every respect. My quibble with the commission was forgotten, and I began to think Ms. Garrett and Prudential-Bache both had been underpaid.

Ms. Garrett said she'd be calling me with good news as well as bad, but I noticed we talked most often during this Angstrom surge, which started in December and continued into January. Though the stock had not yet reached the four-dollar level she'd predicted, my spirits were buoyed by her frequent mention of "an announcement of a big government contract" soon to come. She also sent me a copy of what may have been the one newspaper article written about the company: "Chemicals Key to Low-Cost Vision," which had appeared in *Automotive News*.

This article made me more confident than ever about Angstrom's prospects. From it, I learned that the company made chemical paints, visible under special light, something like the hand stamps used at racetracks and discotheques. Apparently, Angstrom's paint had attracted the attention of major tire companies, the U.S. Post Office, and dressmakers in Hong Kong. That Angstrom was expanding its markets without a sales department impressed me particularly.

Plus the fact I was at the laundromat one day and a copy of the *Wall Street Journal* had blown off a table, leaving a loose page with the word *Angstrom* staring me straight in the face. I'm not a superstitious person when it comes to investments. I've heard of people who tap the newspaper a certain number of times before turning to the stock tables, or who close their eyes and take furtive peeks at the daily quotations as if they've seen a train wreck, but I think they're silly. I'd be the first to agree that how you read a stock price has no effect on the actual ups and downs. But when the great U.S. financial journal spread open by itself on the laundromat bench below the soap dispenser, leaving "Angstrom, $2\frac{1}{2}$ bid, $2\frac{5}{8}$ ask" in plain view, it had to be a glorious omen. Four dollars per share seemed a certainty.

If only I could have shared my joy with Richard Bermont of Drexel Burnham Lambert—the man who in my private thoughts had become "the other broker." I still hadn't told him I'd opened a separate account and was dallying with a competitor. Sneaking around has become common investor practice. I'm told that thousands of clients at regular firms satisfy their wilder impulses with the discount brokers. Some of them actually stoop so low as to take Merrill Lynch advice, and then buy the recommended stock at Charles Schwab, where they pay less commission. At least I couldn't be accused of that cheap trick. I'd gone off with another high-class house, and every bit as expensive as Drexel. Still, like a cheating husband, I was deprived of the pleasure of bragging about my success with the one person who could best appreciate the improvement.

TEN

HOW THE EXPERTS
PICK THEIR STOCKS

I HELD ANGSTROM INTO THE NEW YEAR, WAITING FOR A BETTER payoff. Meanwhile, I began to interest myself in various stock market newsletters as a possible way of charting my next move. As my chosen stock went up in price, so did my pleasure in reading what other experts had recommended. Several friends showed me their copies of the latest *Zweig Forecast, Market Logic,* and *The Prudent Speculator*. I also saw a sample of the *Dick Davis Digest,* which runs excerpts from all the other newsletters. That there's a newsletter of other newsletters proves how complicated this business has become.

Dick Davis and his helpers edit, print, and mail out a bimonthly twelve-pager from an office in Miami Beach. I went there one day and dropped in on him. He told me that he was an ex-stockbroker who soured on that profession twenty years ago. "I was being unfair pretending I knew all the answers. Why not just admit that I didn't know all the answers?" With that in mind, he became a financial journalist and started one of the earliest and most successful Wall Street television programs. After that, he began to write his syndicated column, and then launched his newsletter of newsletters.

"Even if you try to say something 100 percent truthful about the stock market, it's impossible," he told me. "There's always an exception, a caveat, a contradiction. You can never end the sentence." I sympathized with Mr. Davis and mentioned that I'd only recently learned to be a successful investor after years of having been victimized by exceptions and contradictions. By the end of our chat, he'd invited me to attend an investment conference in Fort Lauderdale, where several prominent newsletter writers—

including Mr. Davis—were scheduled to speak. He even provided me with a free ticket and a press pass.

The conference was held in late January at a Marriott hotel and marina. This hotel was built on the edge of the intracoastal waterway and was surrounded on two sides by cabin cruisers the size of World War II destroyers. On some of these boats, helicopters were strapped to the decks where the rubber dinghies are usually found. Antique furniture and grand pianos were visible through the cabin windows. Gorgeous women in string bikinis tanned themselves on deck, and you could smell the coconut oil halfway down the pier.

A more stimulating environment for a discussion of investments could hardly be found. I remembered Mr. Del Dotto's message from Leonardo da Vinci, "Consider the ends first," and here several were tied up to the dock. I also thought of an exposé on stockbrokers I'd seen in the library: *Where Are the Customers' Yachts?* The author hadn't found any—which was the point of his argument—but these luxurious vessels I could see with my own eyes. After watching a few of the one-sixteenth-dressed, piña-colada-scented deck hands, I promised myself I'd invest in a boat as soon as I could afford it.

(Later, I was disappointed to learn that the yachts parked outside the Marriott were owned by people who had nothing to do with the conference, some of whom may have enriched themselves in a business I'd rather not mention.)

Inside the hotel, down the corridor just beyond the lobby, were 20 or so booths where you could learn about investment opportunities in jojoba beans, cashews, rare coins, diamonds, German windmills, oil-gas leasing, thoroughbreds, the New York futures exchange, rental movie projectors, and preferred rarities, as well as stocks and bonds, plus "free financial analysis," computer trading systems, and more. In the hallway I overheard one exhibitor enlisting recruits for an investor's tour of South Africa, where you'd meet some contented gold miners and see the positive side of apartheid ignored by the media. Another exhibitor was explaining how to depreciate stallions over five years. Another was touting cancer-cure stocks and precious-metal stocks in alternate breaths. "Have you ever tried pistachios—not as a snack, but as the chance of a lifetime?" asked the nut-farm syndicator.

To me, the most interesting person in the exhibit area was Rita Jenrette, the ex-wife of ex-Congressman John Jenrette. The two of them once admitted making love on the Capitol steps, after which he'd been sent to jail in the ABSCAM case while she appeared nude in *Playboy*. To find her sitting in the booth for Bridgewater Securities was a pleasant surprise. She looked a little chubbier than I remembered from the photos, but attractive enough so that the Bridgewater Securities booth never lacked for an audience. While Ms. Jenrette signed copies of her recently published novel, her co-workers explained the advantages of a well-managed portfolio of foreign bonds.

To the side of the booth was a cardboard raffle box, where you could put in a coupon to win a free dinner with Ms. Jenrette. After depositing several chances to show my good will, I introduced myself to her and asked how she came to be interested in foreign bonds. She told me she'd passed her Series 7 exam to become a licensed stockbroker after a friend suggested that career one day after church. She said being a stockbroker was preferable to being married, especially to Mr. Jenrette, who, she said, still had a girlfriend living near Fort Lauderdale. "I'd never ask for alimony," she confided. "That would only give John another chance to manipulate me. It's much better to have financial independence."

A few hours after we'd had our conversation, an emissary from Bridgewater ran up to tell me I'd won the dinner. I was thrilled until I found out that almost everyone who'd put in a coupon had won the dinner, and that Bridgewater had reserved a special dining room to accommodate a large party of men. They'd also planned some special entertainment, which, I think, was a slide show about deutsche mark–denominated debt instruments.

I decided against sharing Ms. Jenrette's company with so many fellow investors and went back to ask her if I could get her views on foreign bonds on a one-to-one basis. She said she worked out of Bridgewater's New York office, and I could call her there.

For four straight afternoons, I attended meetings with hundreds of other conferees. The majority seemed to be retired. We wandered from lecture to lecture, picking up advice on Australian interest rates, the importance of the M-3 money supply relative to industrial production, topping actions, and the advance/decline plurality. Between meetings, I sat and drank rum and cokes while my colleagues read Sidney Sheldon novels on plastic lounge chairs. When asked about their holdings, most were tight-lipped, though several admitted to owning tax-free municipals. I told everybody I met I owned Angstrom.

Whenever possible, we sidled up to the financial celebrities among us, treating them at first with simple respect and later with giddy adoration as the Dow industrials broke through 1558 for the first time. I was excited to see several forecasters and publishers of newsletters whose names and faces I recognized from television. Thanks to the televised financial programs, these once-obscure advisors now reached millions of average investors and sometimes moved entire markets with their predictions. Not long ago, a sell signal from Joseph Granville caused the Dow averages to fall as many points as they had on Black Thursday, 1929, the day of the so-called Crash.

One of my former brokers became a disciple of Mr. Granville's just as Mr. Granville started getting everything wrong, so I was just as glad Mr. Granville wasn't here. Among those who did show up there was Bert "Worry-free Investing" Dohmen-Ramirez, Stan "Don't Be Dow Crazy" Weinstein, Norm "Contrary Opinion" Fosback, Charles "Nobody Knows Where the Market Is Headed" Allmon, Mark "Buy at the Sound of Cannons" Spangler, Robert "10 Percent Correction" Nicholson, Ray "Watch the Falling Dollar" Dalio, Robert "Life Is But a Wave" Prechter, Robert "Elf" Nurock, and Al "Undervalued" Frank. Also, I. W. "Tubby" Burnham, the head of Drexel Burnham Lambert, showed up at lunch to tell everybody it would be a great year for stocks.

Between our meetings and at nightly cocktail parties, we were well supplied with free canapés and pigs-in-the-blanket. After filling my plate, I lurked behind the celebrities and rotated my ears in their direction, to better pick up what they were saying, especially to each other. I overheard Bert Dohmen-Ramirez predict a 2,000 Dow in the coming year; Charles Allmon and Robert Nicholson were worried; Stan Weinstein saw a "choppy near-term"; Norm Fosback was bullish. Ray Dalio told somebody to "watch the cap utilization rate"—whatever that was—and Mark Spangler told somebody else that "all the bad news is out in Hong Kong." Eavesdropping on these experts had the same result as watching them on financial television—the longer I tuned in, the more befuddled I got.

During the formal sessions, the audience wanted to hear hot tips from the speakers, while the speakers preferred to teach their methodology. This reminded me of the adage, "If you give a man a fish, he'll eat today, but if you show him how to fish, he'll eat forever." I regret to report that many of us were looking for a fish, and couldn't have cared less about the fishing lessons. The speakers seemed to understand this, and they deliberately held back their hot tips and best bets—until the end of their lectures. That kept us in our seats.

I was amazed at the forethought and calculation that goes into the picking of stocks. It's gone way beyond just asking the neighbors. In fact, a long-standing doctrinal dispute between two stock-picking camps provoked as much debate as you'd get at any interfaith retreat or ecumenical council. These rival camps are called the Technicians and the Fundamentalists, and both were well represented here. That you shouldn't go near the stock market without choosing sides was one of the few points of universal agreement, and it was news to me. I didn't even know if my stockbroker was Catholic or Jewish.

From what I could gather, the Technicians believe that the best way to foretell the future direction of any market is from the market action itself. Many of them study market action with graphs and charts, so they're also known as Chartists. At the conference, the Chartists could be recognized by the piles of graphs that they'd lug around and hand out to the audience. Those zigzags in the Dow Jones averages that the rest of us take for artwork in the business section, the Chartists study and restudy, to help them predict the next zig or zag.

It doesn't have to be the Dow Jones averages. It could be an individual stock, a pork belly, the interest rates, the Transportation Index, or anything else that can be expressed in wiggles, and a Chartist can interpret it. I saw them do it several times. They'd pull out some graph, take a quick glance at the wavy lines, and say things like: "This one is ready for a breakout to the upside," or "That one is falling below its moving average," or "This head-and-shoulders pattern is a sure sign of disaster."

Without even knowing the name of a company or what it makes, a Chartist can look at a chart and tell you if the stock is in a holding pattern or an accumulation, whether it has made a double top, whether it is being distributed or consolidated, whether it has bottomed out. After talking to various practitioners, I learned there are four stages in a stock cycle: accumulation, markup, distribution (smart money sells to the dumb), and panic liquidation (dumb money gets out at a loss). Give a Chartist any stock chart, and he'll tell in an instant what stage a stock has reached. There are even charts within charts that show when the underlying trend is the reverse of the obvious. This is called "divergence," for which Chartists are always on the lookout.

Reading charts was an ancient practice, and chart-reading for investment purposes is at least two centuries old, although nobody knows who started it. The charting of stocks was a popular practice in America as early as 1840, and stock-chart publishing was a mature industry long before other market research existed. Back when Wall Street was controlled by a few sneaky tycoons—Daniel Drew and Cornelius Vanderbilt, among others—the average investor relied on charts to figure out which stocks were being driven up or down by manipulators.

Now that we've replaced the few sneaky tycoons with "market forces" to explain the ups and downs of Wall Street, charting is more popular than ever. There are charts in every magazine and newspaper, more charts are shown on TV, and every home computer can make its own charts. Lately, there's been a steady gain in Chartist converts, as well as in other categories of Technicians who study investor sentiment, daily trading volume, the ratio of advancing stocks to declining stocks, and other clues.

Among the numerous Chartists and other Technicians billeted at the conference were several celebrities, including Stan Weinstein and especially Robert Prechter, Jr., whom I cornered at poolside. Mr. Prechter was in his early thirties, but a wiggly line had yet to appear on his face. In fact, he looked angelic, and by all reports from his many friends and admirers, he's a delightful character as well. I thought so, too—as soon as he granted me an interview. We sat together at an outdoor table, surrounded by several of his fans.

Mr. Prechter told me he'd graduated from Yale and took the familiar path to Wall Street, though earlier he'd stumbled onto the curious and forgotten research of a man named Elliott. Mr. Elliott had reduced all stock market movements to a series of waves, similar to the light waves in physics. Along the way, he'd also reduced all wars, depressions, plagues, holocausts, conquests, migrations, and the other important events throughout human history to a series of waves. Through this cosmic zigzag, Mr. Elliott could explain everything that happened on our planet back as far as the Assyrians, plus foretell the future from here to Armageddon.

Mr. Prechter was intrigued, and continued to study Mr. Elliott. Though he had no way of proving whether waves had defeated Attila the Hun or Napoleon, he tried to use the wave theory to predict the closing number on the Dow Jones transportation average in a certain week during 1975. To his delight, it worked. Unfortunately, Mr. Elliott had died in 1948, so Mr. Prechter could not go directly to the source for further instruction, but he found a latter-day disciple, A. J. Frost, who taught him the refinements. Mr. Prechter has devoted his life to the waves ever since. He follows the investment markets in a newsletter, *The Elliott Wave Theorist*, which he publishes from his offices in Gainesville, Georgia.

Laugh if you want, but Mr. Prechter's predictions have been frequently prophetic. Of the hundreds of competing publications, his newsletter consistently ranks in the top five in the profitability of advice, according to the *Hulbert Financial Digest*. (Hulbert's *Digest* is a well-known newsletter devoted to rating all the other newsletters, another example of how complicated this business has become.)

I asked Mr. Prechter whether the average investor had much of a chance these days, and he said he doubted it. "If anything, the mass psychology is getting more pronounced. People think that mutual funds will protect them, but in the end, whether they invest for themselves or they do it through a mutual-fund manager isn't going to make much difference." (I reminded myself to investigate the mutual-fund business later.) His advice to me personally was to keep my money in the bank and to work harder at my own job, which he called "investing in yourself."

He'd never heard of Angstrom, but he did show me his latest wave chart on the future of the stock market in general. After all the doubt and confusion, it was a great relief just to be able to see clearly where we stood. We had reached the upside of a third mini-wave of the five-wave stock market cycle. Soon there would be a short downward dip, but Mr. Prechter said it wouldn't last long. After that short dip, the stock market would begin an extraordinary rise, almost straight up to a peak of 3,440 on the Dow Jones industrial average. Then we'd have the terrible decline, worse than the Crash, worse than the 1930s, when stock prices would suffer a complete collapse. I thank Mr. Prechter in advance for this Useful Tip Number 11:

After the Dow hits 3,440, get out

Before I leave the Chartists, honesty compels me to mention the scientific evidence that chart-reading is as useless and unreliable as reading pigeon wings or pig's bladders. This I learned from the rival camp of Fundamentalists. They swore that a famous nineteenth-century French mathematician, Louis Bachelier, already proved without a doubt that no statistical pattern repeats itself except randomly. This Random Walk Hypothesis, as it's called, should have put an end to the Chartists as surely as Pasteur put an end to goblins in the bloodstream, but it hasn't.

A vehement critic of Chartists, who asked to remain anonymous, showed me a book called *The Pitfalls of Speculation*, written in 1906. The author warned against charts as "untrustworthy, absolutely fatuous, and highly dangerous" even back then. Recently, a Yale professor has proved once again that the past zigs in a line have no bearing on the future course. The Chartists continue to dismiss such objections as academic.

The opposing camp of Fundamentalists in residence had a passing tolerance for the Chartists, and the two sides commingled in the buffet lines. Fundamentalists could care less about graphs and wiggles. They concentrate on corporate earnings, the economy, and events in the real world that affect investments.

One Fundamentalist I cornered right away was Al Frank, a massive Zero Mostelian presence in purple pants bunched at the waist with a drawstring. Mr. Frank had a gnomelike face and an appealing diffidence. On television, I'd seen him many times apologizing for himself, saying things like "the market just confuses me." I'd hardly shaken his hand before he apologized for his bad breath. He said he hadn't had time to brush his teeth on the airplane.

I took him aside and invited him to lunch, where he told me his remarkable story. He'd been a professor with a master's degree in American studies, who in the early 1970s began to manage an investment portfolio of a few hundred dollars as a hobby. He found he'd done so well that by late 1977 he put $8,000 into this account, and borrowed another $8,000 on margin, and devoted himself to making it grow. In 1982, he quit his job, and went into the investing business full time.

Contrary to Mr. Prechter's suggestion, Mr. Frank had disinvested in his own career and pinned his future hopes on the few thousand dollars he'd put into stocks. I told him that I'd recently done the same, which made us kindred spirits. The difference was that Mr. Frank's portfolio had grown to $1.2 million to date, which made me sorry I'd invited him to lunch.

Mr. Frank reminded me he'd added a couple of hundred thousand to his account along the way—so it wasn't exactly rags to riches—and also that it took ten years for him to reach the $1.2 million. Still, it was an impressive gain, the kind I'd hope for myself. He told me that halfway through the effort, he began to send out a mimeographed newsletter explaining his methods and tracking his results. He was going to call his newsletter *The Pinch-Penny Speculator, a Fortnightly Epistle on Investing*. Later, he simplified it to *The Prudent Speculator*.

To date, *The Prudent Speculator* had attracted a substantial following: several thousand subscribers at an annual $175 each. Mr. Frank showed me some sample copies. It was the only market letter I'd seen that quoted Robert Byron, or Tacitus, or Kipling. For several years it had ranked in the top five newsletters in the country for profitable advice, according to Hulbert's *Digest*.

As to Mr. Frank's reputation for charm, candor, and humility, you'd get no argument from me. When I congratulated him on his good fortune, he quickly reminded me that good fortunes can change. When I asked if I should subscribe to his newsletter, he cautioned that "picking the right newsletter for all markets is no easier than picking the one right stock." He said many strange and wonderful things, such as "maybe I'm paranoid," "beware the tautology," "I have a curious appreciation for the logically absurd," and "I've never raped anybody."

This latter remark preceded an invitation to visit his room, where he promised to share some Fundamentalist beliefs. I was delighted to accept the invitation. As soon as I settled into the far chair, with Mr. Frank sprawled across the bed, the phone began to ring. It rang incessantly throughout my visit. The magazine interviewers finally had caught up with him, and for that, he of course apologized.

While Mr. Frank was being interviewed, I thumbed through The Book, a thick record of his current holdings, with evaluations of 130 or so companies whose shares he owned. I could see by the dates that many of these shares were purchased years ago. "Buy and hold" was one of his Fundamentalist rules.

Looking through the A's and disappointed not to see Angstrom, I spied Amfesco Industries, the closest thing in spelling. "What does this Amfesco do?" I asked Mr. Frank after he hung up the phone. "Who cares?" he said, bobbing on his bed. "I never remember what half these companies do." According to him, only an amateur would buy shares of Hershey because he liked Hershey bars, or invest in Subaru because he drove a Subaru, or choose any stock because of the company's reputation. This made me feel better about having bought Angstrom before I could remember its name.

Mr. Frank scoffed at Charting, though he admitted to having friends who were Chartists. Instead of wasting his time with wiggly lines, he searched the earnings reports for "undervalued companies," then bought their stock and waited for the companies to become "fully valued." When I asked what this meant in layman's terms, he said, "Find something that sells for 20 cents that you know is worth a dollar. Buy it for 20 cents. Sit back and wait until you get your dollar for it."

"How do you know if something's worth a dollar?" I asked, thinking he'd tell me to take calculus. But according to Mr. Frank, the Fundamentalist approach to picking stocks is simple, and any idiot can learn it. The important numbers— such as earnings, sales, and book value—all can be found in the annual reports that you and I toss into the garbage can. Mr. Frank actually opens these reports. Specifically, he looks for stocks that "sell at ten times earnings or less, with a price-to-sales ratio of about 20 percent, and cheaper than the stated book value per share. Such bargains are hard to find these days, but it's not impossible."

The most important of all Mr. Frank's numbers is the price/earnings ratio, or "P/E." A big advantage of the P/E rating on each stock is that it's published daily in the stock tables of the newspaper. To understand the P/E, Mr. Frank said, first you have to realize that the "earnings" of a company are different from the "dividends." A company may declare no dividends at all on its stock, but if the company earns a lot of money the stock could have a favorable P/E ratio. On the other hand, the company could declare a huge dividend and yet have paltry earnings and an unfavorable P/E ratio. In searching for his stock market bargains, Mr. Frank ignores dividends and concentrates on earnings.

The P/E of any stock is simply the current price of the stock divided by the annual earnings per share. As Mr. Frank explained it, if a stock is selling for $10 a share and the company earns $1 per share during that year, then the P/E ratio is the $10 stock price divided by the $1 earnings, or 10. The more money a company earns relative to the stock price, the lower the P/E. The lower the P/E, the better the bargain. Mr. Frank prefers to buy stocks where the P/Es are 8 or below, but there's no strict rule.

The P/E of any stock can be compared with the P/Es of other similar stocks to help determine which is the best buy. Also, the entire stock market has an overall P/E—a good indication of which way the market as a whole might be headed. When investors are optimistic, the overall P/E is bid up as they pay higher and higher prices for shares. When investors are pessimistic, the P/Es fall so low that nearly every stock is a bargain. That's what happened in 1974. While I was learning to throw a fish net to insure my family a protein supply during the coming economic collapse, Mr. Frank was busily buying thousands of shares of stocks that have tripled, quadrupled, or sextupled in value since.

At the time of our conversation, the overall stock market P/E was hovering around 14, a medium-high range, with a few bargains yet available. Mr. Frank said that in earlier bull markets, such as a famous one in the 1920s, the top wasn't reached until the overall P/E reached a euphoric 30. For that and other reasons, he was convinced the market would go higher, maybe as high as a 3,000 Dow, though he couldn't vouch for Mr. Prechter's 3,440.

Mr. Frank's low-P/E approach is only one branch of Fundamentalism, which no doubt I've oversimplified. Some Fundamentalists I met paid little or no attention to P/E ratios. Some invested in growth stocks, often in new companies with P/Es as high as 80, on the theory that great earnings would pile up later. Some picked stocks for the dividends. Some bought stocks in the so-called cyclical industries and sold out again at the end of each economic boom. Some bought stocks for asset value, usually in real estate, oil, or metals. Some took chances on companies that were restructuring. Some bought shares in companies that were destructuring.

As to the schism between Fundamentalists and Chartists, there seemed to be little hope of reconciliation. Both sides agreed that each investor should believe in something—whether it be asset values or P/E ratios, head-and-shoulder patterns, or advance-decline lines—and should find a broker who shares in that belief. A Fundamentalist investor cannot be properly represented by a Chartist broker who reads wiggles. Equally horrifying is the Chartist investor whose broker buys stocks with low P/Es.

If only I'd known this earlier, I could have asked my broker the basic question: Chartist or Fundamentalist? Then again, maybe it wouldn't have mattered. Based on my interviews, I'd guess most brokers would claim to be both Chartist and Fundamentalist until they could feel out the client.

If brokers favor any side of this debate, it's Fundamentalism. Apparently, it's easier to be a Fundamentalist when explaining losses. Those grievous events are more troublesome to Chartists, who must admit either that their charts were wrong or else that they misinterpreted the wiggles, both of which sound like mistakes. On the other hand, a Fundamentalist broker can simply say, "Your stock went down because its fundamental value is not yet recognized by the marketplace."

Though I never asked Ms. Garrett to declare herself, I called her several times to report on the conference and to get information. For instance, after meeting with Mr. Prechter, I asked her to send me the chart on Angstrom. She said she didn't have a chart, but would try to get one. After leaving Mr. Frank's room, I phoned her again, to inquire about Angstrom's current price/earnings ratio. She said she didn't know it offhand, but would try to find out. Between "very high" and "very low," she guessed it would have to be "very high."

A high P/E ratio would make Angstrom an emerging growth stock, as opposed to one of Mr. Frank's undervalued stocks. Although I'd been swayed momentarily by Mr. Frank, I left Fort Lauderdale convinced that the high P/E, emerging-growth scenario was the scenario that really made sense.

I'd hoped to make a second successful investment by now, but having seen all the trouble the experts go through, with nothing but widespread disagreement at the end of it, I was feeling a bit unsure of myself. Also, Angstrom had begun to slide almost immediately after I'd learned at the conference why I'd picked it. This is one more sorry example of how a little knowledge can be a dangerous thing.

In early February, the stock price fell from a high of 2¾ to 2⅜ in a single day, losing 10 percent of its value. Maybe a lot of other people had just been taught what to look for in a growth company and decided all at once that Angstrom wasn't it.

I shared my concern with my broker, Ms. Garrett, who volunteered to check her source in Philadelphia, the man who recommended Angstrom in the first place and who'd been following it all along. I still didn't know his name, only that Ms. Garrett said he was very clever. She called back to report what he'd said: that the drop was due to "general market conditions" and "the smart money is holding on." There was a rumor that Angstrom was about to announce a big government contract, which the smart money must have believed, while the dumb money was getting out.

It's amazing what the phrase "smart money is holding on" can do to an investor's perceptions, turning the tangible evidence of failure, i.e., falling prices, into a sign of success. The dumb money must have continued to get out, because Angstrom dropped from $2\frac{1}{4}$ back toward $2\frac{1}{8}$, hurtling me closer to the familiar "break even" point. By the end of February, my 5,000 shares were worth $9,687.50, according to my monthly statement, which gave me a paper loss of $455.75. I took this to mean that smart money was in shorter and shorter supply.

My resolve to hold on was continually tested in the ordeal of more dumb money selling more shares. I went back over the list of time-tested rules, and was comforted by: "Don't panic, be patient, never sell too soon." In my anxiety, I began to sneak into the neighborhood office of Dis-Com Securities, a discount brokerage, to peck the symbol for Angstrom (ATSI) into their countertop Quotron machine. That way, I could watch the price going down every day.

Each time Angstrom reached a new low, I'd call Ms. Garrett, who I noticed was no longer initiating calls to me. She'd phone her source and call me back with various updates, such as: "delays in the big announcement of the government contract," "a bit of infighting in the company soon to be resolved," "continued general weakness in the market," and the especially promising "Gabelli may be buying."

Mario Gabelli, a.k.a. the Great Gabelli, was a famous investor of smart money, frequently quoted in *Barron's*. This Gabelli story was only another rumor, but I found it reassuring. If Mr. Gabelli liked Angstrom and had the patience to suffer through the actions of its dumber shareholders, then so should I. Ms. Garrett also told me that neither she nor anyone in her office had sold their shares.

In yet another phone call, which began to remind me of the tranquilizing talk-downs on cocaine hot lines, Ms. Garrett mentioned "more sellers than buyers" as further explanation for our short-term setback. "More sellers than buyers" was a phrase I'd heard from other brokers as well. This time, as I lay awake worrying about Angstrom at 3:00 A.M., I realized it made no sense. After all, for every share that's sold there has to be somebody who bought it—so how could one side of the transaction outnumber the other?

After pondering this for a few hours until daybreak, I had to admit I didn't understand why stock prices go up and down. You'd think I would have learned it by now. You'd think that any average investor could explain such a simple thing, but I polled a few friends and they drew blanks as well. At the investment conference in Fort Lauderdale, they never discussed the mechanics of stock prices. Maybe millions of people have bought stock without having the slightest idea why they paid the prices they did. For their sake and for mine, I decided this mystery ought to be cleared up.

I returned to the library to research the matter and met up with one of the unfortunates described earlier, who called himself Bannister. Mr. Bannister told me he slept under the stars, if possible on a public bench, waiting for someone to supply him with some venture capital so he could eat. I invested a few dollars, and then asked him if he knew why stocks went up and down. He surprised me with this answer:

"It's like an auction, man. Think of it this way. You ever been to an auction? A couch, a chair, whatever, sold to the highest bidder. With stocks it's the same, except the old merchandise gets brought out again and again, and gets sold over and over."

After leaving Mr. Bannister, I found several books that more or less confirmed his view. Thinking of the stock market as an auction, I tried to imagine what must have happened to my Angstrom. At $1^{15}/_{16}$ per share, which is where I bought it, there must have been a crowd of buyers, but not so many sellers. Then some anxious buyer must have raised the bid to $2. This extra little profit coaxed out a few more sellers, but still not enough to satisfy all the buyers, until the latest anxious buyer raised his bid to $2^1/_{16}$. This $2^1/_{16}$ price attracted a few more sellers, but supply must have dried up quickly, because a subsequent buyer was forced to raise his bid to $2^1/_8$. It kept going like this until the stock price reached $2^3/_4$, its high to date.

At that point, there were many sellers delighted to give up their shares for $2^3/_4$, but the buyers disappeared. The most anxious of the sellers had to drop the price to $2^{11}/_{16}$ to attract the next buyer. Other sellers, seeing that no more deals could be made at $2^{11}/_{16}$, were willing to lower their price to $2^{5}/_{8}$. After the buyers disappeared at that level, somebody offered to sell for $2^{9}/_{16}$. Meanwhile, people who'd refused to part with their Angstrom at $2^{3}/_{4}$ were scared by the downturn and were dumping their shares at much lower prices.

When the price got so low that nobody was willing to sell—which I hoped would be soon—new buyers again would be forced to raise their bids in order to entice new sellers. This would cause the whole process to reverse, the stock would start moving in a favorable upward direction, and the smart money would be vindicated.

Soon I realized that the phrase "more sellers than buyers" only means that more people want to sell than to buy at the current price. If only I could contact the would-be sellers of Angstrom, to convince them of the big government contract in the works, they might stop driving the price down. If only I could find the people who sold me my 5,000 shares in the first place, I could tell them what I knew that they didn't, and maybe they'd get back into the stock.

It occurred to me that stock and bond sales are among the few transactions where one party is unable to meet the other party directly. Over cars, furniture, houses, clothes, jewelry, baseball cards, and other general merchandise, we're allowed to haggle face-to-face—buyers asking sellers why they are selling, sellers giving their reasons. Why couldn't we do the same with our equities? What's to stop us from gathering up shares from our safe deposit boxes, laying them out in the yard with the stereos and the roller skates, and putting up cardboard signs that say: TODAY ONLY, IBM AT 135 $^{7}/_{8}$, 100 SHARES, or GENERAL MOTORS, SPECIAL PRICE, 50 CENTS OFF AT $65? What's to keep us from driving our stocks to the flea markets and trading them for water skis, or selling them outright for cash, and absent the broker's commission?

This idea got me so excited I called the Securities and Exchange Commission in their New York office and asked if it was legal to sell my shares at a garage sale. I was connected to a helpful attorney named Robert Anthony. "There's nothing to prevent that," he said. "Nothing, that is, if you are going to do it once. But if you make a habit of it, and start buying and selling stocks as a business, then you have to be registered as a securities dealer. Those are the facts of the situation."

Before I could get any further with this, I saw a TV ad for *Barron's* magazine in which the editor said: "You buy a stock convinced it is going to go up. The trouble is, the person you bought it from is just as convinced it's going to go down." I realized then that the garage sale idea was impractical. If I met the sellers of Angstrom face-to-face, they'd probably tell me it was a lousy company with no sales department and no hope of getting a government contract. We'd argue and argue and never come to any agreement, or if we did agree, then there'd never be a stock sale.

If I were trying to sell you my Angstrom, for instance, then you'd want to know why. If I were honest I'd have to tell you I didn't like the P/E ratio, or the charts looked rotten, or whatever, and then you wouldn't want to buy. I couldn't get away with "I'm tired of this stock," or "I change my portfolio every two years," or "I'm moving away," which are the common excuses we use to sell each other our cars, houses, or furniture. A car sale or a house sale may benefit both parties in the transaction. In a stock trade, there's one winner and one loser, and it's soon obvious which is which.

Perhaps the official stock markets—the New York Stock Exchange and so forth—only exist to keep buyers and sellers from any direct contact, or else nobody would want to trade any stocks. Perhaps that's why each party in a stock deal engages a separate professional to interpret what is going on, so my broker can tell me "the smart money is holding on," while the seller's broker, with equal conviction, can congratulate his client for "dumping a dog."

These late-night suppositions had gone far enough. Since everything I'd heard about the stock market so far was secondhand, and some of it quite curious, I decided to travel to Wall Street to see for myself.

ELEVEN

A FOOL AT THE STOCK EXCHANGE

I MADE MY TRIP IN THE MIDDLE OF WINTER, LATE FEBRUARY 1986. By now I expected to have made enough paper profit to afford a room at the Plaza Hotel on Central Park South, but given the circumstances, I sublet an empty apartment on Ninety-sixth Street from a friend who charged a merciful monthly rate. Instead of the Burberry coat I'd hoped to purchase, I came up with a five-dollar thrift-shop cashmere. The moth holes were scarcely visible except in direct light. I consoled myself with the thought that soon I'd be surrounded with firsthand knowledge of the kind that the average investor only dreams about, and this could only improve my fortunes.

Avoiding an expensive cab, I took the Lexington Avenue subway downtown. The general appearance of the riders improved at each successive stop, until only the people wearing recently dry-cleaned Burberries, carrying unscarred briefcases, and reading the *Wall Street Journal* were left. At the Wall Street stop, they all got off in a clump, and I followed.

Still below ground, we trudged past a glass display case that tells the story of the stock market. I paused to consider the details, causing a minor traffic jam, and a few curses were hurled in my direction. I ignored these and read on. Here it confirmed that our earliest investors bought Revolutionary War bonds. These war bonds, along with the first stocks, were traded in coffeehouses and under the trees along Wall Street. It sounded like the stock exchange did start out as a flea market and might have continued in that way except that the brokers decided to organize. The pioneer brokers wrote up a Buttonwood Agreement, a sort of Wall Street

79

Magna Carta. It was their historic defense of a basic human right: "the establishment of regular commissions."

This Buttonwood Agreement was apparently signed on May 17, 1792. The brokers were greatly relieved. From there, they moved away from the outdoor flea market under the sycamore tree in front of 68–70 Wall Street, and occupied several temporary indoor homes. In 1863, the present New York Stock Exchange was opened for business. In 1867, the first tickers were installed, and on December 15, 1886, the Exchange had its first million-share day.

Before I finished taking notes on all this, I suffered the additional curses from more impatient people stuck behind me, as two or three more subways disgorged hundreds of additional passengers carrying *Wall Street Journals*. Finally I joined the crowd, which launched me up the stairs and onto the cold sidewalk.

If you've seen the TV advertisement where the investor stands here alone at the crack of dawn, anxious to get the jump on his competitors, then you already know that the much ballyhooed Wall Street is actually a narrow, crooked way. I'm told that there once was an actual wall, built to hold off wolves, raiders, or any other enemies who might attempt an unfriendly takeover. Such protection is no longer necessary and the wall has long since been removed. From today's investment news, you'd think that all the raiders, wolves, and enemies who attempt unfriendly takeovers have been absorbed into the regular business routine.

At one end of the crooked way is the Trinity Church and graveyard, at the other end the East River, and in between the financial masses scurry to work, pressed briefcase-to-briefcase like rival thoroughbreds squeezed at the eighth pole. I wondered how many old college friends were among them, people I once chided for wanting to be rich instead of happy, now earning $350,000 plus per year and not demonstrably the worse for it. I read in the paper that one such old friend, John Brim, was named a managing partner of Salomon Brothers, the huge and powerful investment house right up the street. If only I'd sent a few Christmas cards or kept up some contact, at least I'd have an excuse to pick his million-dollar brain.

As it was, my first Wall Street contact was with Anatoli, who runs the candy stand outside the New York Stock Exchange building on Broad Street. (For some reason, this whole financial district is full of candy vendors.) Anatoli is an ex-mechanic from Russia who says he makes $25 a day selling jellied fruits to millionaires. "Heard any good tips?" I asked him. Anatoli smiled a big smile, and I could see his inflation hedge in gold teeth. "No tips," he said, "no tips." He insisted he'd never bought a share of stock in his life. Give him time. He'd only been in this country two years and was just learning to speak English. Soon he'll know enough to read the business pages.

Behind Anatoli, I saw several men and women loitering at the side door of the exchange building. They were dressed in colored lab jackets with large plastic identification badges pinned to the pockets. These people could have been taken for research chemists or a janitorial service, but they turned out to be traders from the exchange floor who do the actual buying and selling of the stocks. I asked a few of them for their stock picks, but they wouldn't answer. Maybe they weren't allowed.

The facade of the NYSE is worthy of a Temple of Minerva. This is no gaudy commercial building, but a sober shrine of white granite. Above the Greek columns is a busy little scene that's so unusual I drew a picture of it. In the middle is a lady with winged ears. Beneath her, two naked guys stare at some babies. Next to the naked guy on the right is a fully-dressed Pilgrim woman, while the naked guy on the left is shadowed by another fully-dressed person holding up a large wheel. At the far corner two more naked guys are absorbed in a game that looks like chess or backgammon, and at the near corner a similar duo seems to be committing arson. Whether this whole scene is supposed to illustrate the perils of investing, or whether it's supposed to be a group of heavenly shareholders who've reached their financial objectives was difficult to tell.

Inside the public entrance, an elevator took me to the third-floor visitor's gallery. This gallery is covered in red carpet from floor to ceiling, and it reminded me of a day-care center in a bowling alley or a padded cell in the bondage wing of a bordello. Educational displays are embedded in the vertical carpet. I studied all the old photographs and punched all the buttons that activate recorded messages. Two advisories stuck with me: "Make sure you have set aside funds for family emergencies before you invest," and "Deal with the facts, not tips or rumors."

In recounting the history of the stock market, the New York Stock Exchange was quite frank in describing the treacherous past, when rumor mongers, shills, and connivers victimized the average investor and took most of his money. About recent times the exchange was not so pessimistic. It told of the remarkable reforms that have been effected, and of the great improvement in the shareholders' chances. "Investment objectives," a recording concluded, "have changed from quick-dollar schemes to savings-oriented vehicles concerned with long-term security."

Beyond the education gallery there's a large overhead ticker tape, similar to the ones I'd seen in the local broker's offices. A crowd of visitors stood at attention, gazing respectfully skyward, and I was happy to join them. How exhilarating it was to watch the march of stock quotes across the ceiling, in the very building these quotes are produced. I was told that every trade of 100 shares or more from every investor in the world, no matter how piddling, gets its blip of fame, flashed here and on thousands of other screens around the globe. For those few seconds after every deal is made, the resulting IBM $133\frac{1}{2}$ or SLB $40\frac{3}{4}$ inspires millions of viewers to groan, cheer, and perhaps to take action. If only you could tell which IBM $133\frac{1}{2}$ might actually be yours!

The tour guide stood on a semicircular platform below the overhead tape and entertained us with interesting facts. She said the New York Stock Exchange had 11 major computer systems that could handle 415 million shares a day, soon to be expanded to 500 million. A 500-million-share day hadn't happened yet but they were preparing for it, just as a 150-million-share day, inconceivable in the 1960s, was the current norm. In the early 1920s they were lucky to have a 150-million-share year. Back then, it took a year to trade as many shares as now changed hands in a week of active sessions.

As to what accounted for this phenomenal increase in buying and selling, I got two explanations. First, there were more shares than there used to be. On the New York Stock Exchange alone there were 51 billion shares in 1,500 companies whose stocks trade here. On the nearby American Stock Exchange there were seven billion more shares, and the over-the-counter markets listed another 30-or-so billion. Add to this the penny stocks and family companies traded in private, and there must be trillions of shares in every conceivable kind of enterprise. Most of these were either kept in a "fungible mass" by the brokerage houses (all the shares of all the customers lumped in an undifferentiated pile), or else stored separately in the safe-deposit boxes and closets of the nation.

In 1959, there were only 10 billion shares loose in the country, a fifth of what was now counted on the New York Stock Exchange alone. A century or so ago, there were a few million shares in everything from coast to coast. The printing of shares had been a very popular business, and more consequential than all our gold rushes and oil rushes combined.

Taken together, our shares in everything were worth several trillions. The companies traded on the New York Stock Exchange had a collective value that exceeded $2 trillion, almost as big as our federal debt. Shares in companies on the American Stock Exchange were worth well over $100 billion, and the over-the-counter market represented a third of a trillion worth of stock.

Not only were there more shares in our safe-deposit boxes and closets, but we also traded them more often. In fact, we frantically shuttled back and forth. More than 35 billion shares switched owners in the latest year at the NYSE. Many of these shares switched owners more than once. Since 51 billion shares were listed on the exchange as a whole, nearly three-fifths of all of them changed hands in a year. Another 28 billion shares were traded across the over-the-counter markets. Add these to the billions traded on the American Stock Exchange, and we reached an epidemic fickleness. And that was just in stocks.

How these facts fit in with the recorded message I heard in the visitor's gallery, that we'd abandoned "quick-dollar schemes" in favor of "savings-oriented vehicles concerned with long-term security," I couldn't begin to guess. If stocks were such good long-term investments, I wondered, then why didn't we stop trading them around and hold onto the ones we've got?

This last question was theoretical, of course. Personally, I was feeling more fickle than ever about Angstrom, and began to delight in the thought of putting it on the auction block with the other billions of shares. After the NYSE tour guide finished her spiel, I stood in line with a dozen or so other investors in America, waiting to peck at one of the three Quotron machines provided for public use. The man ahead of me did a delightful little jig to the up-to-the-minute price on his stock. I pecked in "ATSI," the symbol for Angstrom, only to see that it had fallen a sixteenth more, from $1^3/4$ to $1^{11}/16$, and further below my break-even point.

My attention was diverted by a man at the neighboring Quotron, who asked: "Do you know the symbol for Brooklyn Gas?" I said I didn't. He was tall and gawky, and he wore a long coat more tattered than mine. When I heard him mumble "It's going down when it's supposed to be going up," I suspected this was a fellow average investor. He identified himself as Lester Schwartz, a science teacher from Brooklyn who liked to visit the stock exchange on his lunch hour.

We walked together up the ramp to the viewer's gallery as Mr. Schwartz related his investment history. It was a sad progression, beginning with: "I made $10,000 on one of those bond-recall deals. That was great." From there, things degenerated from "great" to "pretty good" to "pretty lousy." Soon, he got to the part about how he'd decided to steer clear of all stocks after a long run of horrendous losses, when he'd been lucky just to break even. "I've got all my money in Treasuries now, and the rest you can forget it," he said. "Except for this one other thing—Brooklyn Union Gas. It's supposed to be going up, and its going down."

As we approached the large picture window that overlooks the trading floor, Mr. Schwartz confessed that he'd been fibbing to me most of the way up the ramp. He admitted that he was still in and out of all kinds of stocks, and not just the Brooklyn Union Gas Company. "Put a bug into my head, I'm a goner," he confided. He also admitted he wasn't a science teacher anymore. He'd only been a science teacher until he got stock fever and quit his job. He was inspired by a close friend who lived out of a suitcase, slept in his Corvette, and played the markets.

"Your friend got rich?" I asked.

"No, actually he didn't," said Lester. "But he had a broker who did."

"Did he recommend stuff?" I wondered.

"Sometimes."

"And did you follow his recommendations?"

"Just as well you don't know. At least I've still got my car, still got my home. You know my ex-wife works down there?" He pointed to the floor of the stock exchange. "She had to get a job. I never see her anymore. She's down there now."

We stood together at the picture window and looked down to where Mr. Schwartz's ex-wife was supposed to be. Below us was the frantic spectacle of the most active marketplace for paper assets in the world. From the ornate walls and the decorated ceiling you'd think this was a nineteenth-century ballroom, cluttered with girders, tubes, and wires, as if a space station had fallen through the roof. Below the gridwork was a swirl of red, blue, and yellow coats, people hustling, people loitering, people queueing up at certain spots like would-be buyers at the ticket windows of sold-out Broadway shows.

A panel of recorded messages explained the scene: the runners and the messengers take buy and sell orders to the floor traders, the floor traders crowd around the specialists. The recorded message said that every share of stock is bought and sold through these lone individuals who stand there on the floor. Apparently, the small transactions are matched automatically by computer, but anything over 100 shares is handled through a specialist.

The specialist for IBM, for instance, buys all the IBM stock that sellers want to sell, then turns around and sells it to the buyers. The entire inventory of that billion-dollar issue is the exclusive franchise of a single vendor. Moreover, that same vendor must handle several other stocks, and there are 400 specialists, working at 14 posts for all the shares traded on the NYSE.

To me, this was an astounding setup. Each of the specialists must move millions of dollars of inventory every working day.

Above the specialists' posts are TV sets, across the floor a fantastic litter of crumpled messages, and the general din and clatter could be heard on our side of a thick picture window 50 feet beyond the action. A giant ticker tape runs its course along the ornate borders of the ballroom, and to the right of the tape is the platform where a bell is struck to start and stop the day's trading. I stood watching for several minutes, fascinated by this eccentric fusion of man and machine—all the global electronics of computers, televisions, and telephones plugged into this anachronistic street-corner bazaar where the lone specialist presides, gesturing with his fingers, scribbling the results of his commerce on tiny slips of paper, not unlike the ancient merchants of Alexandria or Khartoum.

"It's a garage sale," I exclaimed to Mr. Schwartz. Mr. Schwartz looked around and shook his head. "All bullshit and garbage," he said. Something he saw on the trading floor reminded him that he's being taken over by the Japanese. "You know," he said, "in my house the only thing American is the kitchen table. Everything else is from Japan, Singapore, Korea. The Japanese, they don't even have a word for *vacation* in their language. The Japanese haven't had a vacation since Japan was started. When they need a rest, they go up into the mountains and sit in cubicles and put electrodes on their heads to think up new ideas. No wonder we're lagging behind.

"We'd better get our act together," warned Mr. Schwartz, waving his arms like Moses to encompass the full length and breadth of the New York Stock Exchange. "This is all bullshit and garbage." He walked down the ramp to the little Quotron machines where he rechecked the price of Brooklyn Union Gas, and that's the last I ever saw of him.

TWELVE

ON THE FLOOR

FROM THE PICTURE WINDOW IN THE VISITOR'S GALLERY, I BEGAN to wonder about how to get down to the floor. Everything seemed to revolve around this handful of specialists, who were running the entire sale for themselves and had been kept so quiet the average investor had never heard of them. If only there were a way of looking over their shoulders and finding out what they were doing. Who knows what useful bit of gossip, or what profitable little fact could be picked up from watching these merchants process their orders there in the middle of the paper debris.

With that in mind, I called up the public relations office of the New York Stock Exchange and requested a floor visit plus a chat with any specialist. Unfortunately, I got nowhere. You'd imagine they'd be more eager to please the average investor, whom they're constantly praising as the backbone of American capitalism, but I was rebuffed. They told me that specialists do not customarily grant interviews and are best kept isolated from the outside world, due to legal problems and that kind of thing.

Not giving up so easily, I redialed the PR department several times and was connected to as many different representatives, and the best response I got was: "Write us a letter." Having no patience for letters, I abandoned all hope of getting official approval. Meanwhile, I came across a *New York Times* article on Wall Street, in which an expert named William Hayes was quoted several times. Though Mr. Hayes said nothing about specialists, he sounded so astute in general that I called him up and introduced myself. In a happy coincidence, it turned out that Mr. Hayes worked for a firm of specialists himself.

Though he said he was no longer active in that part of the business and couldn't guarantee he could get me onto the trading floor, he offered to get me at least as close as the New York Stock Exchange dining room for lunch.

Even for that, we had to pass through a security checkpoint downstairs, and I had to seek visitor's clearance to enter an elevator. We got off at some upper level, and Mr. Hayes led me out into a dark, aristocratic room that oozed walnut varnish and smelled of leather armchairs. It reminded me of the Yale Club, or the New York Yacht Club, or the lobby of "21." Old men in blue blazers had taken up positions in this quiet, snobbish preserve, which seemed far removed from the shrieking, arm-waving yahoos I'd seen in the big ballroom. Going from there to here was like reaching the U.S. ambassador's residence after escaping a riot on the streets of some chronically unstable country.

Mr. Hayes and I walked to the edge of the dining room, where a maître d' escorted us to our table. To a man, the waiters looked and acted as if they'd come straight out of old Pullman dining cars. Around the walls were the stuffed heads of many former wild animals plus the bodies of several big fish. It occurred to me that they ought to replace these with busts or wax replicas of certain investors, especially the unfortunate ones who've been bagged enough times to have paid for this walnut paneling, these leather armchairs, and all the hunting trips to Africa.

My new friend told me as much as he could about specialists. It turns out they had exclusive franchises from the New York Stock Exchange. Mr. Hayes called it the "ultimate inventory biz." He said a specialist must "make the market" by having enough stock to sell to every willing buyer, and by buying back all the stock from every willing seller. In pocketing an eighth of a point or so in each direction, a specialist could make a very nice living.

For decades, these were mom-and-pop businesses, with a few families controlling the franchises. Sons took over from fathers, just as they did in the neighborhood grocery stores, pharmacies, or newsstands. Lately, said Mr. Hayes, the old specialist families had been selling out to bigger firms. Most of the business was now handled by well-capitalized trading houses like Spear Leeds or Wagner Stott, who were likely to operate at several specialist posts at once, rotating their personnel and making the market in dozens of different stocks.

To me, the most interesting part was that each specialist carried a "Book" on each stock. The Book was a record of all the orders that came in from various buyers and sellers, mostly from big institutional clients who dealt in thousands of shares. Mr. Hayes said that the Book enabled any specialist to tell at a glance "who's selling big or who's buying big, and at what prices, and where's the available supply."

I thought having a Book like that would be a wonderful advantage. Mr. Hayes agreed up to a point, but also cautioned that specialists can lose money even with a Book, that "their biggest fear is one-way markets when they can't reverse their positions," and that "they see only part of the puzzle." Even so, I figured they had to see a more useful part of the puzzle than I was seeing from the business pages or from *Barron's* or *Forbes* magazine. In fact, after my lunch with Mr. Hayes, I was more determined than ever to visit a specialist in action.

He tried to help me with a phone number of an active specialist he knew, but when I called that individual and explained what I wanted, he referred me to the public relations office, which put me right back where I'd started. By now I was willing to try anything, including the following ruse.

I'd learned earlier that the New York Stock Exchange is connected by a corridor to the New York Futures Exchange, a related organization that trades futures, options, and other mysterious vehicles I was determined to avoid. I was tipped off to the existence of this corridor by Daniel Gressel, a professional futures trader and also the husband of Claudia Rosett, the book-review editor of the *Wall Street Journal* who, if she's still there, ought to know I think she's brilliant and has a great flair for reviewing books, and might want to consider this one.

Anyway, her charming husband told me that futures traders routinely hop over into the regular stock exchange to "hedge their positions," and that there was a lot of wandering back and forth through the passageway. He offered to get me onto the floor of the futures exchange. From there I planned to sneak through to the stock exchange on my own.

To get into the futures exchange wasn't much trouble, except I had to wear a tie and jacket. Those I borrowed from a security guard. Mr. Gressel came out to meet me at the door. He was curly-haired, in his early forties, and could have used a shave. He was wearing a red lab coat, with a lapel badge that said EGG. Long rectangular cards, similar to bingo cards, stuck out of his pocket.

"What are those cards?" I asked.

"My trades. You have to keep a record."

"Does *EGG* mean something."

"My trading acronym. Everybody has one on the floor. That's how we identify each other, by *BOY,* or *FOX,* or *ZIT.* Sometimes it means something. I'm *EGG* because my father traded egg futures. I was brought up on egg futures."

"You still trade egg futures?"

"There are no egg futures anymore. There wasn't enough liquidity in eggs. Too much squeezing the market. I wish I was still trading egg futures sometimes."

I followed Mr. Gressel to the edge of a futures pit, where some of his fellow traders were jostling and screaming. There was a sudden price swing that demanded Mr. Gressel's full attention, which turned out to be lucky for me. He handed me off to a colleague named Gollner, who was hanging around a telephone at one of the booths set up on the perimeter of the room.

Mr. Gollner was a likable young man. He began to explain the futures business, but I could hardly hear him above the noise. By putting my ear closer to his mouth, I picked up that Mr. Gollner was one of those people who bought futures, then dashed through the corridor to buy stocks, then dashed back again to reverse the process. This was the chance I'd been waiting for. During a lull in the yelling, I asked if I could tag along on his next round-trip.

Soon the two of us were trotting through the corridor, shoulder-to-shoulder with a large herd of traders on the move. Mr. Gollner led the way. When we reached the floor of the New York Stock Exchange, I gave a private little whoop of joy at having outflanked the public relations department.

Already, I could see that the stock exchange floor was relatively sedate compared with the futures floor, but still louder than most nightclubs. Mr. Gollner had gone into a circular holding pattern and seemed to be awaiting signals from his hip-pocket beeper. We passed various "posts" where stocks were traded and the resulting prices were shown on TV screens overhead. There were numerous kibitzers in solid-colored jackets. Mr. Gollner told me which of these people worked for brokerage firms, which were messengers, which were trading for their own accounts, which were observers, and which were security police for the exchange.

Every now and again we'd pass a phone attached to a metal pole just like you'd find on any street corner. Mr. Gollner would answer it, and it would be for him. How he knew it was for him, and how the other party knew of his exact location on this huge floor I could never figure out. Anyway he'd talk for a minute, hang up the phone, walk toward one of the trading posts, make some odd flapping motions with his hands, turn back toward me and announce:

"It was just filled."

"What was just filled?"

"My order."

"What order?"

"Holiday Inn, $57\frac{3}{4}$."

"I didn't see it."

"Next time maybe you'll see it. Just watch and listen."

Mr. Gollner wrote the results of his supposed trade on a little card that he gave to a guy in a gray jacket. There in front of us was the specialist in Holiday Inn. I'd say he was in his mid-forties: tan pants, madras shirt, Reebok jogging shoes. He had the Book in his hand. I'd love to have peeked into it, but I couldn't get close enough. Between me and the specialist was a crowd of buyers and sellers, haggling over shares. I tried to jump up and down and wave to get his attention, but he seemed to be staring out in space, oblivious to my signals.

"See that?" said Mr. Gollner.

"See what?"

"That man there. Just made an offer to buy. The order came from one of the outer desks, probably from a brokerage firm. Ten thousand shares at $57\frac{7}{8}$ he stepped up with. There, it was just accepted. See? Now it's being recorded." He pointed to another man in a gray jacket who was punching the results of the trade into a nearby machine. Soon it was flashed on the television set above us: 10,000S HOL, 57⅛.

Again I hadn't seen a thing, except the recorder in the gray jacket and the price on the television screen. It began to dawn on me that lingering on the trading floor and hanging around a specialist wasn't a good way to pick my next stock. Though Mr. Gollner patiently explained how the buyer approaches the specialist at the post, how the offer is made, how the specialist responds, and how the order is recorded, I still couldn't tell who was selling what to whom. Blocks of thousands of shares were moved on wiggles, blinks, mumbles, stares, and hand signals, flashed quicker than the common eye could follow. Mr. Gollner said this was a calm day.

Anxious to return to the futures, Mr. Gollner escorted me back through the corridor and deposited me at the guard station where I'd come in. I gave back the coat and tie and headed for the street, more befuddled than ever.

THIRTEEN

MY SECOND INVESTMENT

FTER MY FORAY WITH MR. GOLLNER, I HAPPENED TO SEE AN article about psychics and astrologers who give investment advice. I might have ignored it, especially after the omen in the laundromat turned out to be wrong, but when something appears on the business page of the *New York Times* you take it seriously. This article told how various seers, mystics, and familiars had branched out from health and happiness to make predictions on the gold market, the general direction in interest rates, and the future prices of stocks.

Mostly out of curiosity, I decided to contact at least one psychic. I wrote down the names from the article and found a couple of likely phone numbers in the local New York directory. After getting some strange messages from answering machines, I finally tracked down Carole Jayson-Koerber at her home in the suburbs. Somehow, the idea of a psychic in the suburbs seemed more reasonable than a downtown psychic, especially the kind that rents office space around the bus stations and the blood banks.

I had called Ms. Jayson-Koerber, intending to set up an appointment, but something about our conversation made me change my mind. It may have been the dogs barking in the background, or it may have been her telling me that she was terrific at finding bodies for police departments. This shouldn't have bothered me, but for some reason it did. When I suggested that perhaps we shouldn't meet in person after all, she told me she was "auric." Being auric is a newfound skill among psychics that allows them to sense truth over the telephone, thus avoiding the expense and bother of a physical visit. Soon there may be no house calls even among the supernaturals.

As we continued to chat about nothing in particular, I began to think that Ms. Jayson-Koerber *was* auric. Frankly, I felt she was crawling into my ear. No doubt this was my own imagination hard at work, stimulated by the fear that Ms. Jayson-Koerber might already have learned some terrible thing about me that I didn't know myself. My nervousness caused me to blurt out: "When you find those bodies, aren't you afraid that the killers will want to come after you?" Ms. Jayson-Koerber said this was a very negative question, and from the tone of her voice you'd have thought that I'd just stabbed her myself. That was the end of any worthwhile exchange between us.

After that, I called Bill Attride, a professional astrologer who lived in Brooklyn. He gave me a free half hour on the phone, for which I'm grateful. Mr. Attride said some very provocative things. For example, he'd studied economics in graduate school and found it to be a sloppy pseudoscience, full of wives' tales and irrational thinking, while astrology had proven to be more rigorous, sensible, and practical in every respect. "That's because economists are only working with the phenomena," he explained. "Astrologers go beyond the phenomena and get right into the numena."

Numena, I found out later, means "the heart of things." Mr. Attride mentioned a client of his, an ex-broker at Shearson, who'd been very bullish on a small bioengineering company until Mr. Attride did a background investigation into its numena. While many analysts had liked this stock, Mr. Attride found unfavorable cosmic alignments. He talked his friend out of buying it, which was a lucky thing, since the company suddenly went bankrupt.

I asked Mr. Attride if he had any numatic explanation for what had happened between me and Angstrom—since to date the stock price was well below where I'd bought it. He said to make such a judgment wouldn't be easy. First, I'd have to call Angstrom and also my mother, asking both sources for relevant birthdays, dates and times of incorporations, days when stocks were split, the exact hour I was born, and other critical details.

If I'd bring all this data back to Mr. Attride, he'd do birth charts for the company itself, for as many principal officers as possible, and also for me. Only then could he analyze the interplanetary conflicts, negative or positive aspects of Saturn or Uranus, the

passage of the sun through four cardinal signs, the relations between the company's solstice and mine. "Even if a company has
a good aspect, that doesn't mean it's going to work out for you to
own it," he said. "Some people aren't cut out for owning stocks
at all. Their charts show that clearly. If they buy something—no
matter how positive it is—some hitch will occur and they will lose
money."

I doubted that this research would be worth the trouble, especially after Mr. Attride said he couldn't do it gratis. Also, I dreaded
hearing that my cosmic alignments were unsuited to any and all
investing, which I feared, given the earthly results, would be his
astrological conclusion. I confessed this fear, and also asked Mr.
Attride if he couldn't recommend a less rigorous and hopefully
cheaper advisor. He recommended Mr. Arch Crawford.

He said Mr. Crawford wasn't so much an astrologer as he was
a student of the ionosphere. He'd heard that Mr. Crawford published an investment newsletter that gave stock market advice based
on atmospheric conditions.

I met Mr. Crawford in a swank little cappuccino shop called
Sacco's at Seventy-seventh Street and Lexington Avenue. He was
10 minutes late, which he blamed on the "options closing at 4:10
and the futures at 4:15." He wore wire-rimmed glasses, corduroy
pants, a button-down blue shirt, and sported a goatee. He had the
red hair and fair skin of an Appalachian, the crumpled look of a
Brooks Brothers academic, and he spoke with a subtle, professorial
Southern drawl.

He said he'd studied math and physics at the University of North
Carolina. Then, in 1963, he'd gone to work with Robert Farrell,
the famous Merrill Lynch technical analyst. "I was marking a chalk-
board at Merrill Lynch, putting up the stock prices. This was before
the days of electronic scoreboards. Then Merrill Lynch sent me
to night school, and I came back to help Mr. Farrell with his charts.
Charting was thought of as witchcraft on the Street at the time,
but now it's gotten quite respectable. So has Mr. Farrell."

Mr. Crawford, meanwhile, went to Vietnam, returned to New
York in 1969 to trade his own account, and made and lost two
personal fortunes. Somewhere in the middle he'd discovered the
electrical forces in the atmosphere. He also discovered that he did

a better job advising others than investing for himself. That's when he started publishing his newsletter.

He ordered a cup of herbal tea and a sweet roll and explained his stock market theory as follows:

The general public is affected by sunspots that send out ionizing radiation, as well as by the phases of the moon. Electrically charged investors turn positive or negative in sympathy with the positive or negative atmospheric polarity, with the moon pulling the air, and also with the planetary alignments.

By keeping track of the planets and the electromagnetic emanations, Mr. Crawford said he'd called every major low point in the stock market since 1977, and within 15 points of the Dow Jones industrial average. Calling the highs had been more difficult, but he had the market going up in 1982–83 and topping out in 1984, all of which came true. If I wanted proof, he said he'd bring me the newspaper clippings from his office right around the corner. If that wasn't enough, he told me to call Wall Street columnist Dan Dorfman, who'd once investigated these results and came away impressed.

Looking into the future, Mr. Crawford took the grim view that "with Saturn and Neptune conjunct with Capricorn and opposing Cancer we could be facing very possibly the dissolution of the banking system." Fortunately, this wasn't going to happen until November 13, 1989. More immediate prospects included a "topping out of the stock market in April-May, and from there definitely a correction and quite possibly a bear market."

Mr. Crawford inspired great confidence, even after he let me pay for his sweet rolls and refused to invite me into his messy office, and in spite of the fact that I didn't believe in electrical beings. Maybe it was his gentle offhandedness. Maybe it was because he wasn't selling anything. (Actually, he did sell advice to sophisticated investors who, he said, paid thousands a year to hear it, but he wouldn't give me their names. Then there was the newsletter, but he volunteered to put me on the free list for that.)

Whatever the reason, I was anxious to hear what Mr. Crawford would do if he were in my position. "Buy calls on the market on Friday afternoon," he said, without any hesitation or uncertainty.

"That's what I'd be doing myself if I had any money." Specifically, he suggested the March 225 S&P-100 call options. I didn't know what that meant, but of all the opportunities that had come my way since Angstrom, this one had the greatest appeal. I made a note of Useful Tip Number 12:

The more befuddled the investor, the more absolute certainty he'll demand from his advisor

---

I didn't check with Dan Dorfman, and I didn't check Mr. Crawford's clippings. As soon as Mr. Crawford left the restaurant I rushed outside to the pay phone and called my broker, Ms. Garrett, long-distance.

"Buy the March 225 S&P-100 call option," I said, repeating it exactly as I'd written it down.

"How many?"

"How many? I don't know how many. How much are they?

"Let me check. They are trading for a little less than 1½. That means about $125 to $150 apiece."

"I'll take five of them."

There was no cash available in my Prudential-Bache account, since the balance of my assets was still held in the savings/checking account at my S&L back home. I rode the bus to the nearest New York branch office and gave Prudential-Bache a personal check for $777.16, the exact amount of my purchase. Then I did some research, to try and figure out what I'd bought.

What I'd bought was called a stock-index option. These delightful investments were only five years old, having been invented in Chicago in the early 1980s. They were not exactly the same as the dreaded options on individual stocks I mentioned earlier, or else I would have had nothing to do with them.

While options on individual stocks made it possible to speculate on sudden price movements of some specific issue—i.e. IBM—the stock-index options enabled the investor to speculate on the larger market, by betting on one of the popular stock indexes. As the Standard and Poors-100 Index was a collective measure of the value of a hundred important stocks all lumped together, so an S&P-100 option was a gamble on the direction that the index might take over a short period of time.

There were similar baskets from rival indexes, and new indexes options were being invented every other month it seemed, but the S&P-100 was the one I picked, following Mr. Crawford's advice.

At the various futures and options exchanges, such as the one I snuck through earlier, they bought and sold contracts on numerous index options at different prices and settlement dates in the future. For instance, a March 225 contract gave me the right to pay $225 for one unit of the index, or "basket of stocks," from now until the moment the contract expired, or in this case, the third Friday in March. During this period, if the stocks in the S&P-100 Index increased in value, then so would my option. If the stocks decreased in value, then so would my option, until eventually the option became worthless.

Actual "baskets" of stocks were never delivered to the holders of options, just as actual pork bellies are rarely delivered to traders in the futures markets. The entire exercise was hypothetical, with buyers and sellers settling in cash sometime before the expiration dates.

Since the reader may also have heard of stock-index futures, I must clarify the distinction between those and the options. A future is an agreement to buy something later at a price agreed upon today. In futures contracts, both parties are obligated to the transaction and committed to the fate of the merchandise in question, whether it be a carload of pork bellies or a basket of stocks. If the prices go against them, they can lose much more than their original investment.

An option is really a contract for a contract. It gives the buyer the right to purchase something that may be valuable—in this case a basket of stocks—without obligating that buyer to carry through with the transaction. If the deal turns out to be unfavorable, the options buyer only lost the price he or she paid for the option in the first place. In this way, buying an option was safer than buying a future. Relative to a future, an option could even be called conservative, since the options buyer could only lose his entire original investment and not a penny more.

In this instance, I'd bought five options on five baskets of S&P-

100 stocks. That gave me the chance to pick up the contracts on the five baskets for $225 apiece (March 225s, remember) until mid-March. If the stocks in the S&P-100 Index were worth less than $225, there would be no sense in exercising the options. If the stocks were worth more than $225, then I'd make money. As I mentioned, the index options were settled in cash.

If this were the whole story it would be complicated enough, but there was also the business of "put" options and "call" options. I hesitate to bring it up, but I must. A call option, which is what I bought, gave me the right to BUY the stock index from somebody else. The put option gave me the right to SELL the stock index to somebody else. You could sell the right to BUY (sell a call), buy the right to SELL (buy a put), sell the right to SELL (sell a put) and buy the right to BUY (buy a call). Perhaps I can resolve this with Useful Tip Number 13:

Buy a call or sell a put:
you want things to go up.
Sell a call or buy a put:
you want things to go down.
When in doubt, do neither.

In trying to better understand this myself, I sought out Mr. Gressel, the futures and options trader who got me onto the floor of the New York Futures Exchange in the first place. Since I'd lost his phone number at the clearinghouse, I had to bother his wife, Claudia, the book-review editor, to give it to me again. If she's reading this for possible review, let me thank her once more for her patience and her cordiality. "I have to warn you," she said. "Gressel might not be in a sociable mood. Last I heard, he was down for the day."

The clearinghouse is where traders go in the afternoons to consider their gains and their losses. This particular house was Wagner-Stott, one of many firms the public never hears about, which occupy entire floors in high-rent Wall Street buildings. The secretary was gone for the day, so I invited myself through the lobby and into the back room.

The back room was full of work tables, and the work tables were cluttered with printouts and styrofoam coffee cups. Men in red lab coats sat back in their folding chairs with their feet on the printouts, watching the overhead Quotron machines while idly punching buttons on the keyboards in their laps.

Gressel soon appeared. I recognized him from our first encounter: still curly-haired, still wearing a red lab coat, still could have used a shave. This time, he looked as if he'd just been forced to witness an autopsy. He nervously fingered the identification badge, EGG, pinned to his lapel.

"Just got killed," he said, "maybe $10,000. Maybe more. Completely, totally, fucking killed. Ten thousand dollars. Can you believe it? I ought to be doing something else. I ought to go back to teaching."

Mr. Gressel paced like a hot horse, hung his red jacket in a closet, and finally calmed down enough to sit at one of the tables underneath a Quotron machine. I sat down next to him. He halfheartedly punched in a few numbers, and the results made him slump more dejectedly into his chair. "Got to get back to teaching," he said. "Really I should. At least they pay you something. At least you get a salary."

He explained that he'd given up a good position in economics at the University of Chicago to come to New York and trade options and futures on the New York Futures Exchange while his wife got her great job at the *Wall Street Journal.* "Some days, Claudia comes home and I tell her to go out and buy all the new clothes she wants. Other days, I have to tell her we've just gone bankrupt. Like today. Today I've been feeding the market. I hate to feed the market."

I said I knew how he felt, since having just bought stock-index options myself I was under a similar pressure. "What do you think about March 225 calls?" I asked. "Is that a good deal?" He gave a rambling, incomprehensible answer that included "laying off options" and "implied volatility" and "what the fuck does it matter when the market isn't rational." I could tell he was in no particular mood to elaborate, and we said our good-byes. At the door, he invited me to visit him on the floor the next day, when hopefully he'd have something to smile about.

Again Mr. Gressel met me at the guard station, but this time I remembered my coat and tie. From the quiet outer hallway, I could hear the screaming and shouting, so I felt like a visitor in the waiting room of an asylum. Mr. Gressel led me in through a crowd of futures traders. Some were milling, some were pacing, and some raced around at full speed, bouncing off one another like excited molecules. We took refuge in a tiny walkway between two trading desks at the side of the room.

Mr. Gressel said it was a slow morning, though I couldn't imagine how things could be more chaotic. He took the time to explain the general surroundings: the options pit on one side and the futures pit on the other. He said the options pit was quieter because options are traded on a specialist system—one person taking all the orders—as opposed to the "open outcry" in the futures pit. Above each pit, the huge quote boards displayed the prices of hundreds of futures and options with various expiration dates. Among these I found my March 225s, and was delighted to see that my $700 investment already had increased to $900.

Mr. Gressel pointed out various types of traders: some who simply process orders from brokerage firms and live off the commissions; others known as scalpers, who buy and sell quickly and profit from the tiny changes in prices; day-traders, who hold their positions to the end of each afternoon; and position players, who take the farfetched view and invest for the long term—that is, a week or two. He introduced me to a number of traders, whom I only remember as REP, TAD, GOB, and HAL. By standing close to them in the walkway and yelling back and forth, I learned that some were ex-schoolteachers and some had Ph.D.'s. Most had become futures traders as a mid-life career change. They told me all it took was a $25,000 investment stake, plus another $700 to buy a seat on the exchange, and a few days of training in the hand signals. What an easy way to make a living, I thought to myself.

Actually, I heard several complaints about this job, which ought to be reported. The three major ones were: sore feet from standing up all day; sore throats, colds, and throat viruses from so much spitting and coughing at close range ("It's a regular disease hole in the pits"); and loss of money. The loss of money was a constant fear, and the only important topic of conversation. "When somebody says he's having an affair, everybody else says 'big deal,' " Mr. Gressel explained. "When somebody has an accident, gets robbed, mugged, or raped, it's the same 'big deal.' But just mention that so-and-so went bankrupt today, and there'll be a great hush and then everybody gasps, 'HOW?' "

Just after he said this, we were interrupted by a great commotion and all my sources scattered. "It's the money supply," Mr. Gressel cried. "The money-supply number's being announced." He rushed away to watch the news on the overhead ticker and returned a few minutes later to say: "The market's going up. The Fed may cut the discount rate. I'll have to see you later. Have to go to work."

Mr. Gressel didn't confine himself to the futures pit or the options pit. I watched him scurry from one to the other, punching numbers into a hand-held calculator and muttering about "implied volatility." What I got from him later was that there are proper prices of the options and the futures, and although the market didn't always know this, eventually it would realize the truth. By realizing it early, Mr. Gressel made his profit. "Waiting for the market to resolve into rationality," is how he put it.

It was soon obvious that the market's going up or going down had little importance to him. In fact, the market was going up, and I watched my little options increase in value. You could see the prices rise from minute to minute on the quote board. Since this didn't seem to please Mr. Gressel, I assumed at first that he wanted the market to go down. This was wrong. The fact is that Mr. Gressel was working on some higher plane.

Most of this I discovered at the end of the day, when we'd agreed to go out for a drink. He suggested that we take the subway uptown instead of a cab, and I knew that things had not gone well for him. Apparently the market was being irrational and ignoring proper prices, which caused him to lose money for the second day in a row.

"Ten thousand dollars," he repeated again and again. "Another ten thousand dollars. Can you fucking believe it?" As we walked down Broadway toward the subway station, he went back over his wonderful life at the University of Chicago, the advantages of academia in general, and the virtues of teaching economics. His nostalgia got him further depressed.

Even the bar he chose, a brassy, ferny Fifth Avenue singles' stop, didn't seem to cheer him. He continued to talk about getting a "real job." I tried to make him tell exciting stories about futures. The only exciting stories he remembered were the orthodox Jew who made a fortune in pork bellies, and the trader who blew his nose in his tie.

We ended up at Mr. Gressel's apartment, where we waited for Claudia to get home from the *Wall Street Journal*. It was a one-bedroom place on Twenty-eighth Street and Fifth Avenue, not at all the penthouse I expected. In the galley kitchen, Mr. Gressel mangled an old loaf of bread and cut off some ragged hunks of cheese. We sat down on a soft couch and ate this appetizer while talking about Latin American politics.

Mr. Gressel had just put some left-wing Chilean folk music on the stereo, so I was surprised when he said he was a big fan of the right-wing Chilean dictator, Pinochet. It occurred to me later that this was a political version of hoping the markets will go up and down simultaneously. The sophisticated futures and options trader lives a very complicated mental life.

After a couple of hours, we turned off the music and turned on the TV to watch the latest episode of *Miami Vice*. Mr. Gressel was still preoccupied with his losses. He got half-involved in the Miami plot, then abandoned the show and headed for his desk, where he sat down to consider a pile of computer printouts. Finally, he made a phone call to one of his fellow traders, which I couldn't help overhearing. For 20 minutes they talked about implied volatility and how a "16" should really have been a "13," and Mr. Gressel's mood was visibly improved. After he hung up, he took out his little calculator, punched in some additional numbers, then turned toward me and exclaimed: "I was wrong! Wrong all the time! I wasn't down $10,000 for the day. Really I was up ten thousand for the day."

The rest of the evening was gleeful. When Claudia returned home, Mr. Gressel told her to go out tomorrow and buy some new clothes. The three of us had a nice dinner at a restaurant.

WHAT THE FED
WAS GOING TO DO

I WAS STROLLING THROUGH WALL STREET WHEN I PASSED A CLEAR-
ing called Liberty Square and found myself facing a large
stone palazzo, the kind the Medicis built in Florence. Across
from this palazzo, workers had parked a couple of beat-up
moving vans and were unloading the contents—pallets of silver
bars—as nonchalantly as if it were a shipment of discount um-
brellas. Silver bars were piled up on the street. I didn't see any
guards, but maybe they were masquerading as bums, who were
thick in the area.

Most bystanders ignored the pile of silver, which goes to show
how unpopular precious metals had become. I reminded myself
not to invest in them.

A bronze plaque on the stone palazzo identified it as the New
York Federal Reserve Bank. This was a branch of the famous Fed
everybody talks about. It is housed in an appropriate building,
since the Florentine Medicis were central bankers themselves.

People all over the city seemed to be asking each other what
the Fed was going to do. Already, I'd seen Mr. Gressel work
himself into a frenzy over a simple Fed announcement. I read in
a magazine that even the midwestern farmers were worrying about
the Fed, as much or more than they ever worried about the weather.
Some of them even prayed for a cut in the discount rate.

Ten years ago, when M-1 was still a rifle and not the money
supply, the average person had never heard of the Fed. Suddenly,
all our bank accounts, certificates of deposit, mortgages, stocks,
bonds, retirement plans, college plans, pensions, and Christmas
savings are being affected by what the Fed intends to do. To me,
the organization was completely mysterious. If I hadn't acciden-

tally come across the building, I wouldn't have known there was a Fed in New York.

Inside the huge, steel-studded double doors was a giant hallway. Except for a metal detector at one end and a statue of a depraved-looking Young Sophocles at the other, it was empty. To the right of the statue was an arch that led to a promenade of video screens where continuous taped lectures were shown. From these lectures, I learned there are twelve Fed districts, that Fed headquarters is in Washington, that the organization regulates the money supply, oversees numerous banking matters, shreds old bills and replaces them with new ones, and clears one-third of all checks written on local banks across the nation.

This particular New York Fed had 200 alarms, a security staff the size of a metropolitan police force (the exact number of security guards was kept classified for security reasons), a bowling alley, a firing range, and a gym. On the wall above my head was chiseled the inspirational Fed motto: TO FURNISH AN ELASTIC CURRENCY.

While loitering around the educational archway, I witnessed a curious, impromptu procession. Through the various displays scurried a pair, then two pairs, and finally a mob of young men in tweed overcoats and with pasty winter complexions, swinging their briefcases like brakemen's lanterns. They were on a mission that so completely absorbed them that when I asked one of the men what he was doing, he mumbled "Salomon Brothers" and jogged along toward a distant anteroom.

I followed, watching intently as the Salomon man and his tweedy cohorts scrambled across a wooden dolly piled with telephones. Each of them picked up a telephone, carried it out to a long bank of waist-high cubicles, and plugged it into a waiting plastic jack.

The instant the connections were made, the phones started ringing and the mob that installed them lifted the receivers. Nothing much was said from this end. Mostly, the men listened and took notes.

Soon one or two of them left the phones and strolled across the room toward what looked like a primitive metal ballot box, the kind used in rural elections. Next to the box was a punch clock, controlled by a woman who sat on a highchair. As the men shoved large manila envelopes into the ballot box, this woman handed them slips of paper stamped with the exact time. They checked these slips carefully on their way back to the phone booths. This process was repeated several times.

Presently, a man in a green tie and a matching lab jacket, wearing the badge of a Fed employee, took out his own Casio pocket watch and synchronized it with the clock on the ballot box. "Three minutes, three," he yelled—causing a new flurry of envelope-stuffing—then "Two minutes, two." As he got down to 45 seconds, the stampers and stuffers raced faster back and forth from the phone booths to the ballot box, until finally the timer said: "Five, four, three, two, one, that's it." On the word *that's,* one last man lunged in with an envelope. After that the 30 or so competitors in this odd marathon put the telephones away, grabbed up their brief-cases, and exited the front door as quickly as they'd come in.

The timer in the lab jacket, who would only identify himself as "Just-Don't-Call-Me-Late-for-Supper," was kind enough to explain what I'd seen. The federal government had just auctioned off $13.6 billion in Treasury bills (half maturing in three months and half in six months). Treasury bills are short-term loans that investors make to the U.S. government.

The men with briefcases were emissaries of big investment houses—Salomon Brothers and Merrill Lynch, among others. They filled the ballot box with competitive bids as to the interest rates they'd accept on the Treasury bills. Their bids were approved over the telephone by their bosses. The box would be opened later that afternoon, when the Fed would sell the Treasury bills to the bidders who'd take the lowest interest rates.

I wondered why there'd been such a rush, and why they used the time clock. "When two bids are the same, the one with the earlier time stamp is accepted," said Just-Don't-Call-Me-Late-for-Supper. "That's why the rush. But this was nothing. If you want to see a stampede, you should be here for the Treasury bonds." Treasury bonds are long-term versions of the Treasury bills, held from two to ten years by the lenders.

Apparently the long-term bond auctions attract crowds of bidders from lesser investment houses, who get their instructions from pay phones outside the building and sprint in from the street. "There's always a lot of competition—though no single firm can take more than 35 percent of the action," my source said. (In the auction I'd witnessed, 35 percent would have been a mere $4 billion).

"Can anybody bid?" I asked.

"Anybody with a ten-thousand-dollar check. Even you could put in a bid if you wanted to."

That any idiot can walk into the Fed and compete with Salomon Brothers in the bond auctions is a wonderful feature of our financial democracy. In practice, my guide said, the average investor rarely bids against the big houses. Average investors can order their Treasury bills at the small-fry window on the other side of the building, where they're guaranteed the median interest rate that comes out of the next ballot box. It's called the noncompetitive bid. That's what you get when you buy T-bills or T-bonds at a local Federal Reserve branch or through your stockbroker.

The T-bill and T-bond auctions occur as frequently as the government spends money it does not have, which lately is very frequent. In fact, most of our multi-trillion-dollar federal debt is owed to the holders of these bills and bonds. As to the quaint way the business is transacted, perhaps you're as amazed as I was. Our entire government is supported by these old-fashioned ballot boxes, and these weekly auctions set the interest rates that affect all the other interest rates throughout the economy.

"While you're here, you should take the rest of the tour," said my guide. "You seen the gold?"

According to him, we were standing on the largest single deposit of gold in the world. I'd have guessed the biggest deposit was probably in South Africa, or maybe at Fort Knox, but actually it sits on bedrock of Manhattan Island, fifty feet below sea level, in the basement of the New York Fed.

A tour had formed in the lobby, and I was allowed to join it. We were herded past security, taken down the elevators, and led through a thick vault door into what looked like typical New York basement storage. There were laundry carts and luggage racks, plastic bins and metal lockers, except these carts, bins, and lockers were filled with gold. In all, they contained 960,000 gold bars weighing a cumulative 12,000 tons. The guide said the gold was worth $120 billion at the "official price" of $42 an ounce, but the official price was an artificial reference point that had nothing to do with the actual price. At the actual price, then $350 an ounce, the gold was worth $1.2 trillion. One quarter of all the gold stored in the free world was stacked like cordwood in these bins.

Apparently, each separate bin belonged to one of 86 different countries that used the Fed as their safe-deposit box. Some moved their gold here during World War I, others during various uprisings and revolutions. The guide wouldn't tell us which bin belonged to which country.

When one country owed money to another, they paid it back as follows: Three people unlocked the bin, an auditor slit the seal, and a number of bars equal to the amount of the debt was removed from the stack. Then the bars were weighed on a giant scale, lugged to the bin of the creditor nation, and added to its stack. All locks were relocked, seals resealed, and the debt was paid.

This method of settling accounts was very arduous, and the gold movers used dollies and pulley systems to aid their efforts. They also wore special shoes and slick coveralls so tiny gold particles wouldn't stick to their clothing. Otherwise, they'd have made a small fortune panning for gold dust in their washing machines at home.

The elevators returned us above ground, to the upper stories of the Fed where the checks are cleared. Did you ever wonder what happens to a check after you write it or deposit it? Chances are it takes a two- or three-day trip and passes through one of the Feds, or a similar clearing house. At the New York Fed, hundreds of bags had arrived downstairs, containing millions of checks to be processed that night. Each bag was hustled up to the counting rooms, where the checks were removed, then sorted one-by-one through the high-speed machines that read the electronic codes. After the counting and sorting, they're bundled up and returned to the local banks where they started out in the first place, which is how we get them back at the end of the month.

Meanwhile, each local bank keeps an account, called a reserve account, at the nearest Fed. These reserve accounts are used to settle all the debits and credits from all the checks that are cashed and deposited across the country. If more money leaves your local bank via check than comes in on a given day, your bank owes something to other banks and the amount is subtracted from its reserve balance at the Fed. If your bank takes in more money in deposits than it loses in withdrawals, its reserve balance is increased for that day.

The Fed also handles cash. It's a sort of kidney machine for the currency—regulating the flow and also cleaning the money. When a local bank has too much cash on hand, it sends a pile over to the Fed. The Fed counts the money in its high-speed counting machines and credits the bank's reserve account for the deposit.

If the bills are clean, they're bundled up and sent along to banks that need more cash, while a corresponding amount is subtracted from those banks' reserve accounts. If the bills are cut, mutilated, soggy, or dirty, they're culled and sent to the shredders. The New York Fed alone shreds $40 million worth of bills a day. Because of the chemicals in the ink and the paper, this shredded money is classified as toxic waste. (The implications ought to be explored, but I'll leave them to divinity students and philosophers.)

To replace whatever it shreds, the Fed orders the Bureau of Engraving and Printing to print up new money—but don't jump to conclusions. The popular suspicion that the government solves its budget problems with a printing press turns out to be unfounded. Actually, the government doesn't need to print money to cheapen the currency. Instead, it simply buys billions of dollars worth of bonds with funds that don't exist.

This is how it works. I use "buy" and "pay" in quotes, since there's no real cash involved. When the economy is moribund or in recession, and the Fed wants to stimulate it with more money, it calls up its favorite bond dealers and "buys" some bonds from them. (These are existing bonds, as opposed to the new ones auctioned off each week in the lobby.) The Fed "pays" for these bonds by adding billions of dollars to the reserves of banks where the bond dealers have accounts. This is as painless as typing some extra zeros onto a bank balance.

With these extra "billions" in their reserves, the banks can loan out more money, making it easier for the rest of us to get credit, and driving interest rates lower. This is great for business, but it is also potentially inflationary.

When the economy is getting out of hand and inflation is on the rise, the Fed often works to slow things down, also known as tightening. When the Fed wants to "tighten," or to pressure interest rates to rise, it calls up the same bond dealers and sells back some bonds. Then it wipes a few billion off the reserves of the banks in question. This reduces the amounts these banks can lend, which makes it harder for customers to get loans, and drives interest rates higher.

No doubt this explanation is oversimplified, but it's already complicated enough. When you hear about "tightening" and "loosening," remember the bonds and the funny way they're "purchased." The less said about clearings and drainings of reserves, the primary and secondary markets, the jumping of Treasury deposits, executing system repurchase agreements, and other functions of the Fed that I'm unable to understand, the better. I did find out that the famous discount rate is simply the interest rate the Fed charges to various member banks that need quick loans.

I was allowed a peek into the special room where the aforementioned bond transactions take place. It's called the open-market room, and almost as closely guarded as the gold vault downstairs. Inside is a large blackboard, similar to the departure-and-arrival boards seen at the international airports of underdeveloped countries. Scribes stood on tall ladders, busily erasing old numbers and filling in new ones. These were the current market prices for hundreds of existing bonds. In front of the blackboard, twenty or thirty phone clerks called around the world to get up-to-the-minute prices from bond dealers. The clerks relayed the prices to the scribes.

The results from a day's work at the Fed—the bond auctions, the T-bill prices, the tightening and loosening of reserves—are critical to Wall Street. The Fed is very considerate in releasing this information. It announces the Fed news at regular press conferences, and none of the interested parties can leave the room before everybody's been handed the press release. That way, the race to the telephones is fair.

Unfortunately, I'd missed the latest press conference, which had been held on a Thursday. I'd stumbled onto the building on a

Monday. They gave me the press packet anyway. It was eight or nine pages of numbers, including the M-1, M-2, and M-3 money-supply figures and the latest total on the federal debt, which stood at $1,586.3 trillion, with the nonfederal debt at $5.1 trillion. To me, this information was no more useful than Sanskrit, so whether I'd gotten it a week late or a year early was inconsequential.

FIFTEEN

GOING OVER-THE-COUNTER

I N EARLY MARCH, THE STOCK MARKET WAS ON THE RISE, AND SO were my options. I bought them on February 21 and cashed them two weeks later for a delightful profit of $400. For this, I was grateful to the astrologer and his electrical beings.

Although I could have returned to Mr. Crawford and purchased more options on his latest advice, I sensed that enough was enough. An evening with Mr. Gressel, a professional trader, convinced me that I'd been in over my head, since even he didn't seem to know if he was winning or losing from one day to the next. I figured I'd had beginner's luck, and so I quit while I was ahead. It seemed more sensible to stick with simple stocks, about which I was relatively well informed.

Unfortunately, the price of Angstrom shares had dropped even further, causing me to lose as much or more than the $400 I'd made on the options in the same period. Though the mottoes "Be Patient" and "Don't Sell Too Soon" had inspired me to hold on, I'd begun to suspect that I should have paid closer attention to "It's Never Too Soon to Sell and Cut Your Losses." Frankly, I couldn't tolerate owning this Angstrom any more than you can tolerate hearing about it. The stories about the big government contract soon-to-be-signed and the infighting soon-to-be-resolved were beginning to sound unlikely.

Before taking any drastic action, though, I wanted to meet some people directly involved in the stock, to get their learned advice. Angstrom, I knew, was sold over-the-counter. Perhaps I could get to see an Angstrom specialist—but where was this counter? I'd assumed it had to be someplace around Wall Street, but that turned out to be false. I asked several ignorant pedestrians on Wall Street before a knowledgeable person told me that over-the-counter headquarters was located in Washington. Later, I learned that "over-the-counter" is the popular name for the National Association of Securities Dealers Automated Quotations, or NASDAQ.

Shunning the expensive Metroliner, I took the slow train down to Washington, then shared a cab into town. The cab let me off in front of a small office building on K Street, which at first I thought was a mistaken address. After seeing the great marble facade of the New York Stock Exchange, I was not prepared for NASDAQ to look like the National Asphalt Council, or any similar run-of-the-mill Washington organization.

Inside the NASDAQ building, there was no checkpoint, no guard, and hardly a lobby—just an empty hallway and a couple of elevators. I took one of these up to the public relations office. There I was met by Enno Hobbing, vice-president of the news department, with whom I'd made an appointment.

Mr. Hobbing was wearing a rumpled seersucker suit, and looked considerably more relaxed than anybody I'd seen in the dining room of the NYSE. As he threaded me through the usual secretarial cubicles, around the file drawers, past the Xerox machine, he told me about his earlier career as an editor for the old *Life* magazine.

Inside his office, Mr. Hobbing described how NASDAQ was catching up to the other exchanges, how the institutional investors were buying more over-the-counter stocks, and how NASDAQ had grown to 4,000 companies, more than twice the number represented by the rival NYSE. He said that NASDAQ stocks were worth a collective $360 billion on the day of my visit. The largest of the companies traded on NASDAQ were included in what Mr. Hobbing called the National Market System. It provided up-to-the-minute transaction reports just as the NYSE did. There was a second tier of less-important stocks, simply called over-the-counter, and finally a third tier of the smallest and least-important issues, called the supplementals. Angstrom, I knew, was one of those.

"Does supplemental mean something's wrong?" I asked.

"Not really," Mr. Hobbing said. "Supplementals are small stocks, not widely followed. These are companies that don't meet the financial requirements to make our other lists, but that doesn't mean they're shaky or insolvent. They're still part of NASDAQ."

"But where are the stocks actually traded?" I wondered. "Downstairs, or on another floor of the building, or where?"

"I'll show you," said Mr. Hobbing. He got up and ushered me out of his office. We walked a few steps and stopped at a narrow table. It was no longer than a regular kitchen countertop, and cluttered with newspapers, catalogs, and the usual office debris. In the middle of the debris was a computer terminal.

"This is it," said Mr. Hobbing, patting the terminal. "Heart of NASDAQ. Got any stocks you want to check, to see how they're trading?"

I told him the name of mine, plus the symbol, ATSI. He sat down at the terminal, typed in a few commands, and there on the screen appeared a list of firms you'd recognize: Merrill Lynch and Goldman, Sachs were offering to buy Angstrom at $1\frac{3}{8}$ or to sell it at $1\frac{1}{2}$, while three or four lesser-known firms were willing to buy at $1\frac{5}{16}$ and to sell at $1\frac{7}{16}$. This difference between the "bid" and the "ask" price was called the spread.

"Those are your market makers," said Mr. Hobbing. "Not many for your little stock. There'd be more for a big stock like MCI Communications." To prove it, he punched in the code letters for MCI, and two screens worth of buyers and sellers, about 30 of them, came up before our eyes.

"But where are the specialists?" I wondered. "Where are they standing?"

"There are no specialists," he said. "That's the beauty of it. Our market makers take the place of the specialists, and they're not standing anywhere. They're spread out all over the country. The computer network is the trading floor. You want to buy some MCI, you put in the order to your broker, and your broker sends it off to the order desk, and the order desk calls up the list of market makers on a terminal, just as we've done here. Buyers and sellers can screen down the list, pick out the best price, and make the deal right there with the keyboard."

"How do you decide which market maker to buy or sell from?"

"First, of course, you'd choose the one that's offering the best price. But if a lot of stock is being offered at the same price, there's a rotation system for who gets the business. There's no trading halts, no imbalances, always somebody willing to buy or sell. Plus there's competition. With more than one specialist, you may have a better chance of getting a fairer price."

As disappointed as I was to find Angstrom still going nowhere— and with only a computer to discuss the problem—I was impressed by the over-the-counter system. There was no frantic trading, no jostling on the floor, no funny sign language, no haze of nicotine, no overcrowding, no litter, and no mysterious specialist standing at the post with his Book. In fact, it was so quiet you could hear the hum of the Xerox machine. Watching Mr. Hobbing at the terminal, I began to think of the regular stock exchange in an entirely new light. With a well-organized computer market, there was no need for a huge building, the overhead TV monitors, the floor brokers, or the messengers. Perhaps the NYSE is a glorious anachronism, similar to the British royal family or the American horse cavalry, that only makes sense as a tourist attraction.

Back in his office, Mr. Hobbing told me the story of over-the-counter's sudden turnabout from the small, primitive market for forgotten stocks into the most advanced form of trade. Over-the-counter trading began outdoors, where stock certificates were sold on long tables set up under the trees, and the prices marked on makeshift blackboards. This also was the origin of the NYSE, but when that exchange went indoors in the nineteenth century and modernized its methods, the over-the-counter market became the alternative market, diffuse and unregulated. Buyers or sellers were often hard to find, and where prices existed at all, they were found in locally published "pink sheets," frequently out-of-date and/or inaccurate.

Mr. Hobbing said the over-the-counter market got better organized in 1939 when the dealers agreed to a formal code of regulations, under the aegis of the SEC. The resulting organization continued to survive on secondary issues and relatively obscure listings, living off the tidbits ignored by the major stock exchanges, until the arrival of the computer. Almost overnight, the disadvantage of this loose collection of far-flung dealers became its greatest asset. Big outfits like the NYSE and the AMEX, having invested so much in their buildings, their trading floors, their seats, their pageantry, and their specialists, were naturally reluctant to trade it all in for a telephone hookup and a few scattered terminals, but over-the-counter dealers were delighted to replace pink sheets with computers. Soon, the NASDAQ had leapfrogged over its once-almighty competitors.

The morning I spoke to Mr. Hobbing, the newspapers were full of stories about a Mr. Dennis Levine, an employee of Drexel Burnham Lambert who'd broken the Chinese Wall. The Chinese Wall, as I understood it, was some sort of gentleman's barrier, an invisible bundling board between people who sell stock and other people who work on mergers or banking and learn things that might affect the price of a stock. Talking across this so-called wall was not only ungentlemanly, but also illegal, and that's what Mr. Levine was accused of having done. The papers said that he and some others made a lot of money they shouldn't have made, as a result of their insider trading.

It hadn't yet occurred to me to try any insider trading of my own, but I asked Mr. Hobbing how NASDAQ handled the problem. Mr. Hobbing said the NASDAQ computer warning system made it very hard for insider traders and other such scofflaws to get away with their misdeeds. He volunteered to take me up to NASDAQ's Market Surveillance department on one of the floors above us, where he handed me off to a Bernard Thompson. Mr. Thompson had just begun to show me the office and to describe the compliance system when the alarm bells went off.

It sounded like nuclear attack whistles, and the whoops and shrieks sent various people scurrying to computer command posts and to the teletype machines. "What's happening?" I asked Mr. Thompson. "Parameters," he said. "Parameters must have been broken."

After things quieted down, Mr. Thompson explained that parameters are the regular limits in the up-and-down movements of any stock, which NASDAQ has figured out for its thousands of issues and programmed into the computers. When any stock price suddenly rises above the upper limit or falls below the lower one, and especially when a lot of shares are bought or sold, the alarm is automatically sounded. In this case, the culprit was a stock called Berkshire Hathaway, which was selling for the incredible price of $2,500 per share, making it the most expensive holding in the world. As I'd entered the room, Berkshire Hathaway apparently had violated its parameters.

"Probably nothing," said Mr. Thompson. "Maybe some bit of news. It'll be checked on our pass-fail system and on the teletype. Usually it's a false alarm."

NASDAQ had twelve people working full time to research these occurrences, and the first thing they looked for was some obvious explanation, like an important public announcement. When there was an important public announcement, such as the signing of a government contract, a stock was expected to move higher on a heavy volume of buying and selling. But if a stock moved erratically on its own, or worse, if it jumped higher on heavy volume before a public announcement, there was reason to suspect hanky-panky. By calling the market makers, investigators could find out who has been trading the biggest blocks of the stock. These inquiries worked their way back through the market makers to the brokers, and then to the individual investors, who might be called upon to explain their perfect timing.

Mr. Thompson said it didn't take long to learn exactly why a stock had broken its parameters, and also who had been responsible. The compliance office was always on the lookout for end-of-the-day upticks and other telltale signs of price manipulation.

After gathering all the facts, the NASDAQ people sent the most suspicious cases to the SEC for further investigation and possible prosecution. Mr. Thompson told me the SEC had already pressed ahead with 100 NASDAQ cases thus far that year. From what I'd seen of the compliance room, it was hard to imagine how anybody could get away with anything, and I was half relieved that Angstrom had never gotten its big government contract, and that recently there'd been no upticks to sound the alarms and rouse the SEC police into action.

SIXTEEN

SEEING THE ANALYST

WHEN I RETURNED TO NEW YORK FROM WASHINGTON, THERE was a message on my answering machine from William Hayes, the man who'd taken me to lunch at the stock exchange. He'd invited me to a meeting of the Society of Security Analysts at 71 Broadway. It was this invitation that indirectly led me to my third investment.

Have you ever thought of calling your analyst? I mean the stock market kind, the one who writes the reports that your broker sends you, along with the little notes that read: "Our firm highly recommends this purchase, as noted in the enclosed." For some reason, I'd never thought an analyst was an actual person you could contact, until Mr. Hayes informed me of the fact.

I attended the meeting—actually a small gathering of one committee within the Society. Frankly, it was depressing. This was a sad group of white-collar professionals in their mid-to-upper forties, all out of work. They talked of being a forgotten minority, which you don't expect to hear from WASPS on Wall Street. They complained of having lost out to younger, more aggressive analysts that brokerage houses now prefer.

Listening to their stories, I found out several useful things: (1) there are 15,000 analysts at large in the country, mostly in New York; (2) analysts at brokerage houses are expected to serve us, the stock-buying public; (3) there are "fundamental analysts" and "technical analysts," who carry on the same debate I heard at the investment conference. There are also "quants," who speak a form of calculus, so nobody can understand a "quant" except another "quant"; (4) most analysts have M.B.A. degrees and are very well informed; and (5) they may be the first to know when to buy and when to sell a stock.

This latter point was very exciting and made me sorry that I hadn't learned any of this earlier. It was a good thing Mr. Hayes thought to include me, because the day after the meeting, I returned to the visitor's gallery at the New York Stock Exchange and got a powerful urge to dump Angstrom once and for all.

The Dow Jones industrial average was up 41 points that afternoon. It was up more than 300 points since I started my journey—a fact I'd been trying to ignore. Worse than losing money in a bad market is losing it in this greatest bull market in history, as some had already called it. My frustration was shared by other investors swearing at the Quotrons in the visitor's gallery. I met several who'd bought small over-the-counter stocks that hadn't moved up with the broad market. They, too, were threatening to sell.

At about 3:00 P.M. I began a frantic search for a public phone. I rushed around the visitor's gallery, checking the hallway and the bathrooms, but there was no phone in sight. A guide who must have thought I was having a nervous breakdown suggested I take the next elevator to the downstairs lobby. There was no phone in the lobby, either. In this way, the New York Stock Exchange resembles a racetrack, where they aren't allowed to install public telephones within so many hundred yards of the finish line.

Outside, I ran past Anatoli and the other candy vendors shivering in the March winds. I tried a couple of open-air phones down the street, but the buttons stuck in the cold, and I'd have gotten frostbite completing the numbers. A heat-seeking instinct led me into the service entrance at 50 Wall Street and from there into a rear hallway. There were some laundry carts filled with trash. It turned out to be computer printouts and other refuse from Drexel Burnham Lambert. Their New York headquarters must have been directly upstairs.

In a corner of the hallway of Drexel's building was a phone booth.

As I picked up the receiver and started to dial Ms. Garrett, I was overcome with conflicting emotions. First, I felt guilty for calling my Prudential-Bache broker from the very headquarters of the firm I'd been cheating on. This feeling quickly gave way to my feeling like an idiot for calling Ms. Garrett under any circumstances. It had not helped our relationship—at least from my side—that Angstrom had gone the wrong way in the greatest bull market in history.

Then there was the dilemma of selling or not selling. Any stock you hold might eventually go up, but the act of selling at a loss forces you to admit you made a mistake. At this painful moment of truth, I thought of the Great Gabelli, and the slim chance that the smart money, i.e., his and mine, should continue to hold on.

I hesitate to mention it, but I also worried that selling the Angstrom might hurt Ms. Garrett's feelings. Then I reminded myself of something I'll leave with you as Useful Tip Number 14:

Don't continue losing money just to keep your broker happy

By the time I'd finished dialing the number, I'd nearly talked myself out of what had to be done. Just as Ms. Garrett picked up, I reached a sensible compromise with my conflicting emotions: sell half.

"What's the Angstrom worth?" I asked.

"$1^{13}/_{16}$."

"Is there anything else an analyst would recommend? I'd like to work with an analyst."

"Funny you mention it. Just a while ago, I was listening to an analyst over the morning call on our squawk box. Gillette. Nancy Hall says it's a buy. She's touting the domestic story."

(The "squawk box" is a loudspeaker in each field office that's connected to the home office. In the "morning call," the analysts broadcast their latest recommendations to thousands of local brokers at once. That's how many brokers get the new ideas they pass along to you.)

"Who's Nancy Hall?"

"Our cosmetics analyst in New York."

I got so excited at this chance to get in early on an analyst's best bet that I put in the Gillette order on the spot. We sold 2,500 shares of Angstrom for $4,289.75, a loss of $781.82, and invested nearly all of it in 53 shares of Gillette at 79¼. I remembered to ask about Gillette's P/E ratio, and Ms. Garrett said it was 14. She guessed that Gillette's 14 was a lot lower than Angstrom's P/E, and I felt confident Mr. Frank would have approved of the switch.

As soon as I'd bought the stock, I called Ms. Hall. Getting through to the analyst in person was easier than I expected. The main switchboard operator at Prudential-Bache connected me right to her line and she answered her own phone. I introduced myself as a writer and a Prudential-Bache client who'd taken a major position in one of her stocks, and who wanted to make sure he'd done the right thing. She kindly agreed to let me visit her in her office.

The part about the major position must have helped my cause, but I wouldn't have said it if I hadn't made a substantial commitment to the stock. If you're wondering how many shares you should own before pestering an analyst with a phone call, I'd suggest you follow Useful Tip Number 15:

Never bother an analyst if you own less than 53 shares

Prudential-Bache is housed in one of the many high-rises at the southern end of Manhattan along Water Street. Ms. Hall's office was located on an upper floor. The waiting room was full of what I'd call fine antique furniture, but I can never tell an original from a copy.

Nancy Hall came through the far door to greet me. She was tall and beautiful, and a thin, lime-colored scarf hung like a dorsal fin along her back. In any police lineup, I would have picked her for the fashion model and not the securities analyst, who I would have expected to be more stooped and shopworn.

She escorted me down a hallway and into her cubicle, which had a wonderful view of the harbor. Atop the usual clutter of pamphlets and magazines were samples of various shaving and menstrual-hygiene products from the cosmetic companies that Ms. Hall analyzes. In fact, she seemed to be running a little drugstore counter in there. Before I was able to sit down, she'd handed me the newest Gillette disposable razor, a brown one that swivels, and invited me to try it out and give her an opinion.

Ms. Hall was as charming as she was attractive. She said she'd been an analyst for only two and a half years, and worked as an editor at *Harper's Bazaar* before that. It was comforting to hear her say that being a securities analyst was a lot like being a journalist. Like the journalist, she worked long hours, 10 to 14 a day. She had a journalist's beat, cosmetics. She wrote "stories" on the dozen or so companies she followed. Less like the journalist, in my experience, was that her base salary fell somewhere between $125,000 and $200,000 a year, plus generous bonuses if her stories turned out to be true.

When it came to Gillette, Ms. Hall congratulated me on a wise choice. Though she might have preferred Avon herself, she was certain that Gillette wouldn't disappoint its shareholders. "We've liked the stock since it was $50," she said, "and we still like it now." She explained that Prudential-Bache had a rating system from 1 to 5, with 1 for "aggressive purchase," 2 for "accumulate," 3 for "average performer," 4 for "swap," and 5 for "sell." Each stock was assigned two numbers, the first for its near-term prospects, up to six months, and the second for long-term prospects, six to eighteen months. Avon was rated a "1-1," but Gillette was close behind at "2-2."

More important than the ratings was the annual estimate of earnings, which for Gillette Ms. Hall guessed would be $5.60 to $5.70 per share. With the stock selling at $80, I worked out the P/E ratio. Dividing the $80 by the $5.60, I got 14.3, just a fraction higher than I'd heard earlier.

Ms. Hall went on to explain that last year's Gillette story was international earnings boosted by the falling dollar, while this year's story would be domestic profits boosted by market-share gains in blades and toiletries, especially if people liked the new brown razors. She mentioned new Dry Idea deodorant products and Brush Plus makeup as big money-makers, said there'd be solid sales gains in the old razors, and predicted that White Rain shampoo, conditioner, and mousse would make a comeback.

Internally, Ms. Hall said, the company was planning to split its shares and had prepared a poison pill to swallow in case of an attack by corporate raiders. This pill business didn't sound very appealing to me, but Ms. Hall insisted it was simply a way of restructuring certain assets to give shareholders better protection. Splitting shares would cut the stock price in half, making it easier for average people to buy more.

Though Ms. Hall made a convincing case for Gillette, I thought it wouldn't hurt to get a second opinion. I mentioned this to her as tactfully as I could, and she kindly gave me the names of other analysts who followed the stock. In fact, she seemed as anxious as I was to find out what these other analysts were saying. "Let me know if you hear anything interesting," she said. "You can call me back any time." To me, this was a strange request, since she had the phone numbers and could have talked to them herself, but I let the matter drop.

The first name on Ms. Hall's list was Deepak Raj of Merrill Lynch, whom I contacted immediately. After I mentioned that I'd visited Ms. Hall, he invited me down to Merrill Lynch headquarters, which is more or less the same set up but without the antique furniture.

As you might have guessed, Mr. Raj was of Indian descent. He was much too agitated for a prolonged, idle conversation. Perhaps if I'd bought my 53 shares through him, he might have had more time. He did tell me that he'd been following the cosmetics companies since 1979, he lived in New Jersey, and he also worked long hours. One subject he seemed delighted to discuss was how early he had recognized Gillette's potential. Analysts call this their "initiation of coverage." Mr. Raj initiated his coverage of Gillette in 1980, when the stock was selling in the twenties, and had recommended it right up to its recent $80. I wished I'd been listening to his squawk box back then.

As to Gillette's future prospects, Mr. Raj was cautious but optimistic. Though he rated Gillette "above average"—which in Merrill Lynch's language fell somewhere below "buy" and above "sell"— he didn't seem as enthusiastic as Ms. Hall. He worried out loud about the competition: "What is Bic doing? What do we hear from Schick? That's the battle, getting market share and losing market share." Mr. Raj had no free samples in his office, and said he hadn't bothered to try the new brown razor on himself.

Perhaps I shouldn't have mentioned that Ms. Hall was anxious to know what Mr. Raj was thinking, but I did. He didn't seem to care what Ms. Hall thought. He was more interested in what Diana Temple thought, and wondered if I'd been to see her over at Salomon Brothers.

I made an appointment to see Ms. Temple, which was easy to get after I told her secretary that Mr. Deepak Raj had suggested that I call. Ms. Temple's office was on the usual upper floor of a Water Street high-rise, though it lacked a view of the harbor.

Ms. Temple was a heavy-set woman who looked a bit older than her two colleagues I'd already visited. This was more or less confirmed when she said she'd been in toiletries for 15 years. Ms. Temple was also less ebullient than the other two, and she didn't seem to like Gillette.

It wasn't that she disliked Gillette per se, but that she thought the company would "lag the market" in earnings. "I wouldn't say 'sell' here, but the earnings growth will be below average," Ms. Temple said. "White Rain, though, has made some good inroads." Her own earnings estimate of $5.60 a share was equal to Ms. Hall's estimate, yet she was cool on the company while Ms. Hall was crazy about it. I found this perplexing.

I brought up Ms. Hall's opinion, but Ms. Temple wasn't really interested. She was more anxious to know what Mr. Raj had been saying. She also mentioned an Alice Beebe Longley at Donaldson, Lufkin & Jenrette, which was where I headed next.

I checked in with Ms. Longley on the usual upper floor. She was as winsome as Ms. Hall, and she had the appealing habit of taking off her shoe and wiggling her toe during the conversation. It isn't the kind of detail worth mentioning in some professions, but on Wall Street, appearances were so well maintained that any sort of aberration was notable.

Ms. Longley mentioned she'd earned a Ph.D. in comparative literature. When I asked what this had to do with being an analyst, she laughed and said, "I used to take poems and analyze them to death." She left a job in an English department for the brokerage firm, enticed by the considerable increase in salary she got for analyzing cosmetics companies instead of Dylan Thomas.

About Gillette, Ms. Longley was halfway enthused, calling the stock a "moderate buy." That put her somewhere between Ms. Temple and Ms. Hall, but at this point, I'd become less interested in Gillette per se and more interested in what the analysts said about each other. I was caught up in their intrigue, fascinated with their odd preoccupation with their colleagues' opinions. Now that I'd been dragged into it, I told Ms. Longley that I felt like a messenger in some diplomatic plot. I explained that I'd been moving from office to office, serving as an unpaid spy for Ms. Hall. Why, I wondered, would such a thing be necessary?

Ms. Longley explained that analysts are not the lonely statisticians, poring over annual reports in the back rooms, that I might have imagined. They are a gregarious bunch and spend most of their waking hours on the telephone. All day they chat with important investors, jockeying for influence, hoping to be first in line with some new bit of information—an unusual jump in shampoo sales, an unexpected loss in the razor sector—that outdoes the previous caller. And although it is not the custom for rival analysts to communicate directly, their jobs may depend on what is being said about them. Each wants to be prepared for the latest gossip before he hears it from a big client's mouth.

To illustrate, Ms. Longley said she'd just returned from a visit to Avon. "I get back, sit down, and call everybody I know who owns the stock to tell them what I found out. That takes half a day." Meanwhile, her competitors like Mr. Raj or Ms. Temple may also have visited Avon, and they, too, are busily contacting the same investors to tell what they've found out. "I may call a client who just got off the phone with Diana Temple," explained Ms. Longley. "I'll hear from that client what Diana has been saying. He might say to me, 'Your earnings estimate of $5.60 sounds low. Diana's projecting $5.80.'"

As to where they got their information in the first place, Ms. Longley said most of it came straight from company headquarters. Each Gillette analyst called Boston two, three, even four times a week, to talk to Milton Glass. Mr. Glass was the Gillette vice president in charge of giving Wall Street the latest scoop on the company's progress, projected earnings, and so forth. After they hung up with him, the analysts quickly phoned the big shareholders, hoping to tell them what was happening before the other analysts got through.

I drove up to Boston to meet Mr. Glass. He was a perfect gentleman. During our chat in his office, he expressed a fatherly affection for the analysts who follow Gillette. Since most of them called him at least once a week, and saw him in person four times a year at the quarterly meetings, he'd gotten to know them quite well.

Over a delicious lunch in the executive dining room, I told Mr. Glass my impressions: how Ms. Hall of Prudential-Bache was ebullient, Mr. Raj of Merrill Lynch was cautious, and Ms. Temple of Salomon Brothers seemed a little grumpy. He confided that Ms. Temple was in a bit of a personal slump, which might explain her negative mood about Gillette, even though her earnings estimate was high. "Last year, she picked our Body Flowers as the product of the year and it failed. I cautioned her I didn't like the product myself," he said. He was delighted with Ms. Hall's "domestic story," because it presented the same information the others had received, but in a more imaginative way.

In a few minutes with Mr. Glass, I began to understand why Wall Street analysts tend to think alike, and why their earnings estimates for Gillette fell in a very narrow range, with hardly a dime separating the optimists from the pessimists. Not only did they get their information from the same source, but Mr. Glass was determined to tell all of them the same thing at the same time, so none would be favored.

"Favoring an analyst would be a very serious matter, and I don't do it," said Mr. Glass. He reminded me of a college professor overseeing the writing of a term paper. His students—Ms. Hall, Ms. Longley, and the rest—worked with the same basic material and were expected to come up with similar conclusions, embellished with a few distinguishing flourishes.

Mr. Glass more or less confirmed that the purpose of an analyst is to explain back to the company what it already knows is happening to itself. Excessive flattery, or criticism, or unusual conclusions might sour an analyst's relationship with a company that he or she must continue to analyze. Although Gillette is famous for its even-handed treatment of all analysts, Mr. Glass didn't doubt that at some companies, the skeptical analyst, like the skeptical newspaper reporter, might fall out of grace with official sources.

All this was so interesting that we got to dessert before I remembered to ask Mr. Glass about the stock. If analysts tell their big clients what Mr. Glass tells them, then I was sitting with the horse's mouth. Trying not to be obvious, I leaned over a coffee cup and whispered: "Maybe you can't say anything because of your position, but do you think I made a good deal at 79¼?" "I don't know," Mr. Glass said rather loudly. " I sold all my shares a couple of months ago at $60."

Back at Prudential-Bache in New York, I revisited Ms. Hall, informed her of all the above, and spent an afternoon plus an evening hanging around her office and following her around the building. She took me upstairs to a fancy buffet party where new stockbrokers were initiated to the rigors of New York. There was plenty of caviar and little pâté sandwiches, and as much liquor as we could drink. After that, she let me sit in her cubicle while she made telephone calls.

Like Ms. Longley, Ms. Hall seemed to do nothing but work. In the morning, she prepared her presentation on the squawk box, plus she helped plan the upcoming "road show" for Munsingwear. "Road shows" are frequent whirlwind trips around the country, where analysts meet local brokers and drum up support for their favorite shares.

Even in the corridor on her way to and from the elevator or the bathroom, Ms. Hall was on the job. She accidentally bumped into a mutual-fund manager, and I saw her immediately seize the opportunity to tell him the Gillette story, and to give him a sample of the new brown swivel razor. She was always on the lookout for potential buyers for her favorite stocks.

To say that the primary duty of an analyst is to analyze a stock couldn't be further from the truth. After spending a few hours with Ms. Hall, I realized that an analyst is first and foremost a salesman. Certainly, sales was the major part of Ms. Hall's preoccupation. Her recommending of Gillette was the easy part of the job. After that, she had to go out and stir up demand, so the price would increase and fulfill the prophecy.

(Apparently, analysts have not always been salesmen. Once, they were more like accountants, but that all changed on May 1, 1975, when fixed commission rates on stocks were abolished. For reasons I'll explain in a minute, the profession was revolutionized, and analysts were turned from introverts into extroverts almost overnight.)

My visits with analysts put a great many things into better focus and helped me understand what the average investor is dealing with. For instance, you may have noticed that it's rare for a brokerage firm to use the word *sell* in any of its reports. The word *sell* is very troublesome for the analyst, especially in the role of salesman. "I don't think you'll hear too many 'sells,' " Mr. Raj admitted to me. "If we say 'sell' at Merrill Lynch, people accuse us of pulling the plug on the stock."

I read somewhere that the ratio of buy recommendations to sell recommendations is 50 to 1 in favor of the former, and after my sojourn I wouldn't be surprised. If an analyst cries "sell," he's likely to lose favor with the company and be bumped from a favorable position in the string of phone calls. Even if he's right and the stock falls into disfavor, the big investors who bought it on his earlier "buy" signal may wonder why he didn't see the trouble then.

I've mentioned the "1-1" and "2-2" of Prudential Bache; the "match" or "outperform" the market at Solomon; and the "average," "above average," and so forth at Merrill Lynch. The various rating systems used by brokerage firms are a form of diplomatic language, similar to the flatteries employed by courtiers to disguise direct criticism. Instead of saying "sell," a brokerage firm is better off saying "hold." *Hold* may be a polite way of advising clients to get out of a stock, without offending and corporate bankers and other principals. Some firms that don't use the *buy* and/or *hold* vocabulary accomplish the same with *positive/neutral,* in which *neutral* takes the place of *sell,* or with a numerical ranking system like the one employed at Prudential-Bache. Other substitutes for *sell* include *might do better elsewhere* and *may underperform the market*.

Sub rosa, the analyst can interpret the hidden meanings directly into the ears of favored clients. One place it's safe for the analyst to use the dreaded word *sell* is in a private phone call to the bigger investors, but the average investor will never know it happened.

SEVENTEEN

A WALK
ON THE BUY SIDE

I'VE OVERSIMPLIFIED THIS ANALYST BUSINESS JUST TO GET US THIS far. There's a further complication: the buy-side analyst. The big investors employ these buy-side analysts just to interpret what the Nancy Halls and Diana Temples have been telling them five times a day on the telephone. That I'd only been talking to sell-side analysts is something I discovered at the end of my investigation.

It happened as follows. During one of my conversations with Ms. Hall, she told me that the biggest investor in Gillette was Citicorp—with something like 1.6 million shares. What Citicorp might be doing with its 1.6 million shares was of great personal interest. If they decided to dump their 1.6 million all at once because some analyst advised them to sell, I assumed it might have a depressing effect on the value of my 53.

When I expressed this fear to Ms. Hall, she gave me the name of the person to contact at Citicorp—their buy-side analyst, Valerie Molter. That's the first I'd heard of the buy-side analyst.

I called Ms. Molter and recited the string of sell-side analysts I'd already seen, as evidence of my importance. She agreed to meet with me. Soon I found myself on an upper floor of Citicorp headquarters on East Fifty-third Street, the building with a piece lopped off the top. There was no fancy lobby on Ms. Molter's floor, perhaps because the buy-side doesn't deal with the general public and can forgo the expensive impression. Maybe they'd spent the money on robots; as Molter and I walked back toward her cubicle, I almost tripped over one as it tried to deliver me some mail.

I warmed up to my eventual question about the 1.6 million shares of Gillette by asking about Citicorp's overall portfolio. Ms. Molter said it currently involved about $39 billion, or roughly the gross national product of Greece.

Ms. Molter was an intriguing combination of youthful assurance, argumentativeness, and indifference. I tried to ingratiate myself by telling her what Ms. Temple, Mr. Raj, and others had been saying. She couldn't have cared less. Not only that, she already knew what they'd been saying. Buy-side analysts are allowed to talk directly to the sell side. In fact, they're *supposed* to talk to the sell side. As Ms. Molter explained it, it's her job to weigh the relative sell-side opinions, to take note of any surprising news and who delivered it, and to rate the enthusiasm and general cooperativeness of the various analysts.

When I confessed that the actual purpose of the buy-side had eluded me thus far, Ms. Molter remarked, "The sell-side sees only the trees, but it's up to the buy-side to see the forest." More specifically, she said she listens to all the gossip, the earnings estimates, and the news not only from the cosmetics group, but from automobile analysts, media analysts, dozens of analysts who follow hundreds of stocks. Then she makes recommendations to the Citicorp portfolio managers as to which stocks they should actually buy.

Here was the final clue to the whole analyst mystery, and especially to why Ms. Hall, Ms. Longley, and the rest worried so much about pleasing their big clients. Ms. Molter was one of those clients, and she gave them all grades just like in high school. It was this grading system that kept the sell-side analysts in constant dread. Not only did they worry what grade they'd get from the likes of Ms. Molter, but also about the grades they'd receive from *Institutional Investor* magazine. I'd already noticed that several analysts had copies of this influential publication on their desks, especially if they'd made the highest ratings.

Ms. Molter called the grades "votes." In her firm, she's given 50 votes to divide among all the sell-side analysts. She said she rarely gives out more than 5 votes to any one person, but might give 4 "if they're always around when I need them," or 3 "if they call regularly plus do something unusual every once in a while," or 2 "if they write decent reports," or 1 "for just existing." "I try never to give a complete zero vote," she said. "Sometimes, I'll give a '1' vote to an analyst just because he's funny."

What makes these votes so important is that they translate into dollars. This goes back to what I mentioned earlier, the day in 1975 when fixed commission rates were abolished. If Ms. Hall, for instance, gets a good grade from Ms. Molter at Citicorp, it means that Citicorp will purchase more stock through Ms. Hall's firm, Prudential-Bache. Prudential-Bache will get a bigger commission, and Ms. Hall will get a sizable bonus. If Ms. Hall gets a bad grade, then both she and her firm will suffer. The annual profits of big brokerage firms like Merrill Lynch and Paine Webber depend on the grades its sell-side analysts receive from buy-side analysts at the big institutions that buy most of the stock.

No wonder so many of the sell-side analysts were gregarious, well-spoken, beautiful, diplomatic, and not at all the back-room types I had imagined. No wonder they spend so much time courting the big clients on the phone. They're constantly struggling for better grades. The only way average investors could compete for their attention is if we sent out report cards ourselves.

Ms. Molter didn't say so directly, but of all the Gillette analysts, I sensed that she favored Ms. Temple of Salomon Brothers. She praised Ms. Temple so enthusiastically that I'd bet Ms. Temple got a lot of her votes. That Ms. Temple had a lukewarm opinion on Gillette should have prepared me for the following disturbing news.

When finally I revealed to Ms. Molter that her firm and I had had something in common—their 1.6 million shares to my 53— she confided that Citicorp portfolio managers had been dumping the stock at a rapid rate and had reduced their holdings to less than 600,000 shares. Maybe 53 of theirs had ended up with me.

"Wiser than trusting in oracles," as Euripides said, "is to be friends with the gods." For some reason, I quoted this to Ms. Molter, which was another mistake. After that, she didn't seem so anxious to refer me to any portfolio manager at her institution, and claimed that all the best ones were either sick or out of town. Anyway, since Gillette had gone up four points and her Citicorp had been selling, I knew somebody equally big must have been buying and it would be nice to talk to them. Ms. Molter kindly gave me the name of Ed Platt, a friend of hers who was a portfolio manager at Bankers Trust.

AMONG THE
BILLION-DOLLAR BRAINS

W HEN I HEARD MS. MOLTER SAY THAT THE SELL SIDE MERELY advises the buy side, and that the buy side merely advises the portfolio managers, I knew I was one step away from the most influential of investors. From what I'd gathered, the 9,000 or so portfolio managers control 75 percent of the shares on the New York Stock Exchange and more than 50 percent of the shares in NASDAQ. They make the investment decisions for mutual funds, banks, pensions, and all the institutions.

I didn't go to see Mr. Platt right away. First, I went to see Michael Lipper, the expert on mutual funds. This was as good a time as any to investigate those popular holdings. Right from the beginning, several stockbrokers had argued that mutual funds are the only way an average person could hope to compete in the stock market. An entire generation of investors had bought into mutual funds in the belief that portfolio managers could do for them what they did for Citicorp or Bankers Trust. Mutual funds had become the average investor's own big institution.

Mr. Lipper was the Duncan Hines, the AAA, the Michelin of mutual funds. His company rated them, analyzed them, and ranked them for performance. If you ever wanted to shop around for mutual funds, the Lipper report, published regularly in *Barron's,* was the invaluable source.

It seemed to me there were so many mutual funds that picking the best one was no easier than picking a single winning stock. This was confirmed by Mr. Lipper in our half-hour interview. By his latest count, there were 2,500 separate funds, including loads and no-loads, stock funds, bond funds, and mixtures, offshore and onshore, specialized and general, foreign and domestic, growth and income. In 1950, there were only 98 such funds in total. There were more mutual funds for sale on the current market than there were stocks for sale in 1965.

According to Mr. Lipper, only 30 percent of these mutual funds had anything to do with stocks. The other 70 percent were invested in bonds, bank certificates, or the money market. These income funds were invented so people could avoid the dilemma of choosing from thousands of competing bonds and certificates of deposit, and now there were thousands of them. There were even mutual funds that invested in other mutual funds. All in all, Mr. Lipper figured that $500 billion was riding on this whole business.

During our interview, I suddenly had this thought: *Suppose your mutual fund decides to dump Gillette, while you've just bought 100 shares of that same stock for your individual account? Maybe you're fighting against yourself. Maybe a dumping of shares by mutual funds has driven the price down, frightening you into selling your individual shares at a loss. Then again, when your mutual fund buys something you already own individually, the purchase could work in your favor.* These complications deserve further study. When average investors complain that Wall Street is run by big institutions, they don't always remember their part in it.

Some of the biggest advances in the mutual fund industry, along with the many new types of funds, were the new ways that fees and expenses could be charged to clients. There were load funds that charge a sales fee up front, back-loaded funds that charge a sales fee later, no-load funds that take their fees during the year, and innovative trailing commissions taken out a little at a time. Mr. Lipper said that during bull markets, most clients were satisfied with their gains and didn't notice the commissions and fees, but in the next bad market, he predicted a rude awakening. "Go back to a period of low returns," he said, "and the expenses of these funds could become a real bother. You could find people shopping for mutual funds on the basis of management fees alone, which they don't do today."

If you are paying a mutual fund manager, especially in a stock fund that promises capital growth and so on, then you expect better results than you'd get on your own. That brings me back to Mr.

Platt, and the question of how well the portfolio managers perform in general.

But after I left Mr. Lipper, I still didn't call Mr. Platt. Instead, I headed over to Salomon Brothers and got a tour of the trading room. Trading rooms are where decisions of the big institutions get carried out, and entire floors of expensive New York high-rises are given over to this activity. Salomon Brothers has one of the biggest trading operations, which is why I was anxious to see it.

This single firm takes a large chunk out of the square footage at 1 New York Plaza. Once I'd arrived downstairs, I got up the courage to visit my old college friend Brim, rumored to be making more than $1 million a year as a managing partner. The waiting room alone was the size of an average house. Actually, this wasn't even Mr. Brim's permanent office. The secretary told me that he worked in London, so what I'd seen was the place he hung his hat on business trips.

The trading room at Salomon Brothers is what you'd get if you suspended a football field 45 floors above the street, and covered it with desks, telephones, and computers. The room itself is at least 100 yards long, with another 30 yards from floor-to-ceiling, so an average punt would never reach the acoustical tile. Tennis lobs could make their full arcs here, and birds would never know they'd been left indoors.

Around the perimeter of the upper wall at both ends of the floor, where a scoreboard might normally be hung, was the biggest ticker tape I'd seen to date. As it moved along, it sounded like an unoiled bicycle chain being pulled across the sprockets. Above the background noise, a loudspeaker announced: "Twenty Million Ginnie Maes," and also "Nine percent at 116, let's go guys" in the same way that shoppers are notified of sales at K Mart. There was an occasional squeal or cheer from traders at their desks, and I could pick out bits of the conversation. "I'll trade out of my fuckin' nickel for a bunch" is one phrase I wrote down.

These traders looked like recent college graduates, so I wasn't surprised to hear various whooped obscenities or to see one practical joker pull a chair from under his neighbor, while another trapped his partner in a headlock.

There must have been 200 desks, some with one computer screen but most with two or more. On a few desks 15 of these television sets were stacked three or four high, some showing bar graphs, others showing charts with wiggly lines, and others long columns of numbers. The computers were cooled with desktop electric fans that seemed quite primitive compared to the electronics.

There must have been 1,000 telephones, enough to service a small town. On some desks, entire switchboards were set up between the stacks of computers. Being escorted around them by a public relations officer made it impossible to learn much, but I did discover that Salomon's traders were buying and selling stocks and bonds around the world, 24 hours a day. Their telephones were hooked up to the floors of various stock exchanges, or else to the offices of brokers and other dealers. If a U.S. market was closed, then London or Rome might be open, and after that there was always Singapore or Japan or Hong Kong. Many employees were busily trading bonds, but those who dealt in stocks took their orders from portfolio managers who sat together around the corner.

It seemed futile to talk to a portfolio manager with all the commotion surrounding us here, so I thanked my escort for the tour and left the building. From the lobby below, I called to make the appointment to visit Mr. Platt.

Bankers Trust is located in a midtown building, just off Fifth Avenue and not far from Grand Central Station. I met Mr. Platt in a conference room, and gave him Ms. Molter's regards. If you put him in a crowd of people and asked me to pick him out today I'd fail, so there's no point in my pretending to recall his appearance. I'm sure he was dressed in a sensible suit. I remember he said he was 40 years old, lived in Westchester, had a nice family, had his M.B.A., did his undergraduate work at Cornell, came to Bankers Trust from Marine Midland, and had worked here seven years. He also mentioned he was an unusual portfolio manager, since he doubled as a buy-side analyst. He got input from the sell side and from the buy side, and then invested the $150 million in pension fund money under his control.

Mr. Platt gave me a tour of the Bankers Trust trading room, a miniature version of the Salomon Brothers setup, with four or five people manning the desks. He said the traders were very valuable as mini-specialists, since they knew where big blocks of stock were located, plus who was willing to sell and at what price. The actual Bankers Trust orders, however, were not executed here. They were routed through the regular brokerage houses so that Bankers Trust could pay the commissions and thereby reward the broker-age-house analysts who'd given the best advice and deserved the highest grades.

I said I'd love to be in his shoes—with all that intelligence behind you how could you lose? Mr. Platt laughed. Then he confided that the portfolio manager is on shaky footing, and must look over his shoulder at the other portfolio managers, plus stay awake nights worrying if he's going to lose his job. In fact, the dozen or so portfolio managers at Bankers Trust had made a recent pact to all buy the same stocks, so nobody would look bad compared with the others, thus avoiding what Mr. Platt called "diverse perfor-mance."

"Our agreement works this way," he said, "I hear from all my sources, make a recommendation on what stocks to purchase, then write it up. The other portfolio managers do the same. Then we get together and vote on our recommendations. Basically, what-ever is approved we put in all our portfolios."

You'd think a portfolio manager would welcome diverse per-formance, but Mr. Platt convinced me they'd gladly forgo the chance at relative glory in return for reasonable job security. They'd rather go up and down together for the following good reason: "If a client hears that another portfolio manager did better than me during the last quarter, then he might consider switching to that other manager. Clients demand results, and results is what they pay us for."

As I got further into Mr. Platt's obvious worries about his com-petition and about quarterly results, I began to wonder if the average investor for all his ignorance isn't better off than these gods of the marketplace. Instead of the conquering ego I'd ex-pected to meet, I got the feeling that Mr. Platt was just as nervous as the rest of us, and often forced by circumstance into following the crowd. In fact, he'd said so much about the foibles of portfolio managing that by the time he told me he wasn't buying Gillette I was almost glad.

When he mentioned that "portfolio managers have a hard time

beating the market averages," I could hardly believe my ears. Did he mean that all these layers of experts didn't get any better results overall than the broad group of ignoramuses out there, investing willy-nilly?

I tried to step back and consider this logically. Here were the sell-side analysts earning $150,000 and up, depending on their grades, for recommendations that had to be reviewed by the buy-side analysts, who earned as much or more. Then the recommendations of buy-side analysts again were reviewed by portfolio managers, who earned an even greater amount to make insecure decisions, the consequences of which they avoided by acting only in concert. In the end, none of this did any good, and most of them failed to beat the market averages.

I discussed the matter further with Mr. Platt and others, and got several explanations. One was that since the general public no longer buys much stock, the big institutions compete against themselves and can't possibly beat each other at the same game. Another was that portfolio managers are judged every three months and can't afford to take chances. Mr. Lipper had mentioned that "most of the large chunks of money are managed by people who think alike, who are trained in the same places, and who serve clients who want to hear the same sorts of things." This so-called group-think, he said, caused many managers to adopt the identical strategy. In this way, many portfolio managers tried to be average, so they couldn't possibly beat the average.

A few institutions had attempted to do away with the sell-side/buy-side/portfolio-manager system. One of those was Battery March Financial in Boston. When I visited Gillette up there, I also visited Battery March. There, the portfolio manager had been replaced by a computer.

Dean LeBaron, a balding veteran of Wall Street who recruited the computer, gave me the tour. As he showed me through the office, I noticed fewer employees than I'd seen at Bankers Trust. Around the perimeter of the large open room were a dozen or so cubicles, occupied by the cheerleaders and babysitters of the big brain, which took up the floor space in the middle.

Mr. LeBaron explained that the Battery March computer picked the stocks, watched the prices, monitored the action, decided when to sell, put shares on the auction block, set the price, haggled with the traders, and in general did the work of an entire Wall Street investment firm. "Once you've blown away the research department, you realize you don't need to run around meeting with companies, which is another relief," he added.

"Another thing we like is that brokers never call us," Mr. LeBaron continued. "They only talk to the machine." He explained how the computer was equipped to do business with 25 human traders in various markets around the world. After these 25 signed on from their own computer terminals each morning, the Battery March brain transmitted a list of what it might want to buy or sell. The humans put in their various bids, and the computer shut down precisely at 11:00 A.M. to consider its response. If it didn't get the price it wanted, it simply took the stock in question off the trading block. If it was satisfied with the price, it came back on line to announce that the offer had been accepted.

As the two of us talked, I watched the computer offer to sell 892,800 shares of Black & Decker at $23¼ a share. It gave no indication of any interest in Gillette.

Million-share days were not unusual for this machine. From 9:30 A.M. to 4:00 P.M. it traded the U.S. markets, then went international for the evenings, moving from east to west along the path of the sun. It bought and sold stocks in London, Rome, Hong Kong, Singapore, and Japan, and then after 21 hours of constant work, it took 3 hours off to rest and to consider what it had done.

At night it labored alone in the office, but if there was a problem it knew the home phone numbers for Dean LeBaron and other Battery March executives. In an emergency, the computer could reach them via beeper. When things ran smoothly, which was most of the time, the employees didn't find out what was bought and sold until morning.

Apparently the computer had no sentimental attachment to any stock or to any country. A babysitter named Mary Beth, who sat next to the machine in the middle of the room, told me it would "sell out entire countries if it decided those countries were unattractive."

Trading by computer had produced a very relaxed office. Neither Mary Beth nor her colleagues in the cubicles had the harried look

I'd seen on the faces of the sell-side analysts. I couldn't imagine what the human employees had to do all day except read novels. Then Mr. LeBaron reminded me, "Somebody has to program it."

It turns out the Battery March people were constantly tinkering with the computer's program, which had gone from a "corporate valuation strategy" to a "dividend discount model" to "a balance-sheet focus," and back to a "dividend discount model." "Just as you might own more than one stock, we've owned more than one strategy," said Mr. LeBaron. "Back in 1982 we favored growth stocks and cyclicals—now we like oil and gas." He put Battery March in the Fundamentalist camp, a sort of high-tech Prudential Speculator.

Mr. LeBaron gave me the results, which lately had been disappointing. Though the Battery March system had achieved an enviable return on investment over 10 years, in the current period the computer had failed to beat the market averages. When I left them, Mr. LeBaron and his colleagues were still debating what went wrong.

I could see that out-performing the overall market was no easy task for computers, any more than it was for hundreds of high-paid experts. In the *Wall Street Journal,* I read that most bond portfolio managers consistently fail to beat their market averages. Similarly, *Business Week* did a cover story on how the managers of stock portfolios hadn't beaten the market averages for three years in a row, with the majority doing much worse than the norm.

Here's a modest proposal for all the institutions and the mutual funds: fire the analysts and portfolio managers and invest in the market as a whole. That would save a lot of trouble, not to mention the millions in salaries and commissions now being thrown at a lost cause. Mr. Lipper told me there are mutual funds that already accomplish this. These funds simply buy all the stocks on the S&P-100 list, or all the stocks that make up the Dow Jones industrials, or all the bonds in the various bond indexes, and they've equaled the market average by definition. Their results are as good or better than what most investors, large and small, are paying extra money to try to achieve.

Whether it makes sense to get out of a specific mutual fund and into one that simply buys market averages is something you'll have to decide for yourself. What I got out of my trip to Bankers Trust was an appreciation for the portfolio manager's difficult job. That Mr. Platt worried about equaling the averages made me feel better about my own record—which so far was nothing to brag about.

ON BECOMING
A STOCKBROKER

T HE GILLETTE BEING FIVE POINTS AHEAD PLUS THE EARLIER GAIN
on the option still didn't make up for the shrinking Angstrom, and by the end of April the $10,920.31 I'd invested
was worth only $9,019.88, a loss of $910.42. At this point,
I began to think I should become a stockbroker.

When I considered the negative income, and added up the hours
it took to achieve it, almost any paying job began to sound good.
First, I realized I'd have been better off picking tomatoes or scrap-
ing boats. Even if I'd volunteered my time to the United Way at
least I wouldn't have been out the $910.42. I remembered that
Ms. Garrett had been making a pleasant living during this entire
struggle. Whatever her personal losses from Angstrom, they were
cushioned by several commissions from me. In fact, being a stockbroker was one of the few proven risk-free methods of investing
I'd encountered so far.

I found out it took four months from the day an aspiring stockbroker put in the application to the day he or she advised the first
client. This compared favorably with six months for licensed beauty-
parlor operators, and two years for plumbers certified to unclog
drains. I could have become a broker twice in the time I'd spent
on this project to date. Surely I'd spent more hours bungling my
investments than it would take to graduate from broker's school.

The aspiring stockbroker is hired by a local branch office like
those I visited earlier. There's three months of on-site training:
processing orders, answering telephones, learning the paperwork,
and studying for the Series 7 exam. The Series 7 exam is given by
the SEC and covers basic rules and regulations of Wall Street.
Sixty percent pass it, so it couldn't be too hard. The survivors are

sent to the boot camps of investing, mostly in or around New York, for three weeks of formal instruction.

Thanks to Ms. Garrett and her connections, Prudential-Bache allowed me to spend a few days wandering in and out of its training center in downtown Manhattan. I was also invited to stay three days and four nights at the Merrill Lynch training camp outside of Princeton, New Jersey. It took many phone calls through several departments to get this permission, but it was worth it. Merrill Lynch was the number-one retail firm, with $2 billion in assets. There were 10,000 Merrill Lynch brokers on the job already, and they trained 1,700 new ones a year to keep up with attrition.

I'd recommend their 300-room, $135-million training facility as a vacation spot. It had an Olympic-size swimming pool, racquetball courts, and a special sub-lobby just for billiards. The firm picked me up in a jasmine-scented Fugazi limousine, and assigned me a delightful double room.

The brochure on the table promised an "informal and relaxed atmosphere." Under "attire," I noted that casual clothes was the appropriate dress during the day, while normal business attire was recommended for dinner. To me, casual clothes meant shirt, pants, shoes and socks, and much less in friendly surroundings, but when I ventured out of my room in sport shirt and slacks I was met with numerous stares and a few titters. Everyone but me was wearing a business suit, and I became known as "that guy with no tie." For dinner, I changed into a blue blazer and slacks—to me, the normal business attire—only to discover that the others had changed into the kind of suit I'd wear to a funeral.

I found it curious that stockbroker trainees—many of whom were not from the monied classes—were required to dress so formally. The theory behind it, I guess, is that a stockbroker who dresses like a million dollars has a better chance convincing a real millionaire to throw some money the stockbroker's way—until the broker attracts enough of it to live up to the wardrobe. This made me think of Useful Tip Number 16:

Never trust a broker whose suit is worth more than your portfolio

---

The food was wonderful and wouldn't have embarrassed the chef at "21" or the Four Seasons. There were ice sculptures on the dining room table (swans, not bulls), succulent little squabs dressed in pastel hula skirts, huge slabs of salmon with slices of cucumber stuck on to resemble the fish's own scales, and a French/ Italian/California wine list as long as a good English novel. We ate while looking at a duck pond.

At that first meal I met several of the trainees and their professors, an affable bunch. Most were bright and well spoken, though some had come straight from the unemployment lines. There was a poet from Southern California, Lance Jencks, who'd been laid off as an 800-line telephone jockey for oil-and-gas leasing schemes. There was a 250-pound ex–football player who used to sell insurance. There were a few ex–car dealers (one, Paul from Wichita, said that investments were just "another vehicle"), a computer salesman or two, a rancher, a ballet dancer, a man who'd burned out on wheat futures, a "syndicator" with nothing left to syndicate, plus some former schoolteachers. Of the 150 in the group, I counted 25 women, 1 black, and the rest white males aged 26 to 60. Of the white males, at least 15 were out-of-work Texans.

After dinner, I watched trainees play billiards until they returned to their rooms to do homework, and then I swam laps alone in the giant indoor swimming pool. I didn't see them again until morning when classes began at 8:00. Since I'd been given a badge that got me past the numerous guards, I could roam freely from place to place. Once in a while a conference director would take me aside to ask me my impressions so far.

The first class I entered was fitted out like a language lab, with phones installed on each desk. These phones were connected to similar phones in the next room, so recruits could call back and forth to practice whatever they were learning. Soon, the phones started ringing and I listened to some conversations that would remind you of *La Familia de Tio Pepe,* if you've ever taken Spanish. These dialogues were in English. I copied one from the training manual, to give you the flavor.

Dr. MacIntyre, good morning. This is Terry Harper at Merrill Lynch. How are you today?

Just fine, thanks. What can I do for you today?

Dr. MacIntyre, many physicians I know feel they are paying too much of their income in taxes. I'm calling today to ask you what you're currently doing to ease the tax bite.

Ease the tax bite . . . hmm . . . well, of course, some of my funds go into my retirement account. That's tax-deferred . . . and my accountant has really been after me about buying municipal bonds, but I just haven't moved on that yet. Listen, I'd like to talk to you about this, but I have a patient on the way in. Can you get back to me?

THINK UP A CLOSING FOR THIS EXERCISE

This sort of practice went on for several hours a day. Since I came in at the end of a three-week session, these trainees were already adept at dialogue. Some had gone beyond the written scripts and could improvise their own openings and closings. They'd learned a new skill called "overcoming stalls and objections." They'd learned how to ask open-ended questions that get the client talking ("What do you think?" "How does that grab you?" "What is your feeling about that?") as opposed to closed-ended questions that allow the client to avoid conversation with yes or no answers. They'd been taught "responding to initial resistance during a sales call." They'd studied the "skill of acknowledging"; "probing for client feedback"; the "skill of bridging" ("earlier, you mentioned . . .").

I also sat in at Prudential-Bache and found their recruits just as well versed in dialogue, though some of the vocabulary was different. There, they talked about "restating the need," "avoiding bunched objections," "identifying the buy signals," "supporting on the same level," and "prospecting for gold in the client's words." Also, they had an elaborate system for classifying clients, which I copied from the manual as follows:

A "lead" is a piece of information. A "prospect" is a "lead" with a voice or a face attached to it. Once you have said hello and have obtained a response, the "lead" becomes a "prospect." A "prospect" becomes a "qualified prospect" with the potential for a positive business relationship. Here's a simple test: if you have a reason to call a "prospect" back, you have upgraded the relationship to the "qualified prospect" level.

A "customer" is a "qualified prospect" for whom you've written at least one ticket.

Soon I began to suspect that I was ill-prepared to become a stockbroker. This had nothing to do with my lacking an M.B.A. degree or my having failed calculus in college. What worked against me the most was never having taken a drama course. The one accountant in the bunch confided that he, too, felt out of place and that his education was a handicap. Throughout the training, he'd had trouble probing for client feedback, and asked too many closed-ended questions in a row.

Lance Jencks, the poet from Southern California whom I befriended, had the greatest advantage. Since he'd already done O'Neill, Becket, and commedia del l'arte, not to mention the scripts for the oil-and-gas leases, he could overcome stalls and restate needs without even thinking about it.

In the daily practice sessions, one trainee would play the broker and another would play the client, then they'd switch, and after that they'd evaluate each other. Were they too pushy? Did they close? Did they build rapport? Once they were a person short on the client end and invited me to sit in. This was fun. It amused me to hear many of the familiar catchwords and arguments from my earlier conversations with actual brokers. Such lines as: "Nothing has changed even though your stock has drifted lower," or "What you're looking for is something with growth potential," or "We're long-term oriented" come directly from the dialogues and were practiced over and over. The new brokers could repeat them in a coma.

Those with poor memories were encouraged to prepare cue cards that could be taken home and flipped during phone conversations with actual customers. I saw cards for how to introduce the tax-free bond, what to say about mutual funds, how to sell the retirement account, and even a card for what to say when the client complains, "But I don't have any money." At Prudential-Bache, the training director, Al Levy (since retired), told me he'd once made a tape on what to tell a client after a loss. This I could probably reproduce myself, though I wish I'd been able to hear his version.

I have broker's school to thank for Useful Tip Number 17:

The newer the broker, the less likely he'll make a spontaneous remark

---

For several years, there's been a trend toward more and more prepared answers, and more dialogues that cover every conceivable investment situation. In fact, while the other trainees were studying, I experimented with adding the Merrill Lynch lines to some of the famous laments in literary history. Among the many scripts, I found a Merrill Lynch solution to every conceivable dilemma:

ELECTRA: Hades, Persephone, Hermes steward of death, Eternal Wrath and Furies, Children of gods who see all murders and all adulterous thieves, come soon, I have no strength, I cannot stand alone under this load of my affliction.

MERRILL LYNCH: I understand how you FEEL [*Indicating empathy*], other people have FELT that way [*Indicating the prospect is not alone*], and they have FOUND that there are a number of investment vehicles that offer considerable stability.

SOCRATES: Do you really think that anyone, knowing the bad things to be bad, still desires them?

MERRILL LYNCH: Many investors rate the need for a broker who cares for their clients as one of their highest needs. What are your expectations?

SOCRATES: Do those who think that the bad things benefit know that the bad things are bad?

MERRILL LYNCH: Due to the size and depth of our organization, we're frequently in a position to offer clients opportunities they may not have access to through their regular investment channels.

MERRILL LYNCH: BOB SMITH (your partner, your boss, your associate, etc.) asked me to give you a call. He thought you might be interested in some of the strategies we're using to (reduce taxes, increase the return on your investments, make money in the market, etc.). Choose one.

KING LEAR: Nothing will come of nothing, speak again. . . .

MERRILL LYNCH: I've been speaking to attorneys in the area about ways to reduce their taxes and increase their income.

KING LEAR: How now! Mend your speech a little lest you may mar your fortunes. . . .

MERRILL LYNCH: I can understand the need to be cautious, and that's why an investment offering safety of principle might be appropriate.

By the third day, I'd almost lost all desire to become a stockbroker. First, I discovered my deficiencies in drama. Then I found out that brokers aren't allowed to open their own mail. Anything that's sent to the office, even a love letter, is scissored by the bosses, who are looking for cash or checks that might otherwise elude the firm's grasp. On top of that, the average broker spent most of his waking hours calling up strangers. This "cold calling" was a familiar feature of the business, but I had no idea how much time it consumed. According to the sample schedule handed out at Merrill Lynch, a broker was expected to spend five hours during three workdays a week plus another hour and fifteen minutes on two extra weeknights dialing for new customers. The minimum recommended effort was 180 cold calls every Monday through Friday.

To find enough new people to call, the broker was encouraged to seek out prospective clients from lists of survivors in obituary columns, from articles about the beneficiaries of large legal settlements, from telephone books in fancy neighborhoods, and from specialized mailing lists. A catalog of lists handed out at Merrill Lynch mentioned: "1.1 Million Affluent Individuals," "Aircraft Pilots at Home with Telephone Numbers," "Arabs Who Gamble and Invest," "Cattle and New Movie Investors," "Blue-chip Stockholders," and "Dentists Who Are Heavy Investors."

At Prudential-Bache, they said forget dentists. Dentists weren't making enough money these days and brokers were advised to ignore them. Doctors were a problem because they never answered their phones, so it was deemed best to approach Mrs. Doctor with an embossed invitation to a seminar. Prudential-Bache brokers were also encouraged to start a "tickler file," with the dates that options expired, dividends were paid, retirement funds were due, and so on, as a guide to which people should be cold-called when.

You may have begun to wonder: *But what about the stock market?* So did I. During coffee breaks from the language labs, only a handful of recruits hung around the Quotron machines, where I spent hours pecking in ATSI for "Angstrom" and GS for "Gillette." Once, I was joined by David Beard of Portland, Maine, who told me he'd burned out on wheat futures before he joined Merrill Lynch. He said he was anxious to start working, so he could make up for his losses. I identified with him immediately.

How many stockbrokers, historically, come from the ranks of failed investors I wasn't sure, though I'd already heard one broker admit that brokers are losers in the stock market. From one of the history books, I'd learned that the earliest stockbrokers were found in Amsterdam in about 1600, but nothing was said about what drove them into this business. In *The Common Sense of Money and Investments,* written by the elder Rukeyser, I'd read that the word *broker* comes from the Saxon *broc,* which actually means "misfortune."

Stockbrokers had suffered a general bad reputation—as bumblers, connivers, or worse. In the rural towns and villages of the 1870s, the summer visit of the stockbroker caused many citizens to "close their shutters in alarm," according to Matthew Josephson in *The Money Lords.* During the 1920s, the same author wrote, "The typical stockbroker was well spoken and well clad in conservative style, but not oversupplied with brains." Recently, and perhaps thanks to the bull market, the broker's reputation had improved. In a Gallup poll on which professions deserved the public trust, stockbrokers came in 16th out of 30. They rated no worse than congressmen and building contractors, higher than used-car dealers, and far below priests.)

To imply that the Merrill Lynch trainees never had a practical lesson in their newly-chosen field, investments, would be wrong.

There were hour-long classes in various aspects of stocks and bonds that I would have mentioned earlier, except inserting them as an afterthought gives you a better idea of their relative importance as against, say, sales.

The purpose of the classes was to put the new broker at least one step ahead of the customers he would soon serve. I sat in on two or three of them, including one on municipal bonds, another on the various ways Merrill Lynch could lend money ("We're going after the banks," said a representative named Mr. Humm), and a third on whether the stock market would go up or down. This last was actually a tape-recorded lecture from Mr. Robert Farrell, Merrill Lynch's star technical analyst. His lesson on "contra-cyclicals and defensive stocks" created as much confusion as it resolved. Some in the audience worried that in three days they'd have their own desks at local offices and people would be asking them if the stock market was going up or down, and what would they say?

In a final class, the teacher asked how many of the new brokers felt qualified to recommend any stock and not one of them raised a hand. He reassured them that they had a terrific firm behind them, and that Merrill Lynch would provide all the guidance and good ideas they needed. Then he showed an inspirational documentary film in which some very nice joggers lead a blind man through a cross-country race, up and down rocks, across fields and around trees, the blind man stumbling along and then triumphantly crossing the finish line. To me, this was an appropriate way to end the session.

To be honest, these recruits didn't expect to be selling much stock, as compared to unit trusts, corporate bonds, limited partnerships, foreign investments, 1,700 varieties of mutual funds, some options, annuities, money-market instruments, plus the various "products of the week" that brokerage firms now promote. To date, Merrill Lynch was offering 150 different products, and half of them were invented in the last five years. The trainees were encouraged to get their real estate licenses and insurance licenses to further expand their product line. They were further encouraged to take a Merrill Lynch self-study course, called the "Donald Regan School," after which they'd be certified as financial planners. (The White House advisor for whom this course was named has since resigned under a cloud, so perhaps they're calling it something else now.)

Did I mention that Merrill Lynch brokers are now known as "financial consultants"? There's been a drift in this direction since Shearson Lehman first called its brokers "financial planners." Before that, they were "account executives" or "registered representatives." "Customers' men" takes us back to the 1920s. From "customers' men" to "financial consultant" you'll notice an elevation in stature, to which stockbrokers are no less entitled than prison wardens who've become "behavioral scientists," physical education teachers who are "sports therapists," and ushers who are "crowd engineers."

The dialogues they practiced so hard prepared them for "consultative selling." If you've been cold-called in the last few months, you'll have noticed it. The new broker, a.k.a. financial consultant, doesn't seem to be trying to sell anything. He seems content to sit on the telephone and chat about financial goals. *"When's he going to give the pitch?"* you may have wondered, but he never does. Even if you tell him you've been dying to buy IBM, he'll discourage it until you've come down to the office and reviewed your financial objectives.

As one of the training directors explained it: "In the old days, the sales-oriented broker would say things like, 'IBM is poised for a move, and we at Merrill Lynch think you should pick up 100 shares.' Now, the financial consultant says, 'Mr. Client, what is your most pressing concern?' "

This gets the prospective client into the office with a complete list of assets, since the "financial consultant" has to know your assets before your objectives can be reviewed. From there, he may offer you a loan from the loan department, insurance from the insurance department, real estate from the real estate department. Ultimately, the purpose of not selling anything is to sell a great deal more, which is the zen aspect of the consultative approach.

Another advantage of consultative selling is that the financial consultant becomes an expert in the client's needs. This, I can see, is much smarter than posing as an expert in the stock market. Even when he makes bad investment decisions, the financial consultant is still an expert in the client's needs, which presumably will be greater than they were before the two of them made the acquaintance.

The last day of the Merrill Lynch course the phones were plugged into the outside world and the recruits went live, using Merrill Lynch's Familiar Quotations to set up appointments back home. I wasn't allowed to participate directly, but I sat in on the impressive chorus of a roomful of brokers, all saying things like, "Hello, this is Jim Reynolds from Merrill Lynch. I'm interested in people with financial objectives who are interested in reaching their financial objectives. Do you have time to talk? . . . How about next week?"

I left the training camp with deep affection for the friends I'd made, but convinced that being a stockbroker was not for me. In that field, there's no time to think about stocks and bonds. I'm glad I realized it early enough to avoid the full commitment. From Merrill Lynch boot camp, I returned to New York, anxious to get back to the subject.

TWENTY

SELLING MYSELF SHORT

T HERE WAS ANOTHER STRATEGY I WAS DETERMINED TO IN-
vestigate: selling short. Selling short was one of those investment terms I pretended to understand without having
the slightest idea what it meant. For more than twenty
years I'd nodded my head knowingly at any mention of it, and no
doubt I wasn't alone in this. Maybe people who actually sold short
didn't realize what they'd done.

I admitted this ignorance to Mr. Gressel the night we listened
to left-wing Chilean music on his stereo. He explained that selling
short was selling somebody else's property and hoping to profit
from it. At first that sounded criminal, and I couldn't see the
difference between selling a stock short and selling the Brooklyn
Bridge. Mr. Gressel quickly corrected my misconceptions.

According to Mr. Gressel, shorting works as follows. You call
up your broker and announce you expect a certain stock, IBM,
for instance, to go down. The broker suggests you short the IBM.
If you short 1,000 shares of it, with the stock selling at $160, then
the proceeds of $160,000 are immediately added to your account.
If you did this a couple of times, I figured, you could become a
millionaire very quickly. What better way to get rich overnight
than to short everything in sight and wake up to a giant windfall
from selling a lot of the stocks you never bought in the first place?

Unfortunately, selling short was not quite as perfect as it sounded.
It turned out that you'd only borrowed the 1,000 shares of IBM.
In fact, your stockbroker had asked around and found an IBM
shareholder willing to loan you the shares so you could short them.
(Any person who shorts stock must allow other people to short
his.)

The person whose stock you've borrowed must get the shares back, eventually, and the way you replace them is by paying the current price. For instance, if you shorted 1,000 shares of IBM at $160, and six months later, IBM was selling for $200, then it would cost you $200,000 to settle the account. Since you were credited with $160,000 for shorting the IBM in the first place, you'd be left with a $40,000 loss in this instance.

You could hold on to any stock you've sold short for as long as you want, or for as long as there was enough money in your account to cover a certain percentage of its current value. That meant you'd have to have a lot of equity in your account before you could short $160,000 worth of IBM to begin with. That you could only short what you could already afford depressed my enthusiasm for what had sounded like a perfect scheme. Another drawback was that all the dividends on any shorted stock went to the original owner, and not to the borrower of the shares.

Of course, when you short a stock you are hoping that the price will go down. In the above example, if the price of IBM dropped from $160 a share to, say, $100 a share, then you could replace the 1,000 borrowed shares for $100,000 and pocket a $60,000 profit.

Mr. Gressel told me there were short-term short-sellers who played for a few quick points and long-term short-sellers willing to wait for some hapless stock to become worthless, so it would cost nothing to replace the shares they'd borrowed when the price was high. If, for instance, you could short 1,000 shares of some company whose stock was selling for $50, you'd be credited with $50,000 that would be yours to keep if the company went bankrupt.

Apparently, it's a good idea to keep track of the short interest— i.e., how many shares have been sold short—in any stock you own. Lists of short interest are published in *Barron's* and other financial publications. When a large number of average investors sell a stock short, it's taken to mean that the short-sellers are wrong and the stock price will rise. Conversely, when only a small number of average investors are shorting a particular issue, it's taken to mean that the stock price will likely go down.

Nobody knows when short-selling was invented, or who actually thought of it. In the early days of the U.S. markets, half the investors sold short. In the original definition of bulls and bears, the bulls were manipulators who finagled the prices up, while the bears were the short-sellers who finagled the prices down. The 1920s was the heyday of short-sellers, including the famous "Sell 'Em" Ben Smith.

In recent decades, shorting has become less popular—perhaps due to the moral misgivings that are difficult to comprehend. There's no ethical difference between betting on a stock to go up or betting on it to go down, yet today's professional short-seller is shunned, despised, and slandered as the rheum of Wall Street. I was fortunate to meet one of the best of them through Mr. Gressel.

"Dump 'Em" Jim Chanos had an office in the same clearinghouse where Mr. Gressel hung his lab coat. From what Mr. Gressel told me, Dump 'Em Jim Chanos was about as popular as keel scum, but to me, he seemed no different from your regular investment yuppie. In fact, he told me himself that he was no different from your regular investment yuppie—Yale graduate, wool sweaters, three children, house in Westchester, job on Wall Street—except for his selling short. For that, he'd been followed, snooped on, and harassed by numerous sleuths and spies sent around by corporations that would love to get some dirt on him, to cause him some public discredit and in effect to short his already terrible reputation.

For his part, Dump 'Em Jim Chanos did everything possible to get dirt on corporations and delighted when he could succeed. His great success was Baldwin-United, which he identified as a loser while Wall Street analysts recommended it at $25. He shorted more and more shares as the stock rose to $50. This was a stern test of a negative belief. You can imagine the despair of selling great quantities of something for $25 expecting it soon to be worthless, then facing the prospect of having to buy it all back at $50. But Dump 'Em Jim held on.

While an investor on the long side is mercifully spared since a stock can go no lower than zero, a short-seller is gambling against infinity since there's no limit to how high a stock can go. Theoretically, a stock could go to $1 million a share, and any shorter of it would have to raise that amount to support the increase, until eventually he'd be forced to sell out and/or go bankrupt.

In the case of Baldwin-United, this required extra courage, and

Dump 'Em Jim had plenty—plus the extra capital to hold on until the stock took a downward turn and finally landed at $2. Also, he didn't sit around waiting for the disaster to happen. Like their colleagues on the long side, short-sellers get out and drum up clients for their bad news, calling the lenders and the big investors, planting negative stories in the *Wall Street Journal,* and telling as many people as possible the horrors of the company they've shorted. Short-sellers, in this way, are Devil's Analysts, and several companies thought Dump 'Em Jim Chanos was the most devilish. "They claim I'm a menace," he protested. "But I'm not a menace. I just want people to know the truth."

Since his success with Baldwin-United, Dump 'Em Jim made a career of selling short, and continued to search for terrible situations. His job was helped along by the hordes of regular Wall Street analysts whom Dump 'Em Jim described as absurdly optimistic, and who he said wouldn't have seen the hole in the *Titanic* if they'd stuck their head in it, and who would only have downgraded the czar's empire from a "highly recommended" to a "strong hold." There was a messianic fervor in his short-selling, which he regarded as a cleansing for the folly in the market, an antidote to the self-serving promotions of the brokerage-house research against which he competed.

"What are you shorting right now?" I asked. "Texas," he said. "If I could short New York real estate I'd do that, but I haven't found a way yet, and so I'll settle for Texas. Texas banks, Texas cafeterias, Texas oil-service companies, and especially all the secondary companies. I'm shorting them all and I can wait."

Shorting required a lot of patience and a lot of money to cover yourself. Since I had little of either, I decided against following the lead of Dump 'Em Jim. Later, I changed my mind, as you'll see.

TWENTY ONE

REFLECTIONS ON MY PROGRESS TO DATE

I 'D BEEN AWAY FROM HOME FOR SIX WEEKS DURING THE MIDDLE of winter, but in the spring I returned home in a bit of a depression. By May, the 2,500 shares of Angstrom I still owned were worth $3,281, for a paper loss of $1,719, while the 53 shares of Gillette had risen from $79 to $88, for a gain of $477. In all, the $10,920 I'd invested through Prudential-Bache had a current value of $9,399, not including airplane tickets, phone calls, and other incidentals.

Meanwhile, the market as a whole had gone up more than 35 percent. My own losses were intolerable per se, and devastating in the light of the general advance. Every front-page article about the great bull market was a sad reminder of the thousands I should have made in these exciting times. No matter how optimistic you are at the beginning of each stock-buying cycle, eventually you'll remember the last time you vowed never to do it again. The stock-player's vow, "Never another share," is taken and forgotten over and over, just like the familiar hangover vow, "Never another drink."

The worst part was that my friends and acquaintances still thought I'd done spectacularly well. The mounting pressure to live up to their expectations was something else I had to face.

If I had it to do over again, I wouldn't have blabbed about the early paper profit in Angstrom, telling everyone within earshot how well I'd done. Also I would never have said things like, "Why bother with the racetrack where there's Prudential-Bache?" These remarks helped convince my friends I'd been a big success. Plus they'd seen the Dow Jones shoot straight up since the start of my journey and envied the way I'd put myself in the right place at the right time. "How great that you hit Wall Street during the boom, the gala, the big chance," many said. That they kept asking when I was moving to Park Avenue only made reality more painful.

Several sought my investment advice. I know I've been giving you useful hints all along, but in the middle of my journey and with these results-to-date, to be regarded as a valuable source of investment counsel was frightening. I mention myself as an example of how little we know about the actual performance of the so-called experts we seek to emulate, from the neighborhood geniuses to the TV financial celebrities.

Since I didn't want to disappoint the believers, I often told them things I'd heard secondhand in my trips around Wall Street, such as: "Abbott Laboratories looks good, it's ready for a breakout," or "Gulf & Western Industries is undervalued at 48," or "Heinz is going straight to 50." This made them much happier than if I'd described my own firsthand experience in any detail.

I'd begun to understand why average investors sometimes lie to each other about money they haven't made. It's as hard to admit failure in a bull market as it is to say you've had a bad time in Venice. Admitting you had a bad time in Venice goes against 800 years of romantic expectations. Friends of the romantic Venice have too much riding on the idea of it to tolerate unhappy reports from people who've smelled the canals and fallen out of love. The actual condition of my portfolio to date made me think of this.

I kept up appearances as long as I could, retreating from "Angstrom's going great, I've doubled my money," to "I'm doing pretty well," to "Things are getting along OK." I hoped this "getting along OK" would discourage further inquiry, but it didn't. At several parties, I accepted the congratulations of admirers who announced: "He never made any money before, but now he's found his niche."

Back home, my wife and children remembered the exciting first weeks when I was proud to own Angstrom. They continued to think I'd prospered long after I'd hit the loss column, though I'd dropped several hints to prepare them for the truth. Fortunately, they never opened the Prudential-Bache monthly statements mailed to our home.

Once I'd told them the truth, I found myself casting about for something or someone to blame for it. First, I tried to blame the system. The worse you've done, the more you're convinced that Wall Street is rigged and the cards are stacked against you. After what I'd seen of analysts with no time to analyze, portfolio managers who couldn't beat the averages, and especially stockbrokers practicing their dialogues, I was prepared to distrust everyone.

Then I remembered that half the country was making money on Wall Street. It's ridiculous to blame the system in a bull market.

Next, I tried blaming the broker. How, I wondered, could Ms. Garrett have lured me into Angstrom on the word of some idiot from Philadelphia? How could she have kept up the storytelling, the optimism, the cheery projections? How could I have picked such a silly broker in the first place?

Before I got far with this, I remembered I'd had too many other brokers to continue this infantile lament. Let's face it. Linda Garrett didn't make me buy Angstrom. I insisted on buying it myself. In my experience, the major complaint against brokers, that they pressure customers and "churn" the accounts to get more commissions, is unfounded. I've always churned my own accounts without any encouragement. It's me who always calls the broker, wondering why something hasn't moved, or suggesting we switch into something more profitable.

Gillette was Ms. Garrett's suggestion, but again I called her. After the first few weeks, I always called her and she never called me. If anything, the broker is likely to wait for the client to commit himself, as opposed to the churning for which they're unjustly accused.

Think of it from the broker's point of view. If he's smart, he'll always agree with what the client proposes instead of pushing his own recommendations. If the client turns out to be right, then the broker looks good as well. If the client turns out to be wrong, the broker can always say, "That one was your idea."

Why was I unable to see my broker as the salesperson I knew her to be? After all, I'd been to broker's school, yet I still held on to the fiction that Ms. Garrett was the expert, and a parental figure who could be blamed for my results. I didn't expect a shoe salesman to know anything about podiatry, so why should I expect the broker to know anything about finance? The whole broker-client relationship was too complex to simply blame the broker.

The third stage of recrimination was blaming myself. Here I concluded that I was doomed to failure, a Midas in reverse, and that everything I touched would soon be bankrupt. This, I'm told, is a common and primitive attitude. I've observed it in many friends who say, "I'm death on equities," "Put me in a stock and the company's a goner," or "With me, every investment is a total loss."

In this deprecatory spirit, I went back over everything—people I'd wronged, deadlines I'd missed, sins I'd committed—as if somewhere I'd find the cause of an obvious jinx. Was I my own worst enemy on Wall Street? I wondered about a fatal flaw, or an angry god, that made my poor performance a foregone conclusion. Why was I still being punished?

It sounds silly, I know, but average investors are left with no rational explanations for their uncanny histories of debits. I met a man who told me he'd bought a computer stock at $4 and watched it go to $50, then was unable to sell at $40, $30, $20, and continued to hold until it dropped to $2. He suspected he'd been mesmerized, and wondered if it had anything to do with not telling his bank of an error in his favor. A woman I knew who bought Schlumberger at $80, only to see it plunge to $30, thought it might have to do with her driving a gas-guzzling car during the last energy crisis.

Once you're in the doomed-to-failure phase, it can last for months. Luckily, it didn't last that long for me. Srully Blotnick coaxed me out of it.

Srully Blotnick! There's a name you couldn't forget. It caught my attention in the card catalog of the local library, to which I'd returned in search of a new approach. His book was called *Winning: the Psychology of Successful Investment,* published back in 1979. It was based on Mr. Blotnick's 10-year study of 1,103 average investors from 1966 to 1976. He followed them through one bull market and one bear market to see what happened to their money and why. (Recent criticism of Mr. Blotnick's methodology in no way diminished my enthusiasm for his findings.)

Of these 1,103 people, only 53 made any sizable profit, and only four did "exceptionally well." Many ended up with less than what they started, which to me was no shock. The why of it is where

Mr. Blotnick made some interesting points. The most compelling to me, given my present state of mind, was that average investors aren't doomed by gods. Average investors are first and last doomed by the stupid ways they invest.

Mr. Blotnick found the biggest losers among the so-called sophisticated players, who got immersed in the Wall Street subject as much as yours truly. That none of his 53 winners was an "anxious student of the market" was an eye-opener. It reminded me that a close relative ignored the General Foods in her safe-deposit box for 20 years, through five market cycles with hundreds of analysts taking it on or off their "buy" and "hold" lists, and recently heard on the radio that General Foods was going to be taken over. She called her broker and discovered that her original $10,000 was now worth $180,000. I learned of her good fortune as I was watching the daily upticks and downticks, which leads me to Useful Tip Number 18:

A watched stock seldom appreciates

Mr. Blotnick could discover no correlation between knowledge of the market—at least in the general public—and successful investing. He said picking a "hot" stock is usually foolish and buying financial publications to get an investment edge rarely pays off. For one thing, you're already out the cost of the publications. I should mention that I now subscribed to the *Value Line Investment Survey* at $400 a year, *Barron's* at $70, and Al Frank's *Prudent Speculator* for an annual $175, plus I occasionally picked up the *Wall Street Journal* for 50 cents. As I got more involved in the subject, the number of newsletters in my mailbox expanded exponentially, while the gains from the advice tended to approach zero.

The most useful of Mr. Blotnick's findings was the one about short-term versus long-term investing. Here, I thought, was a root cause of my problem. I bought Angstrom hoping for a short-term profit, but after its immediate rise, I held on to it, hoping for a long-term gain. When it went down, I sold half of it, reminding myself I was a short-term investor at heart.

Then again, I bought Gillette hoping for a long-term profit, but the minute it went up a few points, I started itching to get out. In fact, I was itching to get out of it after three weeks.

When I found out Mr. Blotnick lived in New York and wrote a column in *Forbes* magazine, I called him immediately. I was sorry we couldn't meet in person, but we had a wonderful half-hour phone conversation. He told me his studies were continuing and as far as he knew, average investors were just as likely to lose money now as ever, although in the current market many had gotten temporarily ahead. I told him I hadn't, and that I'd put in hundreds of hours of effort with little to show for it.

"The first 500 hours don't make a great deal of difference," he said.

"No?"

"People who study the market often don't realize this. Five hundred hours of knowledge can be a dangerous thing."

"I can see that."

From here on, Mr. Blotnick sounded more like a guru than an investment counselor. His advice to me was: Know yourself.

"Short-term traders can make money short-term trading," he said. "Long-term traders can make money long-term trading. There are many ways to play the markets, and each one will work for some people but not necessarily for others. If there's any certainty, it's this: People who know who they are and invest accordingly can make money. People who don't know who they are can never succeed. You have to find the method that's right for you and stick to it."

I thought about this hard, and realized the one time I'd made a profit and taken it was the short-term option suggested by Mr. Crawford. It occurred to me that perhaps I was better suited to this sort of short-term trading than I'd imagined.

TWENTY TWO

ON TO CHICAGO

I WAS SITTING AT HOME, THINKING ABOUT MR. BLOTNICK'S ADVICE, when I saw some intriguing ads on TV. These had to do with futures and options, the very short-term investments I wondered if I should pursue full time. One said, "Investor doubles money in three weeks," while another claimed "120 percent profit in two days." A third mentioned "unlimited upside potential with predetermined risk," and a fourth challenged: "Only those who dare have truly lived." Each of them ended with the phrase: "past performance is no guarantee of future results."

The trading companies mentioned in these ads were based in Chicago. I took a chance and bought a plane ticket.

Chicago is no longer the hog butcher for the world. Hasn't been since 1959, when they closed the stockyards. Pigs are already kielbasa by the time they reach Chicago. Neither is Chicago a stacker of wheat, except in the pancake houses. Lately, it's the hog future of the world, put-maker, seller of soybean straddles, and the nation's commodities-hedger: stormy, husky, brawling, city of the reverse head-and-shoulders pattern.

I got there in mid-July, and I took a room at a cheap downtown hotel. The man at the desk told me his brother was a futures trader. Friends of my wife's family who live in Chicago had umpteen relatives in commodities. On the street, almost everybody I stopped knew the location of the Mercantile Exchange, a glassy riverfront high-rise where the trading pits were located.

Reminding myself that a future is a contract to buy something later at a price agreed upon today, I headed to the Mercantile Exchange to open an account with Lind-Waldock. Maybe you've seen their ads: instant access, professional service, operators standing by 24 hours a day, only $25 per round-term trade. I could have stuck with Prudential-Bache, since every big-time brokerage firm has a futures branch. But savvy short-term traders don't waste money on commissions, and Lind-Waldock was a discount broker.

Barry Lind, the president of Lind-Waldock, was trying to become the Charles Schwab of pork bellies. From the lobby of the Mercantile Exchange building, I reached him directly on the telephone. Try that with Mr. Merrill, Mr. Lynch, Mr. Prudential, Mr. Bache, Mr. Shearson, Mr. Lehman, Mr. Dean, Mr. Witter, Mr. Paine, Mr. Webber, or even Mr. Schwab. Right away, I sensed the accessibility, the informality, the friendliness of the futures and options people in Chicago.

Mr. Lind said he was Lear-jetting it out of town, so he passed me to his assistant, Chuck Epstein, the public relations director of the firm. Mr. Epstein's office was on the 17th floor of this glorified greenhouse. His walls were decorated with unusual posters, one of which asked: HOW COME THERE'S NO PEKING DUCK EXCHANGE? and another, HOW COME THERE'S NO HAVANA CIGAR EXCHANGE?" These depicted silly-looking Communists sitting around with nothing to trade, and had been commissioned by the Mercantile Exchange to show the advantages of free enterprise. I wanted to get some copies for myself, but Mr. Epstein said there'd been some complaints and the posters were discontinued.

We stood at a window while Mr. Epstein pointed out where the Fulton Street marketplace used to be. The egg stalls at the Fulton Street marketplace, Mr. Epstein said, had been the last remnants of the actual physical commodities that once made Chicago famous. Those were the days when an onion was an onion, and a bushel of corn had tangible properties. Now a bushel of corn had become a "form of settlement." So had hogs, and lumber, and baskets of stocks. What used to be called "farming" was dismissed as the "cash market."

Every futures contract was still called a "car," short for "carload," in memory of the days when commodities arrived here by rail, though the trains don't stop here anymore. Cattle traders make their living from "cars" of cattle without ever examining a cow. Soybean traders don't have to know a soybean from a rabbit pellet. Ask the local wheat trader where his cereal originates, and he'll point west toward Iowa or Nebraska, get a bewildered look on his face, and shrug. "What's happened," says Mr. Epstein, "is that trading became an end in itself."

Here from an office in the Merc building, you'd think that the only thing growing in the whole Midwest was the futures business. Mr. Epstein showed me a diagram of the trading floor somewhere below us, where 900 people bought and sold contracts on baskets of stocks in the S&P pits, or bonds in the Treasury-bond pit, and behind that the deutsche marks, with cattle next to yen, francs next to lumber, and so on. In 1960, he said, four million futures contracts were traded in the U.S., mostly in agriculture. In 1986, 160 million futures contracts were traded, 40 times the old volume and representing $10 trillion worth of theoretical goods.

Mr. Epstein reminded me that most of these $10 trillion worth of bushels, baskets, and carloads were never delivered. Everything about this business seemed to be theoretical. "It's a wild market down there," he said. "Free enterprise at its best."

I left Mr. Epstein and headed down La Salle Street to visit the rival Chicago Board of Trade, housed in a famous art deco building. For decades the Board of Trade was the premier exchange, until the Mercantile Exchange caught it napping and ran ahead with the first currency futures and the first baskets of stocks. Soon the Board of Trade caught up with its Ginnie Mae futures contracts, and the T-Bond futures. Recently, it added a huge new annex, stuck onto the back of the original just for the trading of stock options and stock-index options.

From brochures I picked up at both exchanges, I learned the following about the history of futures. The first known futures transaction took place on Bahrain Island more than 2,000 years ago, when a merchant took goods on consignment for later sale in India. The basic premise of all futures—"Buy now, settle up later"—was accepted from earliest civilization. The Greeks and Romans traded futures. In medieval times, so-called forward contracting was common practice at country fairs.

The Japanese began to trade rice futures around 1730. The English followed with cotton futures in the late 1780s. In North America, the idea caught on after the Civil War. Although the Chicago Board of Trade, the oldest U.S. exchange, opened its doors in

1848, it was only to sell physical oats and physical corn in the primitive cash market. It wasn't until 1865 that management at the Board of Trade thought of paying for corn now and having it delivered later. This was the "to arrive" contract, the forefather of the modern American future.

It wasn't long after that before somebody thought of selling corn he didn't own. This was the founding "short position." From then on, hundreds of commodities have had their futures traded in the pits of the Board of Trade and/or the Mercantile Exchange.

Until 1919, the Mercantile Exchange was pretty much limited to butter and eggs. Then it added cheese, potato, and onion futures. In 1945, it added turkeys. The postwar turkey contract was the first future in anything approaching a fully developed organism. Its success led to the adoption of a frozen-egg futures contract four years later. Frozen eggs had the advantage of not rotting, which appealed to anyone contemplating an actual delivery.

In 1954, the Mercantile Exchange added iron and scrap metal, among other inedible futures. On the edible side, it started an apple-futures pit. In 1961, when interest in any and all of the above had flagged and traders reverted to playing pinochle in the afternoons, the Merc launched the now-famous pork-belly contract. What was a pork belly, anyway? I'd always imagined it was a pile of entrails, and wondered why anybody would pay money for one, much less risk having it delivered. As it turns out, "pork belly" is another way of saying "bacon"—unsliced, uncured, and packed in frozen slabs.

After the Merc succeeded with its pork bellies, in 1966 it began trading the whole animal via the live-hog-futures contract. Feeder cattle followed in 1971, and there was a full gamut of futures up and down the food chain. Then traders got bored. Everybody got bored. The Exchange might have disappeared from Chicago if it hadn't been for economist Milton Friedman, who helped it make the transition from live hogs to deutsche marks. By 1972, there was futures trading in seven foreign currencies. Over at the Chicago Board of Trade, the general apathy in corn and soybeans inspired another economist, Richard Sandor, to invent the futures contract on Ginnie Mae bonds. This was the first known financial future in the world.

The more the futures business evolved, the less agriculture had anything to do with it. In 1982, the Board of Trade added its stock-index futures. In New York, the Comex and the New York Futures Exchange improvised their own financial futures, then options, then options on the futures. No longer could you tell by the official name of an exchange what its business was. The Coffee, Sugar, and Cocoa Exchange traded Consumer Price Index futures.

The action in the last 10 years made the previous 100 seem but a lazy prelude to furious and spectacular advancements. With trading volume up fivefold across the industry, at last count there were 53,000 registered salespeople working for 383 brokerage houses, 6,000 floor brokers, 1,200 commodity pool operators, 2,100 trading advisors, for a total of 65,000 professionals in futures. This was what I was up against.

TWENTY THREE

OPENING A COMMODITIES ACCOUNT

I'D HARDLY SETTLED IN CHICAGO BEFORE I ARRANGED WITH MR. Epstein to open a commodity account. This was normally accomplished by calling the 800 number or walking into the numerous brokerage houses found along the streets, but Mr. Epstein took a personal interest in my case and agreed to walk me through the paperwork in the sales department on a floor above his office.

The sales department was abuzz with cold callers, prospecting for clients from their desks, using some of the quotations I recognized from Merrill Lynch. In passing, I heard the following snippets of conversation: "I'm calling for somebody," "You told me to call you back in May," "It's up three-tenths of a cent," "What markets might you be interested in?" and "We're the largest discount commodities broker in the world."

Mr. Epstein sat me down at a long table and handed me several booklets that explained the futures markets, plus an application and some other legal papers. As I reviewed this material, he paced behind me. Apparently, the government had added to the burden of paperwork, which is why he kept mumbling, "Government, government, government." To me, the paperwork seemed minimal. I had to fill out my name, address, and estimated net worth— no more than they ask on an application for a check-cashing card at a supermarket. Then I had to sign two forms stating that I understood I could lose more money than I started with, that I could be wiped out, reduced to penury, subjected to "margin calls" and other unlikely disasters that, if taken seriously, would discourage anyone from trading futures, just as the thought of actually having to inflate a life vest would keep us all from flying.

I tried to sign before I'd read the text, but Mr. Epstein made sure I went back and informed myself of all the unpleasant details. The whole filling-out process took 10 minutes.

Then it was time to put in the money. Lind-Waldock requires a $5,000 deposit to open an account, and I didn't have it. Mr. Epstein checked with the lawyers, who said they'd make an exception, being that I was writing a book, and would settle for $2,000. I offered a personal check. Mr. Epstein again consulted with the higher-ups who said the check would have to clear before I could "initiate a position." This might take three days, which a motivated investor could never tolerate. I called my hometown Centrust S&L long-distance and asked them to wire the funds, but they refused. A clerk said he didn't recognize my voice and had no proof it was really me. "For your own protection," he explained, and I hadn't even told him what I was doing with the money.

Mr. Epstein and I explored this predicament together and had the same brainstorm at once, trading futures on a credit card. The credit-card idea seemed logical enough, but the higher-ups said they weren't set up for it. It did, however, lead us to the actual solution, which, if you're ever short on cash in Chicago and anxious to trade a future, I'd recommend. Traveler's checks.

I found the American Express travel office on Michigan Avenue, a few blocks from the Mercantile Exchange. I presented my credit card to a very pleasant Mrs. Riley and received $2,000 of investment capital in less time than it would have taken to buy a plane ticket. "Have a nice trip," she volunteered as I was signing the backs of the checks. I returned to Lind-Waldock, endorsed the checks over to them, and got my account approved. Mr. Epstein gave me my personal trading code, plus an 800 number to call anytime I wanted to put in an order, 24 hours a day.

The next problem was what futures to trade. On this matter, Mr. Epstein was helpful as usual—and so was Bill Murshel, the public relations man at the rival Chicago Board of Trade. From the two of them I gathered up all the brochures and booklets that anyone could carry, and then I holed up in my cut-rate hotel to study the material. Some titles I remember include: "Writing Puts, Straddles, and Combinations," "Call-Option Spreading," "The

Bearish Vertical-Call Spread Worksheet," "Method Trading," "The Trader's Scorecard," and "Meet the Buyers and Sellers."

For several hours I reviewed the menu of investments that took up both sides of a legal page and listed more than 100 different futures plus the options on those futures, further complicated by different delivery months, expiration dates, and the varying sums of money (margin) put up to secure each contract. Margin was the key element in the futures business, making it both very risky and potentially very profitable. By investing a relatively small sum— say five to ten percent of the value of any given commodity—the investor could control the entire amount represented in the contract. For instance, a $500 margin was required to purchase one silver futures contract, enabling the buyer to control 1,000 ounces of silver. As of this writing, 1,000 ounces of silver was worth $7,000. If the price doubled during the life of a contract, the investor would make a $7,000 profit, or 14 times his original $500. On the other hand, he'd also lose $7,000 if the price dropped by half.

Still uncertain as to how to proceed, I made a trip to the visitor's galleries at both major exchanges, hoping to pick up some important clue. Both galleries were suspended above the trading floors and offered a full view of the proceedings below. The tour guide described it as "one half acre of economic action, the heartbeat of an international economy, where risk meets opportunity."

At the several video terminals, the visitor was invited to sit down and make mock investment decisions ("to sell your stock press 1, to hold your stock press 2"). I pressed a number of buttons in different combinations, and always ended up with the voice that said, "Just as you feared, the stock market is coming down. Bad News?" Not if you'd bought futures or options to protect your stock portfolio!

From the press-box vantage, I watched the action in the 24 different trading pits, and the hundreds of people in sneakers and solid-colored blazers milling around the perimeters. Toward the center of each pit was the heaviest density of arm-flailing fanatics. The financial pits were the densest, and in Treasury-bond futures at the Chicago Board of Trade it was hard to see how people could breathe in there, much less determine who was signaling what to whom. A bystander told me that he'd once seen the crowd sway back and forth in unison, setting up a dangerous wave pattern that sent all the traders toppling to the floor, some of them continuing to buy and sell as they went down.

The agricultural pits—live hogs and cattle, corn and soybeans—were populated with middle-aged men and women who could have been the parents of the traders in the financial pits. Many stood around reading their newspapers and seemed to lack for things to do. The foreign-currency pits lay somewhere between bonds and agriculture in general mayhem and in the age of the participants.

Around the circumference of the crowded pits, a ring of bodies faced the wrong way—that is, with their backs to the action. These people seemed to signal in a forward direction, then turned back to peek into the pits. A tour guide told me they were messengers who communicated between the pits and the trading desks, which could be identified by huge vertical placards that said LIND-WALDOCK, PRUDENTIAL-BACHE, MERRILL LYNCH, HEINHOLD COMMODI-TIES, among others. Between their peeking and gesturing, the messengers launched handwritten notes that sailed like frisbees and magically landed on the proper desks, 10 to 15 yards away.

I left the visitor's galleries to revisit Mr. Epstein and to report on what I'd seen. He gave me an overview of the caste system on the floor: at the lowest level, the messengers, many of them college dropouts, who were paid a modest salary for signaling and card-flipping, hoping someday to move into the pits; at the next level, the recorders and inspectors, salaried employees of the exchanges; then finally the traders, divided into various categories of risk and reward. The most conservative were floor brokers, who bought and sold for outside clients and lived off their commissions. Next were scalpers, who took small risks, buying and selling futures for quick profits. Then came the day traders, who took longer and riskier positions but were out of the market at the end of each day. Then there were position players, who rode favorable trends for weeks or even months. On top of that, there were spreaders and straddlers, who hedged their bets from one pit to another, moving between futures and options just as Mr. Gressel had done in New York.

"Ultimately," said Mr. Epstein, "it's a zero-sum game. Somebody wins a dollar, somebody else must lose a dollar." With all these people trying to make a living, and with each person's profit being some other person's loss, this was no friendly business.

As to what I should do, Mr. Epstein said he'd definitely "go long" with Japanese yen if he were me, although being him he'd avoid trading anything at all. He also showed me an advisory bulletin published by Lind-Waldock, with one or two best bets of the day. The firm was recommending something called a deutsche-mark straddle—long the 48 call and short the 49 call simultaneously. From Mr. Epstein's explanation, I gathered that a straddle is roughly the same as arm-wrestling with yourself. Actually, he said I'd make money if the deutsche mark itself increased in value—but if it went up too much I'd lose.

Though Lind-Waldock hadn't mentioned pigs as a best bet, I told Mr. Epstein I'd always been fond of pigs, and therefore would prefer investing in a live hog option over the yen or the deutsche marks.

For further input, I made an appointment to see Ralph Silverstein, a veteran of the agricultural pits and a friend of a friend of the family. He had an office on an upper floor of the Chicago Board of Trade. As I waited in the anteroom, I heard several people whooping "New highs in the beans, new highs in the beans."

Mr. Silverstein was a pleasant, middle-aged man who no longer competed in the pits, and said he was happy to leave that ordeal to a younger crowd. Like many of the older traders, he'd moved upstairs to follow the action on computer screens. He was a confirmed wiggle-watcher, and got up several times during our interview to peer at the graphs on his monitor.

The same schism between Fundamentalists and Chartists exists in commodities as it does in stocks. Fundamentalists study weather reports, feedlot reports, silo utilization, grain sales, and so forth, while Chartists like Mr. Silverstein dispute the relevance of such facts and take their trading cues directly from squiggly lines. Minute to minute they watch their monitors, and in their spare time they pore over weekly charts collected in oversized binders, measuring peaks and valleys with their calipers the way sailors might lay out a course.

Soybeans were preoccupying Mr. Silverstein the day we talked, but I asked him about corn, since I'd eat corn over soybeans any time. He told me it would be a great year for corn, a bountiful harvest, and, more to the point, that corn had a beautiful chart. "That means you'd recommend I buy corn futures," I assumed out loud. "Of course not," he corrected. "You shouldn't be a buyer. You should be a seller."

What he was suggesting was that I "sell" some corn futures, which was the commodity equivalent of shorting a stock, i.e., getting paid for something without actually owning it and then hoping the price would go down. This had certain appealing ramifications I'll discuss later, but what puzzled me at the time was: if it was going to be such a great year for corn, then why should I want to bet on the short side of the market?

In that regard, Mr. Silverstein explained an important difference between commodities and stocks. When a company does well in real life, its stock price goes up on the stock market, whereas when a commodity, say, corn, does well in real life, its futures price goes down on the commodities market. The worst thing that could happen to a commodities investor on the positive, or long, side of the corn market was a bountiful harvest. The best thing that could happen was a drought, a plague, a fire, a hurricane, an earthquake or some similar disaster that will kill off the physical commodity and, in the resulting scarcity, drive the price up. Since this was just the opposite of what I'd learned on Wall Street, I wrote down Useful Tip Number 19:

The worse things get, the better their futures

For further confirmation on Mr. Silverstein's advice to short corn, I got in touch with Jordan Hollander, a famous corn trader whose family held the oldest continuous membership at the Board of Trade. He'd also graduated to an upstairs office, but I didn't see a computer there. I saw a kidney-shaped formica table and a girlie calendar from an auto-parts store, plus several other items that you'd expect to find in a time capsule from the Eisenhower administration. Mr. Hollander wore snazzy suspenders and looked as if he might have served in the Eisenhower administration as well.

Mr. Hollander turned out to be helpful and especially well informed. He told me that his father, Oscar, had traded in the corn pits as early as 1919. My Mr. Hollander had been trading since he left the Air Force in the mid-1940s. He also had a son in the business, which made three generations of Hollanders in corn.

I asked Mr. Hollander what it was like in the old days of physical corn. "The boxcars came into Chicago to a central inspection point at the railroad yard," he said. "The state would inspect the shipment. There'd be a sample of corn taken from each car and put into a paper bag. The paper bags were brought to the trading floor at the Chicago Board of Trade and put up on the flat marble desks, one desk for each separate carload. After the corn was bought and sold, we'd take the bills of lading and send the trains on to their final destinations."

Today, Mr. Hollander continued, the corn never reached Chicago. Instead it was inspected at the point of origin and the orders were placed by telephone. Corn was a form of settlement. A single bushel might be hedged and speculated 25 times in its theoretical life. I asked if there were futures traders who'd never seen an actual carload of corn, and Mr. Hollander supposed there were.

As to my investment, Mr. Hollander agreed with Mr. Silverstein. He, too, was optimistic about this year's harvest, which made him bearish on the futures. "Don't be long," he said. "Be short. Short the September 170 contract." I carefully wrote this down.

After I left Mr. Hollander, I heard about another family, the Schneiders, with four generations in futures. The great-great grandfather, Sam, sold eggs, while the latest Schneiders traded gold, T-Bills, and Eurodollars. Mr. Epstein told me that several Chicago families had followed the same evolution from the cash market to the futures, from edibles to currencies, from the pits to the computers. The skill of trading hadn't changed, and Mr. Epstein suggested it may even have been inbred.

I narrowed my investment choices to the Japanese yen long, the corn short, the deutsche mark spread, and the live-hog option. After going over it back and forth for another half hour with Mr. Epstein, he suggested that for my $2,000 I could pick up a small contract on each. He also arranged for me to follow my own buy and sell orders down through the pits. This would have been impossible at the New York Stock Exchange and was one more example of the openness and generosity of this wonderful city.

Mr. Epstein took me down to the entrance of the trading floor at the Mercantile Exchange. There we met up with Ryman Flippen, the balding director of all Lind-Waldock floor operations, a man with the nervous energy of a roustabout. With Mr. Epstein and Mr. Flippen at my elbows, I was issued a visitor's badge and escorted through the security checkpoint. I could see the need for security. Without it, it would have been easy for any stranger to print up a phony trading badge, amble into the pits, start hollering and waving, and end up owning half the nation's farm output or billions of dollars in Treasury bonds.

To the left of the main door was a bulletin board with a list of names of people who'd been fined by the Mercantile Exchange for wearing cutoff blue jeans, throwing gum on the floor, eating on the floor, and flipping cards improperly. By the nature of these violations, it was obvious that many traders were hardly more than teenagers. The only other places I'd seen such rules were in college dining halls. "You can get fined for many other things," said Mr. Epstein. "Including biting. That actually happens in the crowded pits."

There was a longer list of people whose badges were revoked and who were no longer allowed on the floor. This wasn't for biting. Mr. Epstein said these recent unfortunates had lost all their money, which he called "crapping out." It happened to 40 percent of the futures traders, he said, especially the newest ones. "They come and go pretty fast these days," he continued, sadly shaking his head at the crap-out list. "It used to be more congenial around here, more like a small town. Now it's getting tougher. It's getting so you hardly know your neighbor in the pits."

We entered the trading area, ringed with overhead quote boards. It was at least as big as the floor of the NYSE. Every few seconds, the public-address announcer would page somebody to the telephone. We found ourselves surrounded by messengers in yellow jackets. Most of them had acne.

Ryman Flippen ushered us past the messengers to a bank of telephones at a Lind-Waldock order desk, where the buy and sell orders were customarily received. Having bypassed the normal step of calling in my order to a broker, and the broker calling the order desk, I told Mr. Flippen what I intended to buy. He wrote it down on a scrap of paper and stamped the paper into a time clock. It was the Japanese-yen option Mr. Epstein had recommended.

The Japanese-yen option worked the same way as the option on the basket of stocks I'd bought earlier in New York. It gave me the right to purchase a futures contract on several million Japanese yen anytime from now until the expiration date. Actually, I sought to buy two yen options with a September expiration, which were selling for about $215 apiece.

"Wanna see your order filled?" said Mr. Flippen. "Follow me." We left the telephone desk and skirted a stock-option pit, which at floor level seemed as lively as a cockfight in Tijuana. The Japanese-yen-option pit was relatively quiet. At most, there were 50 traders standing in the ring, with the greatest density toward the center.

Mr. Flippen handed my scrap of paper to a man with a ponytail who wore badge K-62. He grabbed the paper, turned away from us, and yelled into the pit: "Two calls. Two hundred and fourteen dollars on one. September. Two calls." After a few seconds, K-62 reversed direction, scribbled something on the paper, and handed it to Mr. Flippen.

"That's it," said Mr. Flippen, who then introduced K-62 as Howard Schless. K-62 shook my hand and started to tell me something, then mumbled a quick "I'm busy" and disappeared into the pit. "He can't talk now," said Mr. Flippen. "But did you notice what he did? Did you see the $215 offer over on the other side? Howard could have taken that, but he waited and bid you lower and got you the $214. That's the sign of a good trader. It's the cripples you gotta watch out for."

As we walked back to the order desk to record our trade, Mr. Flippen explained what he meant by cripples. A cripple was an indifferent trader who got less than optimum prices for his clients, either paying too much on the buy side or asking too little on the sell. Though I hadn't even seen the actual trade, I was grateful that K-62 Schless had saved me the dollar. Already, I was begin-

ning to sense that putting my orders into the pits was like holding
up bread to the seagulls.

Mr. Flippen stamped in my yen purchase, offered his congratulations, and we repeated the process with the deutsche marks.
At the deutsche-mark pit my transaction was handled by Ron
Englund, a hefty and affable fellow. He quickly bought one September 48 deutsche-mark call while simultaneously selling the September 49 call, thus creating the straddle—whatever that was.

Since Mr. Englund wasn't busy, we had a brief chat at the edge
of his pit. He'd worked as a telephone repairman, fought in Vietnam, and then tried the pizza business before joining Lind-Waldock.
There he'd started out in gold and drifted into deutsche marks. In
his spare time, he helped raise three children, sang in a church
choir, and umpired at Little League baseball games. One thing he
never did was invest in deutsche-mark options, preferring to make
a modest living by executing orders for high-rollers like me. "When
I gamble I always lose," he confided. "I learned that about myself
a long time ago." I admired his self-discipline, though with all the
fantastic fortunes being made around him, I felt he was missing
out.

We took our deutsche-mark spread, logged it in at the order
desk, then marched on to the live-hog-option pit. This pit was as
small as a backyard Jacuzzi and so completely deserted you could
follow all the steps. Mr. Epstein said this was one more example
of the piteous decline in U.S. agriculture.

Mr. Flippen, Mr. Epstein, and I must have stood alone for nearly
two minutes before a man with a red beard and an orange-and-
white checkered jacket sauntered over from the direction of hog
futures. His jacket would have attracted whatever business happened to be around, but in this case there was only me.

The man in the red beard introduced himself as Sonny Hersh.
He seemed to be a thoughtful person, sober even, in contrast to
his wardrobe. He looked to be about my age—40. Mr. Flippen
handed him my order for one hog call.

"Pay 80 on one," Mr. Hersh yelled out to an empty pit. There
was no immediate response. Soon a couple of idle traders moseyed
over to sniff at the opportunity. "Eighty-five," Hersh yelled. Suddenly a young woman with badge LQ-001 appeared and made the

deal. Mr. Flippen took me aside to explain what happened: Mr. Hersh tried to bid 80 and found no takers, so he'd come up to 85 to attract the seller. This 85 was short for $285, what I'd just paid for one option on a contract for live hogs, good until October.

The young woman who'd sold me this option left the pit immediately and disappeared into the adjoining live-hog futures. "Probably laying off her risk," Mr. Flippen said. There's a great interplay between hog futures and hog options, just as I'd seen between stock-index futures and options back in New York.

"What does my $285 represent?" I asked Mr. Epstein. He looked it up on a little tally sheet. "About 30,000 pounds," he said. My option gave me the right to a futures contract for that much hog until October. Considering the average size of a hog, which I figured to be 500 pounds, this gave me a potential controlling interest in 600 animals. Right then, I vowed to eat more pork chops and bacon, and to call my friends to beg them to do the same. Working together, maybe we could drive up the price.

Mr. Flippen pointed out a woman with a walkie-talkie who reported my trade to a central control booth. A few seconds later, the number 85 appeared on the hog–quote board and was flashed across similar quote boards all around the world. Seeing it above my head was as thrilling as seeing my byline in a magazine. "That's my 85!" I yelled to Mr. Flippen, and also to Mr. Hersh. Since hogs were slow, Mr. Hersh had returned to join our conversation.

I asked Mr. Hersh why hogs were so unpopular. He said a government report was coming out the following Monday, and smart money was holding off on any commitments. There was something wistful, even sad, about this quiet man in his orange-and-white checkered coat, but I couldn't stick around to find out what. Mr. Epstein was anxious to get back to work, and Mr. Flippen informed me the corn pit would close in 30 minutes at the Chicago Board of Trade. We left the floor of the Mercantile Exchange as quickly as possible and said our good-byes at the security check. I took a brisk walk over to the Board of Trade.

The interior of this art deco landmark was as impressive as the exterior. It had marble walls, decorated with intricate metal filigree, and lit with ships' lanterns. An ABC television crew was interviewing wheat-futures traders in the lobby for a documentary film on the effects of drought in the Southeast. The traders on the long side of wheat looked very happy.

At the security check near the entrance to the trading floor, I was met by John Sullivan, badge sjj, Lind-Waldock's man over here.

I think Mr. Sullivan had been warned that an eccentric Lind-Waldock client was coming over to follow his own corn trade around the room. He tried to be as nice about it as possible, even after I told him I wanted to "sell one September 170" and then asked what it meant. Mr. Sullivan patiently explained that I was selling one corn contract, representing 5,000 bushels, to somebody else for $170 a bushel. Hopefully, I could buy it back cheaper before the contract expired in September, or else I'd have to come up with extra money or with the corn.

He escorted me onto the trading floor, and over to the corn pit to meet with Lind-Waldock's corn person, Marty Dickman.

"Beans are rallying," somebody yelled. There were so many shouts from the adjacent bean pit I had to lean far into the corn pit to hear what my corn bidder was saying. "Don't stand in the pit, stand back," Mr. Sullivan admonished, grabbing me by the sweater. I stood back while Mr. Dickman wiggled his fingers at twenty or so companions until one had bought my corn.

Mr. Sullivan informed me I'd sold my 5,000 bushels to Cargill, one of the biggest agricultural conglomerates in the Midwest! This was my second great thrill of the day. Selling this much corn made me think of my mother, struggling in her summer garden. Here I was in Chicago, having always refused to help my mother with watering and especially with weeding, getting paid for more bushels of my own corn than she could grow in a lifetime, and doing business with a giant in the industry. It goes to show that farming doesn't have to be drudgery, if you do it the modern way.

My elation was short-lived. Perhaps Mr. Dickman, the corn trader, had seen me smile. Anyway, he had some rather negative things to say, which I wrote down as follows:

"When I first came down here, I was Mr. Big Ego. I had a law degree and here were all these ex-cops and truck drivers and people with 200-word vocabularies trading in the pits. I figured I'd make a killing, right? With this competition, how could you lose? Then

I get the shit kicked out of me. Then I get the shit kicked out of me again. You know what I've learned down here? Humility. Discipline. You come into this business with any sense of superiority, and you're dead.

Sooner or later, you find out who you are. That's what this game is about, finding out who you are. People say the market's this or the market's that, and they begin to think they can understand it. They discover they're wrong. They can't understand it. The market is . . . the market is God."

With that extraordinary speech, Mr. Dickman disappeared into the center of the corn pit. Mr. Sullivan, who'd been standing by quietly, returned me to the trading desk to record my corn sale. I'd sold 5,000 bushels, with the proceeds already credited to my account.

I went upstairs to the visitor's gallery to watch the closing of the grain markets. A few seconds before the 2:00 P.M. closing bell, the entire trading floor went berserk, as if all traders had suffered simultaneous epileptic seizures. After the bell rang, it was silent as prayer. On the overhead quote board, I could see the price of corn had already dropped a tenth of a cent. What was bad for the physical farmers was good for me.

MY KILLING
IN COMMODITIES

I F YOU WANT TO KNOW THE TRUTH, I HAD SECOND THOUGHTS about everything I'd done. These doubts were helped along by the message that awaited me when I returned to my hotel from the corn pit. It was from Lind-Waldock, telling me I was already $2,500 over my head and subject to an immediate margin call. A margin call occurred when the price of a commodity had gone against you, forcing you to put more cash in your account to cover the debit. If you didn't put up more cash, then your positions could be liquidated—in my case less than an hour after I'd taken them.

I called Lind-Waldock immediately, and the phone clerk and I tried to unravel this mess. Had pork bellies plunged in the time it took for me to walk from one exchange to the other? Had the deutsche-mark straddle collapsed around us? Together, we determined that the problem was the yen option. Each contract involved ten times more yen than I'd thought. Mr. Epstein and I had missed a decimal point on the menu of investments.

Controlling 12 million yen instead of 1.2 million was a heady prospect, but it meant that the option had cost $2,140 and not $214 as I'd supposed. Since I'd only put $2,000 in the account to begin with, there wasn't enough margin to cover all of my four commitments.

Even if I'd wanted to cover my investment in yen, I didn't feel like walking back to the American Express office to buy more traveler's checks. I asked the phone clerk what to do, and he suggested we sell out my yen position immediately.

He called a few minutes later to tell me that the yen had gone up in the hour or so I'd owned it, so I ended up with a $25 profit after commissions. This was my first triumph in Chicago commodities, and I was proud of it. Meanwhile, I was still short the 5,000 bushels of corn. Also, I still owned the option on the 30,000 pounds of live hogs, plus the mysterious deutsche-mark straddle.

Between all the debits and credits in my account, including a credit of $437.50 for selling the corn, my actual cash outlay was $1,417.50. That left me another $600 worth of buying power.

Even with the yen problem cleared up, something was bothering me. I reviewed what had happened so far and realized what was wrong. From the traders I'd met, I'd seen no evidence of the great fortunes made in commodities. Where were the millionaires, the high-rollers with expensive cocaine habits, the owners of Caribbean islands that we associate with this fantastic business? Where was the champagne and the caviar? Where were the Lear jets bound for Paris? In all the various pits and the offices above them, I hadn't noticed a single fat bankroll, nor had I heard anybody mention easy money. The stories I'd heard so far were about humility, struggle, and disillusionment.

Perhaps these traders were just being cagey. The day after I took my positions, I returned to the pits, hoping to find at least one trader would tell me what he'd done with his millions, or else introduce me to others who'd made it big. I stood at the security check and had my new acquaintances paged off the floor.

They couldn't locate Howard Schless, the yen man, but I'd sold my yen, anyway. Ron Englund, the deutsche-mark man, was happy to see me again. He mentioned he was on the exchange education committee, and that he'd just come from a training session for prospective traders. There was a new session every week, starting on Monday. After an hour and a half of mock trading on Wednesday, and a short written exam on Thursday, the recruits were installed in the pits on Friday, gambling with real money, in business for themselves.

I asked Mr. Englund for names of traders who had gotten rich. He said there were some, but he couldn't think of any I could interview right then.

Over at the hog-option pit, empty as usual, I hailed Sonny Hersh in his checkered coat. He still looked downcast, and I'd barely said hello before he dropped the bombshell he'd been unable to reveal before. "I lost $140,000," he said simply. "And I'm still trying to make it back." He told how a decade ago he'd been making decent money in the agriculture pits, but was lured away by the action in the stock-index-futures pits. After an initial success there, he risked more money on stock-index futures, and even borrowed to add to his stake. One day, the market moved against him and wiped out everything he had. "It took ten years for me to work up to it, but only a single day to nail myself," he said. "One day is all it took."

Since then, he'd been reduced to working for commissions, saddled with the double burden of supporting a family and also paying off his debts. He blamed his troubles not on the sudden, unexpected move in the stock-index futures but on a flaw in his character. This he thought he'd corrected. He hoped someday to trade livestock futures for his own account, the way he'd always done before he self-destructed.

This was the second time I'd heard something psychological—first from Mr. Dickman in the corn pits ("sooner or later you find out who you are") and now from Mr. Hersh ("it only took one day to nail myself"). I was beginning to sense that regular traders didn't see these markets as pits of gold, but rather as a harsh form of reality therapy in which their defects were revealed and they were financially punished for same. The best they could hope was to settle down and make a modest living. This was a long way from the giddy road to riches presented to the general public, and I saw the hardship in the faces of the humble Mr. Dickman, and the soft-spoken and congenial Mr. Hersh.

Meanwhile, LQ-001 walked by, the woman who'd sold me my hogs. I called her to a halt and she introduced herself. "Elizabeth Quattrocki," she said. She was tall, dressed in a tweedy business suit, and looked all of 25. I asked what she was doing in live-hog options. "Trading for the summer," she said. "On my father's account." Her father was an former Shakespeare scholar whom she said I'd find in the live-cattle pit, though Ms. Quattrocki warned me not to go over there. "Don't try to talk to him today," she advised. "You should have talked to him yesterday. The market was limit up yesterday, but today it's off 80."

Ms. Quattrocki guessed that her father made more money off

cattle futures than he ever made off Shakespeare, and in fact had changed careers to better provide for his family. For her part, she'd begun to trade hog futures to make tuition at Yale Medical School.

Yale Medical School is not cheap—and that fact, coupled with the fact that Ms. Quattrocki had taken the opposite side of my own long position in hog calls—led me to ask her point-blank if I'd done the wrong thing. "I hope so," she said. "Since if you win, I lose. This is a zero-sum game, you know." Mr. Epstein had said the same, but it hadn't really sunk in until I heard it on the rim of the hog pit, and from the mouth of a rival.

I caved in then and there and offered to sell Ms. Quattrocki the two hog calls I'd bought from her at cost so at least we'd both break even. She politely refused. She'd heard that Merrill Lynch was coming in and "crushing the market with paper," which she predicted would depress the hog prices, so she was happy to sit with her short positions and let me get stuck on the long side.

After a second day on the floor, I still hadn't met any high-rollers. The most successful person I'd encountered was Ms. Quattrocki, and even she had to worry about tuition. Whenever a trader told me a story about some other trader who'd made an absolute fortune, the lucky person had always quit the exchange, disappeared from town, left no forwarding address, or else the storyteller couldn't remember the name.

Mr. Epstein introduced me to Jeff Zaret, a 25-year-old who had chosen the stock-index-futures pit over college. I visited Mr. Zaret at his office on an upper floor, where I think I woke him up from a nap on the couch. He had a good-natured twinkle in his eye, a hint of a pot belly, and a two-day growth of beard. When I asked if he knew any millionaires, Mr. Zaret said he once stood next to a guy in the stock-index pit who'd made $650,000 in three hours. Just like the others, Mr. Zaret couldn't recall the guy's name. Soon, he was telling me the story of his own struggle to survive in the business, where it was "getting harder and harder to make a profit."

"There's so much competition at the margins, so many people chasing the last little dollar," he said, "that it's getting thinner and thinner for locals like me. I still rent my seat on the exchange from somebody else. I'd like to own my seat, but I can't afford it." Mr. Zaret said he might move to Singapore and trade there. Or he might go back to school.

The great bugaboo of the futures trader was the out-trade. That's when you'd made a profitable deal during the day, but in the afternoon sorting of buys and sells, the other party to the transaction denied it ever happened. There were regular hearings to resolve such disputes, but often it was impossible to prove who signaled what to whom, especially in the crowded pits. Out-trades were rare in the days when traders knew each other as friends and there was honor among them. Now, out-trades were common.

The more I learned about this business the more perilous it seemed. If it was so difficult for the full-time traders to make money here, then what chance did the average investor have? Everything I'd seen and heard seemed to contradict the advertisements.

Again I went back to Mr. Epstein at Lind-Waldock to share my concern. He'd been honest and forthright from the start. As he explained it, things were even worse than I'd thought. "It's a hard way to make an easy living," he said. Attrition had inspired the Mercantile Exchange to create new categories of membership, making it easier and cheaper for people to become traders. "They've got to have warm bodies in the goddamn pits!" Finding new losers was a growing problem. The public relations people called this "providing liquidity." "Somebody has to take the other side of the trade," Mr. Epstein continued.

The average investor provided quite a bit of necessary liquidity, for which the exchanges were very thankful. In fact, Mr. Epstein guessed that between 85 and 95 percent of the average investors lost money in futures and options. Maybe it was as high as 97 percent. These were people like you and me, who occasionally got a great idea—silver's going up or corn is going down—and called their brokers to buy a few contracts.

Ninety-five percent losers was more than you'd ever see at roulette wheels, slot machines, jai alai, dog tracks, horse tracks, or any of the other activities we call gambling! I was so amazed by this estimate that I checked it with several other people. Bill Murschel, the public relations man at the Chicago Board of Trade, figured that 70 percent of the average investors lost money in futures. Others mentioned 80 percent, 85 percent, and 90 percent. What's more, they tossed out these figures as if they were of no particular concern.

Nobody in the futures industry seemed to keep statistics on how many losers and winners there actually were. I contacted Mike Smith at the Futures Industry Association in Washington, who said he didn't know of any studies on the subject, and also called it "a privileged type of information." He mentioned a study from the University of Illinois that claimed 90 percent of the investors in commodities lost money, but it was done in the 1950s. "To determine such a thing today would not only be impractical, but an infringement on our fiduciary responsibilities to the industry," said Mr. Smith.

From him, I received some general market surveys commissioned by the futures industry. These were most interesting for what was omitted. In one, the researchers asked everything from "What periodicals do you read?" to "Do you enjoy talking to your broker?" but they never got around to "Have you made or lost money?" The closest they came to the apparently troublesome question was: "Are you satisfied with your performance?" and "Do you plan to make future investments in commodities?" Thirty percent of those interviewed said they had no plans to make any further investments, and from that I presumed they lost money. If Mr. Epstein's estimate was correct, then losing money was no deterrent to another 60 percent of the unfortunates who stayed in the market.

I held my futures and options for 48 hours as I learned of the odds against me. I called the trading desk at Lind-Waldock to review my progress and discovered that my $2,000 had grown to $2,265 in two days.

This $265 increase wouldn't have impressed me otherwise, but given what I'd lately discovered, it seemed like a remarkable achievement. I was only too happy to sell out immediately—live hogs, deutsche-mark straddle, and corn. Though I'd planned to hold my positions much longer, I now knew there was an 80–95 percent chance I'd end up a loser, while my $265 profit put me in very special company with the tiny clique of winners. In fact, in carrying this $265 out across an entire year, I realized I'd made the equivalent of a $47,500 annualized return, or a 1,500 percent gain on my investment. Actually, my gain was closer to 2,000 percent, but I'd rather be modest than exaggerate.

Measuring my success against the disappointing stories I heard from professional traders, I'd have to say I made a killing in commodities. I'd gladly volunteer for one of those TV ads, as long as they mentioned my Useful Tip Number 20:

Past performance improves with age

TWENTY FIVE

MY DOUBTS ABOUT FUTURES

L EAVING MY OWN INVESTMENTS ASIDE, SEVERAL PERPLEXING questions about futures and options needed to be answered. For one thing, if 90 percent of the investors were losers, and this was a zero-sum game, then where did all the money go? I asked around Chicago, and began hearing the same handful of names: Richard Dennis, Ray Friedman, Joel Greenberg, Aaron Itken, Barry Lind of Lind-Waldock, Leo Melamed, and Joe Ritchey. I tried to contact these people, but either they were out of town, on their way out of town, otherwise engaged, or else they simply refused to talk to me.

Richard Dennis was well known for having made millions in commodities and for giving some of it to liberal causes. I considered myself a liberal, but his refusal to be interviewed sent me directly to his counterpart on the conservative side, Joe Ritchey. Little was known about Mr. Ritchey's politics, since he kept a low profile, but he was rumored to be a religious fundamentalist.

I heard other rumors about Mr. Ritchey, as follows: Ten or fifteen years ago, he was a sheriff's deputy in DuPage County, Illinois, presumably making a few thousand a year. He and his brother-in-law started a commodity trading firm which had since made them multimillionaires. It was called Chicago Research and Trading (CRT), and had become one of the largest futures and options firms in the world. CRT had 400 employees, occupied two entire floors of the Chicago Board Options Exchange building, and was about to expand to a third. There was an in-house industrial psychologist, a computer system that rivaled NASA's, a cafeteria that served fresh salmon, and a private gym. Mr. Ritchey and associates were buying up the farmland of Illinois—a final triumph of theoretical agriculture over the real thing.

I tried to confirm all this with Mr. Ritchey, but he never responded to my numerous phone calls. I did get through to Thane Armstrong, his stepson, who volunteered to show me around CRT. Mr. Armstrong was a huge tight-end of a man, as good-natured as a koala, who worked summers at CRT on his breaks from college. He corroborated most of the above, beginning with Mr. Ritchey's having started out as a sheriff's deputy. He also told of Mr. Ritchey's stint as a bus driver for the Chicago Transit Authority, his great genius for math, his first success at trading silver in the early 1970s, his playing the soybeans against the soybean meal, his joining forces with friends and relatives to trade gold, then bonds, then Treasury bills, and his subsequent conquest of the various markets of the world.

CRT was rumored to be so big it bought and sold half the Treasury bonds in the Treasury-bond pit, and often did more bond-futures business than the famous Salomon Brothers or Goldman, Sachs, billions of dollars a day. Mr. Armstrong said he didn't know about that, but he took me to see one of the bond traders, who requested I not use his name. I'm allowed to mention that he wore a loud Hawaiian shirt, which served the same purpose as Mr. Hersh's orange-and-white-checkered jacket. The bond trader confirmed that he handled huge quantities of bond contracts, a big responsibility for a 27-year-old. He said he lived on a farm and drove into Chicago early every morning to get the jump on his competition. The only thing that bothered him about the job was the swearing. "I didn't used to know how to swear," he said. "I learned it in the bond pits."

Mr. Armstrong and I must have walked a half mile up and down corridors, between desks, and around computers as we talked. He told me about the family atmosphere at CRT, and that many employees were graduates of the nearby Wheaton College, a no-nonsense, God-fearing campus. It sounded as if these were young, close-knit, hard-working Jesuits of finance, making millions at a furious pace.

Though much has been made of Mr. Ritchey's alleged fundamentalism, from what I could find out, his success had less to do with religion than with math. In the few articles where he'd been quoted, he called it "picking up money off the floor." Apparently, he and his associates were not pure traders so much as they were arbitrageurs who avoided risk. Never would they have taken the positions I did, leaving themselves naked on one side of the market, whether short or long. They bought and sold both sides simultaneously à la Mr. Gressel, but in a much more complicated way.

Arbitrage is making an investment in one direction, covering yourself in another, and locking in a sure profit. Everything CRT did apparently was counterbalanced: They'd buy gold on one exchange and sell it on another, exploiting a tiny difference in price. They'd do the same with Treasury bonds, soybeans, or silver, looking for a guaranteed return—a tick here, a tick there—in each turnaround. With their own employees trading in the pits, with computers to track the prices, and with millions of dollars to pour into every arbitrage, CRT and Mr. Ritchey were getting richer and richer.

How rich I don't know. But great fortunes were being made by a handful of people in Chicago. If they weren't so shy about publicity, we already might know them as the latter-day Vanderbilts, the Jay Goulds, the Carnegies and Astors of our time. The more I learned about the few winners and many losers in commodities, the more I was convinced that never have so many given so much to so few. Futures and options may have created the greatest voluntary transfer payment in U.S. financial history.

My next question was: Why do we have these futures markets in the first place? Not having come up with a satisfactory answer for myself, I asked many of the exchange spokesmen. Their answer was "hedging." A great to-do was made of this hedging—which supposedly separated the futures markets from the racetracks and the roulette wheels, and gave them a social utility, an economic justification, and a noble sense of purpose, not to mention the numerous tax advantages this business had enjoyed over the years.

Booklets from both major exchanges went on for page after page with examples of hedging. I'll relate one. Let's say you're the Hershey company and worried the price of cocoa is going up.

A higher price for cocoa would reduce your profit on your candy bars. You "hedge" against this threat by buying cocoa futures. In effect, you've contracted for a later delivery at today's prices.

On the other hand, if you're the cocoa farmer and worried the price will drop before you bring your cocoa to market, you do the reverse. You sell the cocoa futures so you'll receive today's prices for what you'll harvest later.

Hedging, also known as price insurance, was the celebrated rationale of the entire futures industry from corn to T-bonds. Both the Chicago Board of Trade and the Mercantile Exchange employed staffs of economists to prove that all the newest proposed contracts—the housing-starts contract, for example—would be useful to somebody in a regular business, and not just to speculators and gamblers. There were workshops on hedging, seminars on hedging, entire courses on hedging that explored every conceivable serious purpose.

Yet from what I could gather firsthand, an actual hedger was sometimes hard to find. Agricultural-commodity futures had been bought and sold for a century, yet farmers were notoriously light hedgers. Though there was little official enthusiasm for a census of hedgers, a recent study from the Futures Industry Association concluded that only 5.6 percent of all agricultural futures were bought by hedging farmers. In fact, many farmers blamed the commodities markets for their economic problems, and the only reason they'd get near the Mercantile Exchange would have been to picket it.

In all the other futures markets, the official word was that 10 percent of the participants were hedgers. That meant that 90 percent were in it for the gambling. I began to suspect there were about as many legitimate hedgers in agriculture, currencies, and other futures as there were owners of racehorses who hedged their investments by betting against their own stable—which is to say, hardly any. What we had, instead, was a giant wagering game disguised as insurance.

On a personal level, I'd met investors in the stock market who hedged their portfolios by buying puts or calls, then pretty soon they'd bought more puts or calls than they needed for insurance, and after that they were sucked into the puts-and-calls business, forgetting the stocks altogether. The same may have occurred with firms like Salomon Brothers, which began buying bond futures to hedge their in-house bond portfolios, but soon found themselves speculating in bond futures as an end in itself.

I brought all this up with Lester Telser, a professor of economics at the University of Chicago and a known expert on the organized futures markets. He was somewhat doubtful that the benefits of the futures markets outweighed the social and economic costs. If the futures markets, as presently constituted, were so important as insurance to big business, then why did various contracts go in and out of fashion, and sometimes cease to be traded? If hedging was so important to the well-being of industry, then why could so many industries survive perfectly well without it? Those are my rhetorical questions, not his.

I also contacted Jim Stone, former chairman of the Commodity Futures Trading Commission, the government agency that regulates the business. Mr. Stone did not hedge his negative opinions. "Futures trading is legalized gambling, pure and simple," was one thing he said. Another thing was, "Growth has slowed down lately, because the suckers are temporarily used up." Another: "These markets are like a dinner. The diners are the traders, the arbitrageurs, the brokers. They feed off the public customer, who is the dinner." Mr. Stone concluded by blasting the "greedy academics" paid huge fees for concluding that futures serve a useful economic purpose—which for them, of course, they do.

Mr. Epstein had mentioned that congressmen and other VIPs are paid a $1,000 fee every time they come to Chicago, just for driving their cars past the futures exchanges. Whether this helped convince Congress that futures serve an economic purpose he wasn't sure.

Another popular theory in the industry was that futures contracts were directly related to the underlying physical commodities, i.e., to real eggs, real pigs, real gold. In my limited experience, I doubted this as well. The people I saw trading soybeans would have gone on trading soybeans long after the last known soybean had been made into tofu. After a few days in Chicago, one's relationship to physical reality is revised. You begin to think like a trader, and you lose interest in tangible objects. On the floors of the two exchanges, I watched very carefully and observed that traders hardly ever looked up to check the cash price of whatever commodity they traded.

I'm sure you've heard about the person who buys onion futures and all of a sudden there's 20 carloads of onions delivered to his or her front door. Even though this occasionally happens, the stories are misleading. A dedicated futures trader probably wouldn't notice if there were onions in the front yard or not. He'd be absorbed in his printouts, trying to figure out if he was up or down for the day.

I reviewed these findings with the public relations people, who reminded me that without real soybeans there would be no possibility of settlement, and therefore the millions of dollars in soybean futures contracts would have no meaning. I thought they had a point. A real soybean was a threat to be held over traders' heads on expiration day, without which they might welch on their obligations. As the business gets more sophisticated, the threat of a real soybean becomes less necessary.

They also informed me of recent progress in eliminating the fraud and abuses suffered by the average speculator in commodities. Both industry and government have joined forces to work for fairer trading. Personally, it was hard to believe that anybody lost sleep over the cheating in an industry where 80 to 90 percent of the participants lost all their money anyway, but there were meetings about this every year, and new rules often came out of the Commodity Futures Trading Commission.

The CFTC was established in 1975 to monitor the 82 different futures bought and sold at eight different U.S. exchanges and to insure that a majority of speculators lose money in an orderly, reasonable, and efficient manner. I visited the CFTC in Washington, at its modest new offices near the headquarters of the over-the-counter market. Down the hall, past the flags and beyond the picture of the president, I saw one or two people wandering about.

While waiting to see Nick Memoli, a staff economist, I picked up a booklet entitled "Commodity Futures Trading Commission: The First 10 Years." It had the drama of a good detective novel, and it gave a better overall sense of the futures business than anything else I'd seen to date.

"Off and Running" was the first chapter, when the new CFTC

opened its doors with 240 confused employees transferred from another agency. As these employees settled into their temporary basement offices, $572 billion worth of futures were traded that they were supposed to regulate. They had to decide how to license 22,000 brokers, trading advisors, commodity-pool operators, and floor traders. They had to find an economic purpose for dozens of new futures contracts.

Meanwhile, they had to do something about Jack Savage. Mr. Savage, of Chicago, was the first person deemed unfit to sell commodities futures, due to an earlier criminal conviction for mail fraud and a permanent injunction that barred him from selling stocks and bonds. Mr. Savage was one example of the attraction of commodities for what CFTC Chairman William Bagley called "some of the worst lie-by-day and fly-by-night operations in the financial world."

In May 1976, soon after the agency settled into its basement, it faced a potato crisis. The New York Mercantile Exchange, an East Coast version of the exchanges I've described, notified the government of a default in the Maine potato contract. Apparently there weren't enough theoretical potatoes to cover the theoretical potato delivery. To attack this problem, the CFTC turned to its staff attorneys, investigators, and economists. How attorneys, investigators, and economists came up with the extra potatoes I'm not sure, but the crisis was resolved to everyone's satisfaction, at least until the following year, when there was a second theoretical potato failure.

After issuing 170 subpoenas and questioning 200 people about the potato shortfall, the CFTC took legal action against nine short traders, five long traders, and the potato exchange itself. Then its attention was diverted to coffee. Two coffee traders held 82 percent of the long positions, and there wasn't enough theoretical coffee in all the world to cover their September 1976 "C" (for coffee) contracts. Physical coffee drinkers could switch to physical tea in a physical shortage, but in futures there was no such recourse. Later, the frosts in Brazil, floods in Colombia, an earthquake in Guatemala, and the civil war in Angola all conspired against the coffee contracts, so there were three more theoretical coffee failures in 1977.

In 1977, the CFTC studied hedging. This may have been a tactical error. After polling the farmers, the agency discovered that farmers don't normally hedge—a troublesome result, as I've said. To make up for this, the study pointed out that 30 percent of farmers with more than $10,000 in annual gross sales follow futures prices as a business barometer—which at least made futures good for something. Later, the CFTC redefined hedging and made a distinction between regular hedging and "bonafide hedging." I've read this over many times and still don't understand it.

In 1976, the CFTC staff pursued the Hunt brothers of Texas for violating the speculative-position limit for soybean contracts. That the Hunts made trouble for soybeans before they made trouble for silver is a little-known fact. The CFTC forced the Hunts to pay a $500,000 fine and banned them from trading soybeans for two years—though the agency relented a bit in the case of Nelson Hunt and allowed him to continue to engage in bonafide hedging. Perhaps the soybean ban drove the Hunt brothers into silver.

A year later, the CFTC turned its attention to problems with the London commodity options. Hordes of unsavory operators apparently had showed up there. One of the most unsavory, according to the booklet, was Mr. James Carr. Apparently Mr. Carr sold options without proper registration, though it was hard to tell since he hadn't bothered to keep any records. He was arrested in Boston. Five days later, the FBI announced that Mr. Carr wasn't Carr at all, but an escaped felon named Alan Abrahams who'd used several other aliases.

By 1978, William Bagley, the original CFTC chairman, resigned. He commented that everything was now running smoothly after the understandable start-up problems.

In 1979 there was trouble with March wheat for the same old reason. The wheat in the futures contracts exceeded the known deliverable supply. There were similar emergencies in potatoes, cocoa, and coffee. The CFTC acted once again to stop the illegal selling of options, continued to aid the prosecution in cases of corn, wheat, and potato manipulation, and filed new charges against the coffee manipulators. With the grain embargo in 1980 came the usual kind of trouble.

Since then, there had been several fresh attempts to license the brokers and fund operators, to audit the traders, to monitor the manipulators, to halt the frauds, and to root out the illegal boiler rooms, as the futures industry had grown tenfold. Meanwhile, the CFTC continued to review a long list of applications for new futures and options, to determine the economic purpose in each instance.

When I got to see Mr. Memoli, the staff economist, he said he couldn't remember the agency ever disapproving a contract.

In the future, then, we're likely to see a lot more futures. The NASDAQ-100 futures, the S&P OTC individual index, the U.S. dollar index, cocoa options, orange juice options, European currency unit options, yen options, three-month Treasury-bill options, copper options, and long-term municipal-bond-index options are already approved. Upcoming are Treasury repos, Treasury strips, the Eurobond index, an information processing index, the petroleum index, the S&P high-tech index, utility index, *Financial Times* stock exchange 100-share index, utility stock index, Japanese stock index, Comex stock index, Canadian market index, PSE technology index, and the NYSE beta index, plus the housing-start future, the retail-new-car-sales future, the five-year U.S. Treasury index, the earnings index, future-price index, and high-fructose corn index. I got this list from Mr. Memoli.

There's also an ocean-freight future. Maybe soon they'll have futures on rainfall, the Democratic primaries, the Nielsen ratings, and hospital occupancy as well.

TWENTY SIX

MY ETHICAL DILEMMA

O UT OF COMMODITIES, BUT STILL IN CHICAGO, I REVIEWED MY progress. By mid-July, I'd made $265 in the Lind-Waldock account, plus the $400 on the stock-index options bought much earlier, thanks to Mr. Crawford. This $715 was the only profit I'd taken to date. I'd sold one half of the Angstrom for a loss of $700, which left me about even. Meanwhile, I still owned the 53 shares of Gillette worth $88 a share—a paper profit of $450—and the remaining 2,500 shares of Angstrom, now worth only 85 cents a share, for a paper loss of $2,100. Overall, I was down $1,650.

I chose to accentuate the positive, the small, albeit miraculous, results from my Chicago trading. Though the $265 didn't cover my hotel bill, I decided to stick around Chicago and look for the next smart thing to do. It didn't take long to find it.

There was news from back home that my wife's broker, Mr. Bermont, recommended she buy Loews stock for her own account as soon as possible. An investment genius named Laurence Tisch, who controlled Loews, was using his company to acquire shares in CBS at bargain prices. Mr. Tisch was making other savvy moves to benefit the Loews shareholders. The stock was selling for about $60 and surely would rise to $80 by the end of summer.

I could have bought the stock, but having become a confirmed short-term trader, I was now interested in the option. I checked with local sources and was delighted to learn that Loews options were traded along with hundreds of similar chances in the new building stuck onto the back of the art deco Board of Trade. These were options on individual stocks, as opposed to options on the stock-index futures I'd bought on the advice of the astrologer.

Personally, I'd had nothing to do with options on individual stocks since the early fiasco I referred to back in chapter I. But after getting the good news on Loews, plus being so close to the place where the Loews options were traded, I felt obligated to give it a try.

Other factors aroused my desire for quick profit. My wife was about to visit me in Chicago. On the phone she said she was thrilled about my success in commodities. Since she was ignorant of the general sorry condition of the rest of my portfolio, not to mention the pettiness of the success in commodities, I thought a big move in Loews might improve things by the time she arrived.

More to the point, since she'd heard about Loews herself, it was unsafe for me to ignore it. If I ignored it, then Loews would surely go up 20 points and she'd ask me how I could have missed it. If Loews went down, there was a measure of protection in the fact that Loews was her broker's idea.

There was one problem. I found out that Loews was basically a tobacco company. It did a lot of other things, such as operate movie theaters, as is the case with normal American conglomerations. But basically, it was tobacco. Years ago, my wife and I promised ourselves we'd never invest in a tobacco company. Without getting too maudlin about it, her first husband had died of lung cancer.

When I informed my wife, via telephone, about Loews and the tobacco, it put an end to her interest in the stock. But by then I'd gotten very interested in the option.

This was the kind of ethical dilemma that made it trickier than ever to invest. Not only did you have to find something that would make you money, it had to be something that wouldn't make you sick. The more you learned about any enterprise—its nuclear involvements, defense contracts, mistreatment of women and minorities, tainted funding, or sales to South Africa—the less likely you could stand to be associated with it.

How many profitable opportunities were missed because of ethics I couldn't imagine. I haven't mentioned it because it sounds self-serving, but during this entire journey I had my eye on Union Carbide stock, which I forced myself to resist out of respect for the victims of Bhopal. The stock, meanwhile, had tripled in price.

I often thought of the profits I didn't make as a kind of subjunctive contribution to the Bhopali cause.

I was determined to shun IBM out of sympathy for South African blacks, since at the start of my journey IBM was still active in that country. Since IBM had gone nowhere as a stock, I was glad I'd had the courage to resist it. One of my former brokers once recommended Philip Morris at $60 and I gave up doubling my money there—which I hope the victims of smoking will also appreciate. This leads me to Useful Tip Number 21:

The better a stock does, the more ethical you feel for not having bought it

---

Centuries ago, there was no such thing as an ethical investment. In those simplistic days, money itself was thought to be unethical, and loaning it out at interest was sinful *ipso facto*. Even into the 1920s, there were few ethical distinctions among stocks, since Wall Street was a known den of thieves and owning any stock was thought to be no better than playing cards for money. In those years, colleges and universities did debate whether to accept tainted endowments from the Rockefellers and other robber barons. Inevitably, though, they voted yes. Most were comforted by the emperor Vespasian's reply to critics of his public-toilet monopoly: *pecunia non olet*, "money doesn't smell."

Only in the 1930s did we begin to see a widespread acceptance of stock portfolios as respectable in general. This marked the beginning of distinguishing one stock as morally superior to another. Religious institutions were the first to act on these distinctions. Certain Catholic dioceses wouldn't invest in birth-control stocks, Protestant denominations refused to hold liquor stocks, Christian Scientists stayed away from medical stocks. Eventually, the union pension funds followed suit, avoiding stocks in union-busting corporations

It wasn't until the early 1970s that large numbers of individuals began to invest ethically. That's when ex-hippies, radicals, and protesters came into money. Many who inherited trust funds or acquired other sizable sources of income refused to support unethical companies. They didn't restrict themselves to single ethical issues, such as birth control or alcohol, but rather sought out investments that were ethical overall. This brought us full-circle from the Middle Ages, when ethical investing was oxymoronic.

Most everyone who started out drawing the line somewhere—at nuclear power, cigarettes, women's rights, or the military—ended up drawing several lines at once. With so much damning information on so many companies, and so many companies becoming conglomerates, it was no simple task to find a likable investment. A few mutual funds began to specialize in ethical selections. Three of the biggest as of this writing were: Pax World Fund of Portsmouth, New Hampshire (no liquor, tobacco, gambling, or weapons-systems stocks), the Calvert Fund of Washington, D.C. (no alcohol, tobacco, nuclear energy, weapons systems, companies doing business in South Africa, environmental scofflaws, or enemies of unions), and the Pioneer Group of Boston (no alcohol, tobacco, or South Africa).

Ethical money-managers began to offer professionally chosen, socially screened accounts. There were socially conscious money-market funds, such as one managed by the Calvert group, which avoided the contamination of U.S. Treasury bills. Instead, its capital floated around with Freddie Mac, Fannie Mae, small business loans, cogeneration, office equipment, hydropower, regional banking, and natural gas. There were socially-conscious investment newsletters, including *The Clean Yield* and *Good Money,* both published in Vermont.

Many who began to invest in this systematically ethical way also found themselves wanting to ethically consume. People who began with good intentions soon had no place to put their money, and nothing to eat or drink. On that score, you'll never catch me buying Chilean grapes or plums. My wife won't buy German cars. My friend Phil Stanford says somebody told him not to drink Portuguese wine, but he can't remember why. After the movie *Z* came out, we vowed never to drink ouzo again. Actually, we never drank ouzo in the first place. I gave up nonunion lettuce—which fortunately happened to be iceberg—just at the time it became fashionable to upgrade to endive.

So in my own haphazard way, I was an ethical investor and also an ethical consumer. With Loews bothering my conscience, I thought back on an interview I once did with Rian Fried, one of the editors of *The Clean Yield*. That interview was unrelated to this project, but it turned out to be relevant.

Mr. Fried was an animated, intelligent, mustachioed ethical detective, feared and loved as the Hercule Poirot of the ethical-investment industry. At a lunch in Northampton, Massachusetts, he told me of his delight at finding the dirt on companies that were popular with ethical investors. For instance, he'd noticed the IBM typewriters in Franklin Research, a socially conscious investment company that would never touch IBM stock.

He said he spent hours a week skimming trade magazines to search for obscure evidence. He caught Lotus—an ethical favorite because it wouldn't sell anything to the military—selling to the military indirectly through another company that sold to Zenith, which in turn sold to the military. He caught another ethically popular computer company red-handed: making a hard disk that could withstand a nuclear attack! Why would they make a disk like that unless they were going to sell it to some military outfit that hoped to stay on line during World War III?

I remembered Mr. Fried's having said, "I don't care what anybody tells you. They may be watching a GE television set and GE is into nuclear weapons. They may want you to buy a Sony but Sony isn't into American labor."

What better person to resolve the ethical question of the Loews option than Mr. Fried? In fact, we had discussed options. First, I'd asked him if it was all right to short an unethical stock—in other words to bet on its downfall. Mr. Fried hadn't been sure: "When you short a stock you want the thing to go down, to punish the company because of what the company did. That's OK. But then you're also profiting from the bad thing."

Then I'd asked: If a stock is unethical, is it all right to buy the option? He'd said he thought it was. An option was one step removed from a stock, which in the case of a tobacco company meant it was one step removed from the tobacco.

Recalling this conversation, I felt I could buy Loews options with a clear conscience. These options were sold right there behind the Board of Trade building, a few blocks from my hotel.

TWENTY-SEVEN

A BOUT WITH LOEWS

THE CENTRALIZED MARKET FOR STOCK OPTIONS WAS OPENED IN 1973, but they'd been traded in small circles for more than a century. Call options—along with various warrants and other gimmicks known as "securing privileges"—have existed for nearly as long as there have been stocks. In fact, call options were more popular with investors in 1870 than they were in 1970, before the new market was established.

The put option was a more recent refinement, but even it went back at least as far as Russell Sage, the nineteenth-century tycoon who profited from puts. Somewhere I read that Daniel Drew, the robber baron, bought puts on 50,000 shares of Erie in 1872. After the Chicago fire, many put contracts paid off big as the stocks to which they were connected lost value. When you buy a put, remember, you want the stock to go down. When you buy a call, you want the stock to go up.

After the Correction of 1929, stock options got a bad name and were nearly outlawed by the government. For 40 years, the business was carried on by an obscure clique of put and call brokers, until the grand opening of the Chicago Board Options Exchange, an independent entity spun off from the Chicago Board of Trade.

Like many great innovations, this one resulted from luck, foresight, and coincidence. First, the rival Mercantile Exchange already thought up foreign-currency futures, which demanded an imaginative response from the Board of Trade. Second, it was wintertime, and traders in the agriculture pits were bored. (That's the unofficial version, told to me by Mr. Epstein. The official version is that "grain markets were looking for new ways to diversify.")

It took two years to convince the Securities and Exchange Commission to approve a pilot program for trading stock options. On April 26, 1973, 911 call-option contracts on 15 different stocks changed hands in a small smoker's lounge off the main floor of the Board of Trade. I couldn't locate the lounge, but there ought to be a plaque to commemorate this speculators' Kitty Hawk.

The response to centralized options trading was so enthusiastic that it took the organizers by surprise. Billions of dollars were soon invested in this market. In one decade, the CBOE moved from the smoker's lounge to its own new building, attached to the back of the Board of Trade like a giant high-rise potting shed. As of my visit, the CBOE sold puts and calls on 140 different stocks, while other exchanges had gone into the options business as a form of self-defense. In fact, the success of the stock options led to the invention of the stock-index options described earlier, and also of the options on cattle, pork bellies, and the live hogs that I'd bought.

Since Lind-Waldock didn't handle stock options, I closed out my account there and called my reliable old Prudential-Bache broker, Ms. Garrett. First, I informed her I was in Chicago. Then, as forcefully as I could, I announced, "I want to buy some Loews options. The stock is going to 80." She seemed impressed with my confidence, in spite of what had already transpired between us. "Do you know something about Loews?" she asked. I wondered if she'd call other clients and recommend Loews as soon as I hung up.

The Loews stock was trading at around $65 a share. A September $75 call option gave me the right to buy a hundred shares for $75 a share until the expiration date in mid-September, about two months away. If the stock went to $80, then the option would be worth $500.

At current prices, Ms. Garrett said, each of these options would cost $150. I bought ten of them, for a total outlay of $1,605.47. That wiped out most of the cash left in the Prudential-Bache account.

By now, I knew enough to realize that I could also sell options I didn't own, and the proceeds would be added to my account on paper. I'd done it with corn, by selling the 5,000 bushels to Cargill. The same could be accomplished by selling a put, or in this case, the September $70 Loews put. Technically, this meant I was offering somebody else the right to sell me the stock for $70 a share anytime until mid-September. More practically, it meant that at the $400 price for these puts quoted me by Ms. Garrett, a sale of ten of them would result in an immediate $3,990.33 credited to my account.

The $3,990.33 credit for the ten puts, minus the $1,605.47 debit for the ten calls, gave me a delightful windfall of $2,384.86, which surely would have impressed my wife if she'd accidentally happened to see the brokerage statement. (In reality, there had to be sufficient assets in the account to cover the value of the put at all times. Ms. Garrett said that my Gillette and my Angstrom would serve as this collateral).

Buying a call while selling a put simultaneously is a sophisticated maneuver that Ms. Garrett said was a form of arbitrage, the "bull spread." Inadvertently, then, I'd taken Mr. Ritchey's million-dollar methods—playing one investment off another—and applied it to my own little situation. "If this goes against me, then I know I've had it," I joked to Ms. Garrett, confident that such a thing could never happen.

After I'd established my bull-spread position, I arranged to visit the Options Exchange through the public relations office and its amiable director, Hank Nothnagel. Stock options were traded in pits, much like corn or soybeans, on the largest trading floor in the world, 45,000 square feet. Mr. Nothnagel said there were more computer screens in this building than at any single location outside of NASA. There were enough telephones for a midsize U.S. city. So much heat was given off by computers and other electronic devices that the trading floor didn't require any furnace, even in the worst Chicago winter. In fact, it had to be air-conditioned year round.

The pits themselves were no wider than most elevators, with options on three or more stocks traded in each. At the Loews pit, I saw four or five of the usual baby-faced lot. They stood ranting and raving as buy and sell orders were dealt like cards from a metal deck in front of them. Each time an option price went up or down, a new batch of cards was brought into play and there'd be another flurry of trading.

The orders came in from all over the country, many from average investors like you and me. When you told your broker to buy or sell you an option, this is where the transaction ended up.

These traders seemed more prosperous than their counterparts in the hog pits and corn pits, perhaps because of all the liquidity that was pouring in. For several minutes, I was transfixed by Mr. O'Hara. He wore loafers with no socks, a striped polo shirt and a jacket that didn't match. He was ebullient, even cocky, as he snapped up puts and calls. During a lull, he told me he'd been trading for his own account for two years and with no complaints. "Where else could a young guy come in with $40,000 and start his own business, except at a hot-dog stand?"

Mr. O'Hara introduced me to a fellow trader, Tony Vesh, and said Mr. Vesh was a "scalper." It seemed to start an argument between them. "I'm no scalper," Mr. Vesh said. "I hold up my leg a lot longer these days. You know that." A "leg" turned out to be one side of an option spread position, such as my own. I asked Mr. O'Hara where he thought the price of Loews was going, and he didn't seem to know or care. His philosophy was simple: "Buy cheap and sell fat." To accomplish that, he relied on the same complicated mathematical formulas used by Mr. Gressel in New York, by Ms. Quattrocki in hog options, and, on a much higher level, by Mr. Ritchey upstairs.

When I wondered out loud if it were possible for an amateur like me to beat them at the options game, both Mr. O'Hara and Mr. Vesh laughed unroariously. "No way," said Mr. O'Hara. "We're down here and we get first dibs on all the profits." They thought of themselves as scavengers feasting on the easy pickings, leaving their competitors the bones and the gristle, or whatever else they hadn't bothered to consume. "You guys can have the risky stuff," said Mr. O'Hara. In the case of my Loews, this turned out to be sadly prophetic.

Loews hit a downdraft that was both severe and unexpected. Instead of soaring toward $80, it fell toward $50. In a single session, the stock price dropped $4 and virtually wiped out the value of my calls. Meanwhile, the puts I'd sold—and eventually would have to buy back—got more and more expensive. This all happened the week my wife arrived in Chicago.

I tried to ignore the Loews and concentrate on our walking tours of art deco architecture. This was difficult, and almost impossible. Things got even more difficult when, on a return to our hotel, I found an urgent message from Ms. Garrett in our pigeonhole. It said something about a "margin call." Fortunately, my wife hadn't seen it.

I crumpled up the message as quickly as possible and later returned alone to the hotel lobby to phone Ms. Garrett from a pay station. "You're in trouble now," she said. "You've got to put in more money to cover your short position." Besides the Loews sinking fast, my Angstrom shares were now considered unworthy collateral by her accounting department. She said she'd cover for me and stall as long as possible, which I appreciated. She left me the strong impression that I'd better send cash right away.

Here I have another embarrassing confession: I wired $4,000 out of the general household funds and never told my wife. In fact, when she reads this I hope I'm not in the room. I'd like to remind her that I'll make it up to her somehow, that I put back $2,000 of it from the closing of the Lind-Waldock account, and that she still hasn't reached the end of the book.

Even after I put up the extra $4,000, I got another urgent message about another margin call. It was partly to avoid such horrible surprises that I suggested to my wife we change hotels because our room was too small. Since I'd been careful not to leave a forwarding address or phone number at the old hotel, I was temporarily liberated from more pink slips from Ms. Garrett's office. For two days, I ignored my troubles and concentrated on the Wrigley Building and the metalwork around the doors at the Carson Pirie Scott department store. I tried to pretend that Loews, the stock market, Prudential-Bache, and Ms. Garrett had never existed.

Finally, I could hold out no longer. After a particularly disastrous session with the Dow Jones average down 45 points, I called Ms. Garrett from another phone booth and put myself at her mercy. "I can't send more money," I said. "Then we'll have to buy back the puts," she insisted. "We have no other choice." I don't think I ever felt worse, but I told her to do what had to be done. Buying back the 10 Loews September $70 puts cost me $8,429.10. At least I wouldn't get any more margin calls.

TWENTY-EIGHT

A HOUSEHOLD CORRECTION

I RETURNED HOME FROM CHICAGO IN WORSE SHAPE THAN EVER, ANG-strom's loss eclipsed by my having dropped several thousand on the ill-fated Loews options in a matter of days. Thankfully, my wife continued to make a decent living in real estate, and had also taken care of the children, while I'd fallen deeper into this hole. Although she didn't know the half of it, I did. This self-knowledge had profound effects on the politics in the house.

In periods when there's some profit on paper—in my case, as far back as the first weeks—the investor in the family is infused with uncharacteristic generosity and does suspicious things, such as buying champagne, encouraging the family members to go shopping, and taking them to restaurants normally off the budgetary limits. These spasms of largess baffle those recipients who are accustomed to Scroogian economics from the investor. Earlier, I mentioned my having bought extra Christmas presents during the brief but happy Brigadoon of Angstrom's being up. Naturally, the family distrusted these gifts and wondered if I'd lost my mind.

The generosity lasts only as long as the paper profits, and then there's the great comeuppance. Not only has the investor suffered investment losses, but he has also run up big credit-card bills on the expectation of gains that lately have vanished. This is a frightening realization, which sends the investor cowering to the side of economic austerity and turns him into a penny-pincher.

For instance, after my retreat from Chicago, I wandered about the house turning off lights and muttering about the electric bill. I complained about the 15-cent charge for calling the operator for directory assistance, and I put the telephone book out on the dining room table for all to use. I also made my teenage daughter pay for the oil change in the car we share.

It got to the point where I'd open the refrigerator and yell, "You bought too much broccoli," or "We already have white rice," or "Why have three new lettuces when one is rotten in the crisper?" I counted the spices and noticed there were three oreganos and complained: "Every time there's a trip to the grocery store, somebody buys another oregano."

Worrying about oregano duplication is a sure sign of trouble with the investments. Other signs are: a sudden interest in energy conservation, questioning the water bill or the monthly garbage service, complaining about greedy charities, and making the children buy their own stamps—all of which can be summarized in Useful Tip Number 22:

The larger the sum you've lost, the smaller the sums you'll worry about

---

I hoped my family would take my frugal campaigns seriously, but they didn't. They knew all along that my moral stand on broccoli had something to do with what had happened in Chicago. Unbeknownst to me, they'd figured out months earlier that my moods went up and down with the stock market. In fact, they could almost predict the Dow Jones by how many household purchases I encouraged or condemned.

Anyway, I was back home with my Loews gone wrong, and feeling worse and worse. Suddenly, I got an urge to get out of the market altogether. On July 29, I called Ms. Garrett and ordered her to sell everything, the Gillette, the Angstrom, and whatever was left of my options, and I didn't care about the price.

A day later, I found out I'd gotten $2,146.91 for the remaining 2,500 shares of Angstrom (a loss of $2,824.66 from the original cost); $4,535.96 for the Gillette (a profit of $308.72); and I'd sold the 10 Loews calls for $895.40 (a loss of $710.07). Altogether, it was a terrible day. Of the entire $14,700 I'd put into the markets since the previous December, I was left with about half, or $7,577.

Yet this costly closeout made me strangely happy! I felt even happier than when I'd closed the commodities account with an actual $265 profit. To say that the average investor is delighted to make money and depressed to lose money is an oversimplification. In my experience, I'd have been delighted to sell a stock for a profit only if the stock price didn't go higher from there. If the price did go higher, then I'd feel depressed and stupid for having sold prematurely. In fact, I was much happier taking a big loss in something that's going even lower than taking a small profit in something that's going higher. This was the great mystery of investing.

"You should have heard our market expert, Larry Wachtel," Linda Garrett told me the day we sold. "The most negative he's ever been. Sounded like we're going into a Depression." I told her I was elated to be out of it. Then she added: "But if people like you are selling everything, then it's a sure sign the market will go up."

That last remark made a delayed impression, and I was only out of the market for two weeks. One advantage of short-term trading—my new specialty—was, once you realized how quickly you'd lost, you also realized how quickly you could gain it back. A long-term drop in a stock price might take years to correct itself, but a loss in options could be covered on the very next position.

I knew I needed to change my strategy, and so I did. In Chicago, I'd bought the Loews calls and sold the Loews puts simultaneously. Since this resulted in the loss, I decided to try something more conservative: buying an in-the-money call and selling an out-of-the-money call against it. I won't try to explain the strategy, since even if I could, you'd be better off not knowing how to do it. But you see how much I'd been learning. No longer could I consider myself an amateur options player.

I searched the newspapers looking for a certain kind of in-the-money versus out-of-the-money spread that would cost $200 or less per contract and might return up to $500 per contract. With this kind of spread, there was hardly a way I could lose. The one way I could lose was if both options ended up out-of-the-money, which could only happen in a severe correction or a bear market. Mr. Wachtel's remarks notwithstanding, the majority of advisors were still bullish. We'd been in a great market for most of the year. Plus, I swore to myself I'd get out at the slightest downward move.

When I called Ms. Garrett again, I didn't mention my recent selling of everything, and she didn't bring it up either. We had a regular conversation, as if my behavior were completely normal.

One of the options that fit my new requirements, ironically, was Loews. Here I was about to buy back something I'd just sold, which proved my confidence in the new approach. I ordered Ms. Garrett to buy eight Loews September 65 calls—which cost me $3,621.88, and to sell eight Loews September 70 calls—which gave me a credit of $1,402.41. She didn't comment on the odd coincidence that the very options that drove me out of the market I'd now reacquired.

I also ordered her to buy 10 Budweiser September 55 calls at a cost of $3,509.63, and sell 10 Budweiser September 60 calls for a credit of $895.40. All in all, these transactions set me back $4,733.70.

A few days after I took the new positions, I was waiting for my car to be fixed in the lobby of a repair shop and called Ms. Garrett to check on our progress. The market had taken a sharp drop that morning. This was bad news for my strategy. The in-the-money legs of both my spreads were dangerously close to falling out-of-the-money, the point at which I'd promised myself I'd sell.

"I think we should sell the Budweiser spread," I told Ms. Garrett. "Things are going in the wrong direction." "Sell the Bud?" she answered. "Are you sure? We like Bud." This was the last bit of advice I ever took from her. I didn't sell, then the Bud went blooey and so did the Loews. I'll spare you the details, but I closed out my Prudential-Bache account a week later and told Ms. Garrett to send me a check for the remains. Of the entire $14,920.13 I'd invested from the beginning, I got back a check for $3,296.56. A discouraging result, but I tried to concentrate on the $265 I'd made in commodities.

Was this the end? Of course not. The next step was to find a new stockbroker. Instead of wasting time on interviews, I went directly to the local Dis-Com Securities, a do-it-yourself brokerage house with lower commissions than even Charles Schwab's.

TWENTY-NINE

IN SEARCH
OF A FORECAST

TRYING TO REMAIN CALM ABOUT THE MOST RECENT SETBACKS, I analyzed the situation and realized I'd been missing something. No matter how good any stock happened to be, the short-term trader had to pay close attention to the mood of the market he was in. A positive market pulled most everything up with it, but in a downturn, the odds were against any stock's gaining ground. It occurred to me that if I continued with my short-term strategy, I'd have to get a better sense of the character of the stock market overall. For the options player, especially, timing was critical to any success.

Predicting the general direction of the markets was the work of another group of experts, the forecasters. Forecasters were hired by the big brokerage firms to ponder the future of interest rates, stock prices, and the economy as a whole. Though not all forecasters were economists, many of the 60,000 economists in the nation were called upon to make predictions.

Knowing that I couldn't afford another mistake like the last few, I began an intense at-home study of what the various forecasters had been saying. In a single week of watching as many of them as possible on television, I heard the stock market described as a psychiatric problem ("lost and without direction"); a football game ("coming back from fourth-and-ten"); a stomach ailment ("struggling to digest recent gains"); and a weather report ("rising pressure and a possible washout"). A succession of experts said that the market was: "correcting," "pausing," "long in the tooth," "accumulating," "overbought," and "tired." Others noted that it was "consolidating," "in a negative mood," "waiting to see what Congress would do," or that it had "overstepped its bounds," "discounted the news," "anticipated the next advance," "climbed a wall of worry," and "cleansed itself with a small decline."

Finding it difficult to interpret what any of this meant, I undertook a careful review of the previous statements and predictions that had more or less been gathering dust in a corner of our bedroom. These happened to be from the forecasters at Drexel Burnham Lambert, the firm of my wife's broker, who thankfully had continued to do well with her money. By going back over what Drexel had forecast, I hoped to get a feel for the vocabulary and for the general way in which forecasters operated.

Back when I began my odyssey, that is to say, the beginning of the great bull market of 1986, the Drexel experts gave a skittish, and even negative, prognosis for stocks. In December 1985, they still hadn't foreseen that a marvelous run-up was about to occur. Instead, they worried that the economy would pick up steam, which for some reason would depress the stock market. That a vigorous economy would be bad for the stock market was the first of several curiosities I discovered in the Drexel pile. (Soon I learned that the stock market was usually one step ahead of itself, so that during a bad economy, it could optimistically look forward to a good one, but during a good economy, it could only anticipate a forthcoming setback.)

In December 1985, with the Dow Jones average at 1450, Drexel's clients got a report entitled *Digestion,* which again suggested that the "potential for further declines in interest rates may be slight" since the Fed was unlikely to ease credit. What the Fed did was an important element in forecasting, as I mentioned earlier. The same report mentioned that many people were bullish, another bad sign for stocks.

On February 24, two months later and 200 Dow Jones points higher, the latest Drexel statement had no explanation for the impressive advance, other than to call it "heady." Instead, the forecasters were nervous, and warned clients of "the possibility of higher interest rates, plus some profit taking" that would drive stock prices lower.

During February-March, Drexel came out with an update entitled *More Records.* Mentioning none of the negatives cited above, this time the forecasters listed the new reasons for optimism in the market. These included a "rebounding economy" and an observation that the "business climate is good." This was doubly curious, since these reasons for optimism were the same as the reasons for pessimism offered three months earlier. The dreaded economic pickup that supposedly caused people to sell stocks would somehow now stimulate a new wave of buying.

On March 3, readers got the *Constructive View* that the recent bond rally was inspired by the cut in the Fed discount rate, the very same cut that forecasters had doubted would occur. The inflation they had predicted earlier was now pronounced "under tight control," with no sign of recession in sight. The Dow Jones average had responded by hitting 1692.

By March 10, under the title *Consolidation Phase*, Drexel was saying: "We feel that the reasons for being bullish are intact," although in reviewing the forecasts one after another, I couldn't possibly tell you what those reasons had been.

In July-August, Drexel blamed a drop in the stock prices on "selling pressure," combined with the fact that inflation was moribund and the economy was sluggish. This sluggish economy, earlier seen as causing the market to rise and then later as causing it to fall, was apparently causing it to fall once again. An economic pickup, so recently a bearish sign, was now eagerly anticipated as bullish. By the August-September Drexel letter, these positions once again reversed: the economic pickup was deemed a bearish sign, while the sluggish economy with low inflation was once more bullish.

Then on September 29, *Building Confidence,* we learned that stock prices were rising because the "widespread fears of inflation"—previously dismissed—were "somewhat mitigated," while on October 6, *Straining,* the muddling economy and the resulting lack of inflation combined to cause stock prices to fall.

Probably we are not supposed to go back and read these reports all at once, which brings me to Useful Tip Number 23:

A forecaster should never look back

Certainly, the twists and the turnabouts from the Drexel reports had thrown me for a loop. This much I'd figured out: a good economy was good for the stock market, a sluggish economy was bad for the stock market, and vice versa. Also, lower oil prices were bullish for stocks only until higher oil prices became bullish for stocks. Since the stock market "discounted" the things it already knew, while it anticipated the unknown, there was no point in thinking too far ahead. And since current conditions changed so fast, there was no use analyzing them, either. Remember this when you pick up the latest forecast from a brokerage firm, and you discover that their year-long "raging disinflation scenario" has been turned into a "raging inflation scenario" overnight. It couldn't be easy, or else these brokerage firms wouldn't have huge staffs of humans and computers to figure these things out.

In my doubt and confusion from reviewing the forecasts, I thought of Henry Kaufman. If you're going to look into the economic future, why not go straight to the dean of the economic forecasters, the famous spokesman from Salomon Brothers, the man whose speeches make the front page of the *New York Times* and whose opinions move the world markets? Rather than continue to muddle around with secondhand information, I decided to spend some money on another trip to New York. There, I could meet Mr. Kaufman, get his short-term forecast, and then invest whatever I had left in some carefully chosen calls or puts, where one big move could make up for everything.

I was back at my friend's apartment in New York, preparing to contact Mr. Kaufman, when I came across a startling blurb in a magazine: "Astrologer Predicts 88-Point Drop." It referred to Mr. Crawford, the astrologer I'd met in Sacco's coffee shop back in March. Apparently he'd anticipated the recent brutal correction that drove me out of options, out of Prudential-Bache, and out of $4,000 worth of assets!

A lot of people are going to say: you can't compare Henry Kaufman with Arch Crawford. Mr. Kaufman is the chief economist at Salomon Brothers, and I figured he was paid at least $1 million a year, plus insurance, for his opinions. Mr. Crawford, I knew, earned considerably less for his. But before I started work on getting an interview with Mr. Kaufman, I thought I'd check in with Mr. Crawford. In fact, after seeing the blurb in the magazine, I phoned him immediately.

What impressed me the most in the article was that Mr. Crawford apparently had been specific. Other forecasters that I'd been following tried to avoid specificity with words such as *likely, scenario,* or *within a context,* but Mr. Crawford not only picked the exact week the market would drop, but also the size of the drop.

The astrologer agreed to meet me at his favorite coffee shop, but then he didn't show up. I called back, and he said I must have gotten the date wrong. I insisted he'd gotten the date wrong, which is a very dangerous thing for an astrologer to do. Anyway, we rescheduled.

He arrived in his same blue cotton shirt and corduroy pants, same thick glasses with tortoise-shell rims, same reddish hair and Appalachian complexion, same overall look of the underpaid professor on sabbatical. Again he ordered tea with no caffeine.

I congratulated him about the wonderful prediction, and said I wished I'd known about it earlier. He said I had known about it earlier. He reminded me he'd been sending me his newsletter, *Crawford Perspectives,* since our earlier meeting. It was the two-page mimeographed job I'd apparently been throwing out with the junk mail.

"With all the other stuff I've had to read," I apologized, "I guess yours got lost in the pile." That I'd held his prediction right in my hands without knowing it was a sad realization. Mr. Crawford tried to cheer me up by offering to run to his apartment, which doubled as his office, to get me another copy. I offered to run along with him so I could see his workplace. He refused, just as he had the last time we'd met, insisting that the place was still messy. In a few minutes, Mr. Crawford returned with his issue of August 30, 1986, typewritten and mimeographed on drab gray paper. The headline read:

SHORT-TERM SELL THIS WEEK!!

LONG-TERM SELL STILL OPERATIVE!!

The text below described a dangerous "massive rolling top formation" and the general sorry state of the markets. "The public has been lulled into thinking that any corrections will continue to be limited," it said. "They will no doubt buy stocks all the way down—the same stocks they are frustrated about missing all the way UP." This was the preamble to the equally sorry state of the heavens, resulting from the New Moon coming in late Wednesday night, the Sun conjuncting with Mercury on Friday the 5th, and Jupiter squaring (90 degrees) Uranus on Saturday the 6th. Two awful configurations would occur on Monday the 8th and Wednesday and Thursday the 10th and 11th. Below this was Mr. Crawford's clear-cut advice:

> Look for the TOP of this move between Sept. 3rd and 11th with the best bet falling on the 4th to the 8th. Roll completely out of long positions and into shorts during this dangerous time. We do not want to own stocks over the next few weeks. We could see a hundred-point down DAY during September. . . . Hoping for one last push into new high ground this coming week, we are unloading all stocks and preparing ourselves against the extremes of early frost. BEWARE!

So he said 100 points, and the actual drop was 88. It was impressive regardless. In six months, he'd made at least two accurate predictions. Along with the newsletter, he'd brought along a chart, similar to a historical time line, which showed his remarkable record, dating back to 1977. For independent verification, he again invited me to call Dan Dorfman, a well-known Wall Street reporter.

I was at the point of asking Mr. Crawford to volunteer his next prediction, but prudence caused me to resist the impulse. Whatever his suggestion I probably would have invested in it, and I decided it would be foolish to rush back into the market for astrological reasons when I'd come all this way to hear from the dean of forecasters, the widely followed and highly respected Mr. Kaufman. When I mentioned to Mr. Crawford that I sought to see the great economist, the astrologer replied: "Oh yes, Henry. In 1982, I put out my buy signal three days before he put out his."

It was not as easy to speak to Mr. Kaufman as it was to speak to Mr. Crawford. Mr. Kaufman probably lived in Manhattan, but I couldn't swear to it. His home phone number wasn't listed, and Mr. Crawford said he'd never seen Henry at Sacco's coffee shop.

I called Mr. Kaufman at Salomon Brothers and was connected to a public relations officer. I was fortunate just to get to talk to this Mr. Brophy. After I explained I'd heard some great things about Mr. Kaufman's predictions, Mr. Brophy said that I might get an interview, but before I made a formal request it would be a good idea for me to read Mr. Kaufman's speeches. He made up a packet of several of them, dating back to 1981.

The packet was left for me at Adams and Rinehart, a public relations firm that represents Mr. Brophy, who in turn represents Mr. Kaufman. While riffling through this material, I wondered what Mr. Kaufman was saying on August 30, 1986, the day that Mr. Crawford issued his planetary sell. The closest thing I found was the speech Mr. Kaufman gave two days earlier at a Federal Reserve meeting in Jackson, Wyoming. In that speech, Mr. Kaufman made a few cautionary observations—such as, the U.S. deficit wasn't going away, our leaders were in a quandary, the financial system needed to be redefined, and so forth—but this was far from seeing the immediate danger in the Sun conjuncting with Mercury and Jupiter squaring Uranus, which had led Mr. Crawford to advise the selling of all stocks.

Not that Mr. Kaufman would have mentioned stocks in particular. Mr. Kaufman was not paid to be a stock-market timer. What he did, instead, was to lay out an overall course for the economy, which had a direct effect on stocks and bonds.

Having found no evidence of prescience in the Jackson speech, I went back to the earliest speech in the packet, April 22, 1981. Among many general statements about "cyclical patterns" and that sort of thing was a single clear-cut prediction. Mr. Kaufman was convinced that interest rates were going higher. "It is safe to say they will go very much higher than levels prevailing currently in all maturity sectors," was what he actually said.

Checking this against the results, I found that at the time Mr. Kaufman gave this speech the prevailing rate for long-term bonds had approached 20 percent, and from there the interest rates went lower. I say this with all due respect, but Mr. Kaufman appeared to have made an error.

Every forecaster can be wrong from time to time, and I assumed from his reputation that Mr. Kaufman was mostly right. Unfortunately, the famous speech in which he correctly predicted a break in interest rates in 1982 was missing from my packet. In my material, there was a big gap between the erroneous April 1981 forecast already cited and the February 1984 speech Mr. Kaufman gave at a financial-outlook conference in New York. There again, he predicted that "short- and long-term interest rates will move up in nearly lockstep." On May 4, 1984, he told a group of Texas bankers that interest rates would move "spectacularly higher," and warned that the Fed soon would be "forced to respond to the flaring of inflation."

Hindsight again is 20/20, but we now know that interest rates didn't go higher but lower, there was no flaring of inflation, the Fed didn't assert itself with monetary restraint and, in fact, did the reverse. In spite of a slight rise in interest rates in the middle of that year, the overall trend was down. Just about the time of Mr. Kaufman's assertions to the Texas bankers, long bonds topped out and the yields began to fall.

In October 1984, Mr. Kaufman gave another speech to the annual bond conference at the New York Hilton. Here he never confided that he'd personally missed the sharp bond rally and decline in interest rates since midsummer, yet he explained in great detail the reasons these events occurred. He called this effort "interest rates: the cyclical perspective." In the end, he warned once more that lower interest rates were a "pleasant interlude" and higher rates would surely follow.

It's easy to second-guess, and we now realize that 1985 brought lower interest rates, a sluggish economy, and more mergers and acquisitions than anybody could have imagined. Mr. Kaufman, unfortunately, stuck to his old story. On May 22, 1985, speaking in New Orleans, he again foretold the bottoming out of interest rates, the economic resurgence, amd so forth. In the middle of that summer, he told the Swiss-American Chamber of Commerce in Zurich that the bonds had already seen their best days, and soon the Fed would tighten the money supply and lift interest rates.

As we know, the Fed did the opposite for most of 1986, bonds rallied, and interest rates fell. In September of that bullish year, Mr. Kaufman gave a lecture on the six major causes of the longest and most consequential interest-rate decline in our postwar history. Again, nowhere did he mention he'd missed the last three or four years of it, or why. He concluded by saying that vigorous economic growth would elude us and the bonds would continue to rally, with as much conviction as if he'd been saying this all along.

Having done my homework on the speeches, and curious as to how Mr. Kaufman could have been wrong at every point Mr. Crawford claimed to have been right, I called Mr. Brophy and requested the interview with his boss. Mr. Brophy said that Mr. Kaufman was a very busy man with an active speaking schedule. I tried to imagine why. Then I remembered that I, too, had come all this way to listen to Mr. Kaufman. Mr. Brophy suggested that I get back to him in a day or two.

When I did, Mr. Brophy asked me if I'd read Mr. Kaufman's book. I was unaware he'd even written a book, but I told Mr. Brophy I hadn't had a chance to pick up a copy. Mr. Brophy said the book answered many of the questions I'd probably be asking, so there was no point wasting Mr. Kaufman's time before I'd gone through it.

Mr. Brophy kindly sent me a copy that same day, by courier. It was called *Interest Rates, the Markets, and the New Financial World,* and I spent the evening with it in bed. There was some excellent analysis of our national debt problems and credit problems, but I skipped over all that and turned to the section on forecasting. Here was a detailed description of the three times Mr. Kaufman had made good forecasts—all from 1982 or earlier. There was not a single mention of the losing streak I'd hoped he would explain.

Early the next morning, I called Mr. Brophy and told him I'd finished the book but still had a few questions. He set up a phone interview with Mr. Kaufman, the best he could do.

Mr. Kaufman had a nice telephone voice, but sounded a bit stuffy. I tried to warm him up by asking how many people at Salomon Brothers helped out with the forecasts. He said that 350 people had some professional input but that the final judgments, up or down on interest rates, were left to him.

As gingerly as I could, I inquired about the overall accuracy of those final judgments. Right away, Mr. Kaufman went back to the major turn in August 1982, which he'd correctly predicted. He also recalled that he was "correctly bearish" in May 1983. When I asked about 1984–86, he freely admitted there'd been some trouble. I jotted down the following phrases: "I didn't see the economic slowdown," "I thought the economy would pick up," "What I recognize belatedly is that it wasn't a typical cyclical setting," "elements of discontinuity," and "rapidly changing financial system." He asked me to imagine how hard it would be to stand in the middle of the block and guess what was coming around the corner.

He confirmed that he continued to head up the Salomon Brothers research department and was still in great demand for predictions, so his reputation hadn't suffered. He said his recent resignation as vice chairman of Salomon Brothers' board of directors had nothing to do with erroneous forecasts. That was a management change resulting, in part, from an in-house disagreement over the worthiness of junk bonds.

I don't mean to belittle an intelligent, well-respected economist. That Mr. Kaufman commanded big audiences and a big salary, plus all the front-page attention throughout his recent losing streak, was proof that forecasting is a difficult business, where errors are commonplace and widely tolerated. I'd noticed from my packet that he rarely spoke twice in the same city or to the same group. I doubted it was deliberate policy, but if I were him, I'd do the same thing.

Let us leave Mr. Kaufman predicting the further fall of long-term interest rates, a further sluggish economy, and continued easing by the Fed, with little risk of inflation in 1987. Perhaps there was a potential Contrarian strategy here—short Mr. Kaufman— by failing that, I'd developed a clear preference for the astrologer. Though I'd been fighting this all along, it was impossible to ignore the evidence, at least from Mr. Kaufman's side, that 350 helpers and the resources of a major Wall Street firm produced such thoroughgoing miscalculation that neither astrologers nor dart throwers could have done worse if they'd tried. Again, I point this out as an illustration of the inherent folly in the general attempt at economic forecasting, as opposed to any deficiency of these aforementioned forecasters in particular.

I called up Mr. Dorfman for a confirmation of Mr. Crawford's genius at picking the direction of the markets, only to discover that Mr. Dorfman had cooled considerably on the astrologer. "At one time he had a terrific record," said the Wall Street reporter. "I wrote him up in my column. After that, I found he would change his mind on any given day. It got so bad I had to accept the premise that Mr. Crawford wasn't very good."

Even after hearing that sour news, I would have taken Mr. Crawford's word over Mr. Kaufman's, and, in fact, I phoned the astrologer to ask for his latest planetary prediction. The trouble was that Mr. Crawford was momentarily befuddled. "If the market goes down the next two days, I'll give a buy signal," he said. "That would last for two or three weeks. But if the market goes up, I'll give a short-term sell signal. Then if we build a better base, I'll give a blanket buy signal." At that, I threw up my hands, and went off to look for Ivan Boesky.

THIRTY

MY INSIDE INFORMATION

SINCE I NO LONGER HAD ANY FAITH IN DETERMINING WHICH WAY the market was headed, which in turn made short-term forecasting impossible, my latest trip to New York was in danger of becoming another waste of time and money. Only as a matter of absolute last resort did I consider a rescue from Mr. Boesky, a famous investor whom I would have hoped to meet on more equal footing. In all the time I'd been losing money, Mr. Boesky was touted by everyone from "Wall Street Week" to my mother-in-law as the champion of all stock-pickers. What my mother-in-law told me was, "If you're writing about stocks, why not talk to a guy who is successful and knows what he's doing?" This had the same effect as if she'd come right out and said, "Ivan Boesky made $400 million in the time it took you to drop $10,000."

Mr. Boesky was part of an elite group of investors called risk arbitrageurs. These people bought stocks in companies that were obvious candidates to be taken over, since takeover bids usually resulted in huge jumps in the stock price, entirely independent of market conditions. In some cases, the risk arbs threatened to take over the companies themselves, a prospect that caused management to counter with defensive measures that often drove stock prices even higher. This is where an options player, with the right information, could realize huge gains in a short time, and without fretting about the general market forecasts.

I had a line into Mr. Boesky through my brother-in-law. My brother-in-law worked for a New York restaurant outlet that sold Mr. Boesky wholesale caviar and salmon, which you can buy in bulk if you're as successful as Mr. Boesky. I told my brother-in-law I'd like to interview Mr. Boesky about the history of the stock market, but quite frankly, I was lying. I really wanted one good tip on a company that was about to be taken over, or some other stock that was bound to go up fast.

This was just before Mr. Boesky was caught and plead guilty to insider trading. Prior to his legal troubles, Mr. Boesky's information was thought to be just as legitimate as everybody else's information—only more valuable.

"You should try to see him in the morning," my brother-in-law said. "I heard he drives in from Westchester in a Winnebago with a satellite dish on the top and already has bought millions worth of stocks before he crosses the river and hits Manhattan." My brother-in-law put in a call to Mr. Boesky, but Mr. Boesky didn't return it. That, he said, was unusual.

I went to Mr. Boesky's office building on Fifth Avenue to try to collar him in person, but there were guards at the elevators. Then I searched for a basement to see if I could look through Mr. Boesky's trash. I hoped to find some scrap of paper that would indicate what he was doing, but I couldn't find a basement, or anything resembling a trash bin around the entire block. In this expensive part of New York, trash seemed to disappear on its own.

Having no luck at seeing Mr. Boesky or even examining his droppings, I did what seemed like the next best thing. I approached some of his competitors. These were other so-called risk arbitrageurs from a reputable firm that asked to have their name kept out of this. I made up a pseudonym, Z. B. Troutman.

To get into the room at Z. B. Troutman where the risk arbs who competed with Mr. Boesky did their trading wasn't easy. First I had to contact a friend of another friend, a respected Wall Street analyst who'd become Z. B. Troutman's éminence grise. Unfortunately, he only liked to talk about what was wrong with the markets. I wanted a profitable hint, while he wanted to bemoan the decline of the morality on Wall Street. He reminisced about the old days when people held on to stocks, when they took their positions based on a faith in industry, when they "invested" instead of "speculated." It was a dark picture he painted, I'll tell you that. Some of the notes I took include phrases like "everything's up for sale," "no honor among thieves," "the word is, 'quick profit,' " and "everybody wants inside information." Most frightening to me was his "bigger fool theory."

"That's what it's come to," my source said. "People buy stocks not because they believe in them but because they think some bigger fool will pay more than they did for them. It used to be that the bigger fool was the public, but now it's the portfolio managers themselves. With institutions controlling the markets, who is going to sell to whom? The big institutions are their own bigger fool."

I tried to nod my head as knowingly as I could, while keeping my ears open for any bit of extra news on which I could base a short-term investment. The only useful thing I heard came in a phone call the éminence grise got from a friend who recommended Centronics Data Computer. I didn't want to buy Centronics Data Computer options, since I owned a Centronics printer and it didn't work very well.

After this depressing discussion, I told my new acquaintance I'd like to meet some arbitrageurs, and he took me to the room where program traders worked. These were people who bought baskets of stocks and sold the corresponding stock-index futures, or bought stock-index futures and sold baskets of stocks, exploiting the price differences just as Mr. Ritchey did with bonds and other commodities. Millions of dollars was poured into program trading, and computers made the decisions. Since I didn't have millions of dollars, program trading was only of academic interest, and I informed my guide I preferred to visit "risk arbitrageurs" who invest in the takeover situations.

Eventually, I reached the head of the risk arbitrage department, a man I'll call Orton. I found Orton to be nervously brilliant, like something out of Yiddish vaudeville. He told me he was a former floor trader who'd decided "the ⅛s and the ¼s don't mean anything anymore."

This meant that to him, the small bits of profit were no longer exciting, which on Wall Street leads not to retirement but to a promotion. Orton was elevated to manager of the $400-million risk arbitage portfolio at Z. B. Troutman.

As Orton escorted me into the trading area, I noticed a British flag on the ceiling, five clocks, and a bank of computers operated by two women and two men. I listened as closely as I could, but didn't hear anybody mention a stock. Orton immediately ushered me into the glass-enclosed office that abutted the trading floor which reminded me of a waiting room for fathers in a maternity ward. I couldn't pick up any of the comments of the risk arbitrageurs from this side of the glass, but I tried to read lips.

In the corner of the room was a beanbag chair shaped like a baseball glove. On the table in front of us was a computer printout of all the stocks in which Orton and his staff currently were invested. I wanted to peek at it, but felt that it wouldn't be polite to snoop. There it was, a pile of potential profit, just inches from my fingertips. I stared at the printout as Orton answered a phone call.

"My mother," he said as he hung up the phone. "My mother asks me for a stock pick, says she wants action. Then I give her a stock pick, and the stock goes down a couple of points and she calls me to complain. What is this? Fuck her." He gave this speech as he paced frantically around the room, furiously chewing a wad of bubble gum.

I asked Orton if he exchanged ideas with fellow arbs, especially Ivan Boesky. "Guys call each other," he said. "Of course guys call each other. Take Viacom. Maybe I can call some guys and find out who is buying the stock. I might call a guy at Goldman, Sachs, and he might or might not tell me who's buying Viacom. Or I might ask one of the floor brokers. Most of the firms use the same floor brokers—who are you kidding?

"Take CBS. I just had dinner with a guy who says it'll go to $180 in a year. It's what, $125 now. You hear stuff like that all the time. The thing is, is it worth it?

"You can sometimes find out what's going on in a particular situation—what Boesky is doing, for instance. Sometimes he buys shares just to convince the rest of us he's on that side of a stock. Meanwhile, he's secretly selling through some other firm, so it turns out we're buying from him. I don't talk to Boesky directly. I don't talk to the Boesky people directly. No way I'd do that. They seem to keep to themselves."

Through the walls of the outer room I heard somebody yell

"31⅝" and Orton got up, said his good-byes, and took the computer printout with him. A replacement I'll call Graham was sent in to continue the discussion. Graham proceeded to give me an example of why risk arbitrage was a tricky business, and too complicated for an amateur.

He told a long story about what happened to the stock of Anderson Clayton, a company that recently was "in play," which is what arbs call it when they're interested. The family owners of Anderson Clayton had wanted to sell, and there were several factions bidding for control, which made the stock a perfect candidate for risk arbitrage. For Z. B. Troutman, buying the stock was the least of it. They sent lawyers to file suits against certain rival bidders, they hired appraisers to evaluate the stock, they analyzed trading patterns, they listened for gossip about who was doing what, and after all was said and done, they still didn't really know what was happening. The entire effort resulted in a profit of $9 per share, from their having bought the stock at $56 and sold at $65.

Graham's point was that you couldn't just expect to buy a stock and wait for it to go up. You had to get involved, and even at that there were no guarantees.

After Graham finished with his story, one of his colleagues popped his head in the door with an exciting bit of news. He'd just gotten off an airplane, where he overheard a woman in a nearby seat telling somebody that Holiday Inn was going to be taken over. He'd just checked the Quotron, and sure enough, Holiday Inn stock was up six points. This caused a great flurry around the trading desk, and Graham quickly terminated our conversation. He showed me to the door.

As much as Graham's speech about the complexities of the Anderson Clayton deal should have impressed me with the sophistication of risk arbitrage, it was undercut by the Holiday Inn incident, from which I concluded that these well-informed professionals listened to the same airplane gossip that you or I might overhear, and acted on it in the same way.

Here also was a great opportunity for me. From the jubilant commotion that followed the Holiday Inn gossip, it seemed certain that Z. B. Troutman would take a major position in the stock. I was prepared to go out and invest my remaining capital on Holiday Inn options, before I stopped off in the bathroom of the Z. B. Troutman lobby. There I heard two well-dressed employees discussing the "Bally takeover." Believing that information gained in the bathroom would prove more valuable than what I'd gotten from a regular interview in the office, I immediately lost interest in Holiday Inn, and decided in favor of Bally. It was just this sort of accidental hint that I'd hoped to get from Mr. Boesky's office, something that occurred naturally in the speculative habitat. I called my new discount broker and bought 10 Bally May 22½ call options. This cost me $2,426.44 and left me with only $800 in cash from my original stake.

THIRTY-ONE

A STREET GONE MAD

THE NEXT THING I KNEW, MR. BOESKY WAS ARRESTED FOR allegedly having traded on inside information that made him his millions of dollars. Apparently the people from one side of the Chinese Wall in various merger and acquisition departments of banks and brokerage houses had leaked information to people on the other side of the Chinese Wall, and Mr. Boesky was a major beneficiary. Being foretold of numerous upcoming takeovers and deals that inevitably would send stock prices soaring, Mr. Boesky made investing look easy.

I could see why he never called me back. He was wired up by the SEC. God knows what would have happened if they'd recorded me blurting out, "Give me a tip. Tell me something, anything, to rescue my portfolio," which is how I'd planned to put myself at his mercy. By now, my mother-in-law was telling me, "It's a good thing you stayed away from that silly man."

Everyone who'd been desperate to see Mr. Boesky all of a sudden was desperate to avoid him. He was in universal disfavor, the whole of Wall Street was shocked, and there was talk of future indictments. This troubled me a great deal. What if I, too, had acted on inside information in the Bally deal? After all, I'd heard it in the bathroom, and from two of the players in the same game as Mr. Boesky's. That would be a fitting end to my journey: the only insider trader to have lost all his money.

To avert potential problems before they came up, I called the Securities and Exchange Commission office in New York and was put through to Mr. Anthony in the legal interpretation section. I'd talked to him earlier about selling stocks in a garage sale, but

I don't think he remembered. This time, and without tipping my hand, I asked him to define "insider trading" as it applied to information overheard in a public place. To my great surprise, he said there was no actual definition of insider trading at all.

"What we always say is, just as you know pornography when you see it, you'll know insider trading when you see it," he said.

Since I still wasn't sure I'd seen it, I returned to my new friend Orton, the risk arbitrageur, to discuss the recent events. In the aftermath of the Boesky revelations, Orton was speechless, but only because he had the flu. Between coughs, he told me the whole investment business was transformed the day after Mr. Boesky got indicted. "The game is over," Orton said. "It's a pre-deal situation. It's like the 1970s again. People aren't talking to each other."

Orton said that his own firm, Z. B. Troutman, lost one-third of the profits they'd made all year during the week the takeover stocks fell in the wake of the Boesky news. He wasn't complaining, though. "Lots of firms gave back their entire year," he said.

"Looking back on it, it was a Street gone mad," he said. "I really believe that. I grew up in this business, and even I didn't realize how closely the merger and acquisition departments worked with some of the arbitrageurs. There was no honor among thieves. The business was filled with people who'd lost sight of all reason.

"On Boesky day, the pendulum swung from all the way to the right to all the way to the left. Suddenly, we're back to the old methods. There will be a lot of layoffs, a lot of lawsuits, a lot less deals, and a lot less money. Lately, it's been so easy to tell other people what you've heard about some stock. Now I wouldn't even tell good friends what I know."

"What about Bally?" I whispered. "What do you hear about Bally? Are people getting in trouble for that?"

"You mean the Donald Trump takeover?" he laughed. "That old news? Last year sometime, Trump made a play for Bally. I'm sure you saw it in the papers. Recently, there've been some lawsuits and speculation that Trump's actually getting out of Bally. It's not one of our deals."

So there it was! I'd bought Bally options on inside information that actually was stale public news. I'd gotten in just as the takeover people were getting out. Sitting there with Orton, I felt as if I'd walked through a jungle, happened upon a magnificent ancient ruin, and run back to trumpet my discovery—only to be told I'd seen the back side of Machu Picchu.

As I write this, my Bally options are still alive. They don't expire for two months, so anything could happen. The stock is selling for $20. If it goes to $40, I'll double my money and come home a winner. If it doesn't, I've lost most of the $14,000 I put in over the months of this journey, give or take a few hundred, and not including all the airplane fares, taxis, meals, and other expenses.

I returned home from New York, ready to admit I'd run out of good ideas, not to mention money. I'd hoped to learn something about the bond market over a dinner with Ms. Jenrette, the expert from Bridgewater Securities, but when I phoned that office they told me Ms. Jenrette had gone away and had left no forwarding address. Having lost confidence in forecasters, except for Mr. Crawford; having learned too much to trust most stockbrokers; having followed the stream of analysts, market advisors, portfolio managers and floor traders, I could only marvel at anybody who succeeds on Wall Street. To make money here, you'd either have to know a lot more or a lot less than I do.

I ought to mention that my wife's portfolio at Drexel Burnham Lambert, under the guidance of Richard Bermont, had continued to do well in the months I'd been off investing for my own account. Her gains made up for most of my apparent loss. In fact, I figured that the two of us together had just about broken even for the year, which is one of the reasons I'm still allowed to live at home.

This brings me back to my good old savings account and Centrust S&L. Looking back on it, I would have collected $1,200 in interest by leaving my entire stake alone in the bank from the beginning. This isn't too exciting in itself, but added to the funds I wouldn't have squandered, I'd be left with a $15,200 windfall, the kind of profit an average investor can only dream about. If you've ever felt stupid for not having participated in a great bull market, remember my example, and also Useful Tip Number 24:

**Considering the fortune
you might have lost,
you'll have to admit
you're rich already**

POSTSCRIPT
Black Monday, 1987

On October 19, 1987, a 508-point one-day drop in the Dow Jones average—the worst such drop in history—wiped out any residual profit that had built up in my wife's account at Drexel Burnham, thus eliminating any discrepancy between my own sorry performance as described herein, and hers.

Who could have suspected that between Friday the 16th and Monday the 19th, the world would be a trillion dollars poorer, or that crowds would collect outside the mutual-funds offices, awaiting news like nervous onlookers to a palace coup? There had been widespread agreement among the knowledgeable that some trouble might occur one or two years ahead, and that the smart money would know when to get out.

On Friday, I paid no particular attention to the market, but at the end of the day, my wife informed me she'd heard on the radio that it had gone down a whopping 100 points. This was especially troublesome as both of us spent the evening with a wealthy friend who'd gotten out of the market a month earlier. Nothing is worse than hearing bad financial news in the million-dollar home of someone who has just gotten wealthier.

It was a nervous weekend, and the phones were abuzz with people reassuring each other that the worst was over.

Monday came and a sixth sense of doom pulled me into the local Thomson McKinnon office, where the elderly spend the day watching the overhead quotron. The market had been open less than an hour and already there was stunning news: the Dow had plummeted another 100 points or so, and some stocks had not even opened. The heavy selling could no longer be accomodated in the normal routine. The retirees, usually talkative, sat transfixed. If you'd have seen them, you would have thought they were the home crowd watching the visitors win a game with a home run in the bottom of the ninth.

"Don't you think it will turn around?" asked a man in jogging clothes. For an hour or so we watched one particular blip—"F" for "Ford"—as it came across the screen again and again, the man's hopes rising and falling with each updraft and downdraft, as if he were cheering on a wounded bird. "Look," the man exclaimed several times, "F is holding, F has turned around," and then F would fall and he'd slump back dejectedly into his chair.

I returned home to see what they were saying on the Financial News Network. By midday, the market was down 250 points. One of the big differences between this Crash and the one that ushered in the Great Depression in 1929 was that you could watch this one happening in your own bedroom.

The financial newscasters, many of whom I'd counted as distant but important investment allies, seemed wild-eyed, unstable. As they babbled on, my wife asked what she should do. The fact that she was asking *me* was further evidence of the total panic into which investors had fallen.

I noticed that at least stock prices didn't look so bad on the TV tickertape, but then one of the announcers mentioned that the tape was running two hours behind so none of the prices were current. I lay down on the bed and watched the progression anyway. I ran once to the refrigerator to grab a beer, which I normally never drink.

An hour or so later, I got in the car and returned to Thomson McKinnon. By now the market was down 350 points, but the audience had cheered up. Gloomy at 200 down, cheery at 350 down—it was the enormity that took them beyond shock into a kind of idiot's bemusement. We all began to take pleasure in announcing how bad it was, especially to each arrival who just came through the door to sit down. "You know how bad it is? You *know* how bad it is? 350 points." Soon that arrival would be gleefully passing on the same news to yet another arrival.

I headed home again and spent the final hour watching television—not the Financial News Network but a game show—while drinking Myers rum straight from a bottle. That evening of the 508-point drop, we got concerned phone calls from all around the country, similar to the ones we receive when a hurricane warning makes the national news. My father reminded me that *his* father, heavily margined, had gone from millionaire to pauper on that fatal October day in 1929. My friends asked me for more advice on what was happening, and, as usual, I gave answers as if I knew. I wondered if the newscasters who were forced to give answers felt as ridiculous as I did.

Our wealthy friend who had gotten out months ago called to say that all her other wealthy friends who hadn't gotten out were staying in, and that only a fool would get out in this panic.

During the late evening and into the early-morning hours, we sat watching one news account after another of markets crashing around the world, until we were convinced it was time to get out, to protect whatever my wife had left. By the morning, my wife had sold all her stocks—near the bottom, of course. The next day's newspaper was full of moralizing about how *this* Crash was a fitting end to our national profligacy, to young millionaire traders on Wall Street, to borrowing and buying abroad.

But on a more human scale, how did Black Monday affect the various brokers, traders, and investors whose acquaintance I had made in my odyssey as an Average Investor? What were they doing on the day of the 508-point drop? Linda Garrett was on the phone at her local Prudential-Bache office, calming nervous clients. Brokers were nervous as well. It was from Ms. Garrett I first heard the news that a disgruntled investor named Arthur Kane, who had lost millions on this one bad day, expressed his displeasure by killing the branch manager of his local Merrill Lynch with a hastily-purchased revolver. He also wounded his broker and then killed himself. This being a Miami story, it later turned out that Mr. Kane was actually somebody else, having been awarded a new identity for pleading guilty to some earlier fraudulence up North. It was unclear where he got his investment capital in the first place.

Chuck Epstein, the Lind-Waldock spokesman who had kindly showed me around Chicago, had since moved on to the New York Futures Exchange and watched the action on the trading floor. "It was frenetic," he said. "All the orders were coming in on one side." (Mr. Epstein meant that everyone wanted to bet on the market's going down all at once.) "I never saw anything like it."

William Hayes, the analyst who took me to lunch at the New York Stock Exchange, spent the day in the offices of his specialist firm and took the drop calmly: "I certainly didn't expect 508 points. A lot of it had to do with the instantaneous network we've created, all over the world. Remember, some real buyers came in that day, too."

Jeff Zaret, one of the young traders at the Chicago Mercantile Exchange struggling to make a living, had moved upstairs and allied himself with the trading department of a large Japanese bank. "There are great possibilities in the global markets," he had said. On the day of the debacle, he revisited his old haunt, the S&P trading pit, where he was happy not to be working: "I saw haggard faces. A lot of guys were elated, true, but then again there were more long faces. Mostly, guys looked confounded."

Donald Trump, the New York tycoon whose *faux* takeover of Bally I'd mistaken for genuine inside information, announced to the world that he'd been out of the stock market for months—probably even at the time I'd invested in his alleged machinations. Other corporate raiders, including Boone Pickens and Sir James Goldsmith, volunteered that they, too, had gotten out of the stock market with profits intact. Many of the prominent billionaires, whom average investors adopted as inspirations in the headlong greedy rush to riches, had apparently closed out their positions—leaving them with all the money, and the rest of us punished for the greed.

Al Frank, genial editor of the *Prudent Speculator,* had been on a diet and had lost a lot of weight, which seemed to parallel the decline in the heft of his portfolio. On his weekly FNN interview slot, he looked slimmer and also more somber than I'd ever seen him, but still he had a sense of humor. What had he learned about this market? the newscaster asked. "Learned about how to get margin calls," he said.

Robert Prechter Jr., the Elliott wave theorist who carries on the entirely illogical but apparently effective zigzag method of forecasting, advised his clients to get out of the market at the high end. It seemed that the technicians and chart readers saw this collapse better than the fundamentalists.

Martin Zweig, a well-respected student of the market and author of the popular *Winning on Wall Street,* also sold stocks and went into cash, at just the right moment.

I tried to call my friend Orton at his risk arbitrage office, but he never returned the call, and the news that his particular firm lost $44 million in a single week gave me the idea he might not be in the mood for conversation.

Daniel Gressel, the futures trader with whom I spent a delightful evening trying to figure out whether he'd won or lost, had moved to Hong Kong, where his wife, Claudia, worked in the bureau of *The Wall Street Journal.* Knowing that the entire Hong Kong Exchange had been temporarily closed, with millions of dollars in outstanding futures contracts in jeopardy, I feared the worst for Mr. Gressel, but his wife informed me that he had taken a job with a British investment management firm. As to his own trading results, "He's still living" was her only comment.

The computer at Battery March Financial in Boston had apparently beaten out most of the competition from the rival firms with the hundreds of paid analysts. Dean LeBaron told me that the computer had outperformed the S&P index by a "couple of percentage points" for the entire year, and that even in the Crash the Battery March fortunes had gone down a few points less than the market as a whole. This was a small but meaningful consolation.

The only real winners in a 508-point drop were the short sellers. Dump 'Em Jim Chanos admitted that "life had been pretty grim" during the entire year and a half of bullishness, but now that everybody else was grim, it was his turn to be happy. "I don't want to quantify things," he said, "but I'm doing just fine. I'm still net short, by the way. I think the bull market is dead."

If only—one imagines—one had sold all stocks on the most recent words out of the mouth of the economist Henry Kaufman. A few days prior to the Crash, on October 9, in fact, Mr. Kaufman made front-page news with a sanguine assertion that veteran Kaufman-watchers should have known was a sure sign of imminent fatality:

One optimistic note was sounded by Salomon Brothers' asset allocation committee, led by chief economist Henry Kaufman, which predicted Thursday that the global bull market will continue into 1988 following recent corrections. Kaufman's outlook includes rising interest rates and mounting inflation risks as economic growth accelerates. Better than anticipated corporate earnings will overcome the drag from rising interest rates.

Burnham Lambert's bulletin of October 19, the very morning of the Crash, dismissed recent downturns as "a dramatic overreaction to poor trade data" and confidently asserted that "economic conditions are good . . . the acceleration in profit growth has just begun." Here was another signal pointing to the certainty of big trouble ahead.

If only one had bothered to read the recent newsletters from my old friend the market astrologer, Arch Crawford, whose predictions I had continued to ignore. In the aftermath of Black Monday I read in a Dick Davis financial column entitled "Some Market Analysts Saw the Crash Coming":

Using a combination of technical, fundamental and astrological factors, Arch Crawford's *The Crawford Perspectives* from New York has made some uncanny market calls. In early August, he said, "Our long-term sell signal is set in stone. Be out of all stocks by August 24th, from which point we expect a horrendous Crash." August 24th marked the Dow high of 2,722. Crawford remains pessimistic . . .

Too late, I've decided to take Crawford's advice. My wife and I have resolved never again to invest in stocks, a resolve which probably will last until too late in the next bull phase, by which time we will doubtless have engaged a promising new stockbroker.

A FOOL'S GLOSSARY

AVERAGE INVESTOR: born loser

BULL MARKET: rising market; a time when your neighbor's stocks are going up

BEAR MARKET: falling market; a time to lose whatever you might accidentally have made during a bull market

CORRECTION: short-term downswing in an otherwise rising market; wishful thinking by investors in a bear market (see also: Russian Correction of 1917, World Corrections I and II, the Bubonic Correction, etc.)

SAVINGS: whatever you had before you invested it

SUCCESSFUL INVESTOR: liar

PORTFOLIO MANAGER: expert who invests huge sums for mutual funds, pension funds; person who is highly paid to underperform the market averages

INSIDE INFORMATION: something you wish they'd tell you; what everybody else has heard

CORPORATE ANALYST: person who studies a company's prospects, predicts future earnings, etc.; expert who tells the shareholders what the bankers want them to hear; expert who tells little shareholders what big shareholders want them to hear; expert who tells the company what it already knows

MERGERS AND ACQUISITIONS: two ways in which companies are combined with other companies; two proven methods of turning various profitable enterprises into one big loser

RESTRUCTURING: modifying a company from within to enhance shareholder value; hiding the biggest mistakes

DIVESTITURE: way in which a company sells off its subsidiaries; getting rid of all the losers from the latest mergers and acquisitions

LEVERAGE: controlling a large investment with a smaller amount of money; betting more than you can afford to lose

MARGIN: borrowing from the brokerage firm to buy stocks or bonds; borrowing to buy the Brooklyn Bridge

LONG-TERM AVERAGE INVESTOR: patient fool; someone who should have sold a little sooner

SHORT-TERM AVERAGE INVESTOR: impatient fool; someone who should have held on a little longer

SELLING SHORT: selling borrowed stock or borrowed commodities, hoping to replace them at lower prices later; selling something you don't own—in the real world, a felony

STOCKBROKER: salesman for stocks, bonds, mutual funds, etc.; a person who will never go broke

FUTURES CONTRACT: a contract to buy something later at a price agreed upon today; an agreement in which one party sells huge quantities of something he doesn't own to another party who hopes it will never be delivered, and where one party ends up with all the money

CONSERVATIVE INVESTMENT: a gamble in drag

CONTRARIAN STRATEGY: investing in things that are currently unpopular, hoping for big profits later; going against the crowd at the same instant the rest of the crowd has decided to do the same

FINANCIAL SECURITY: perpetual care enjoyed by insurance companies, brokers, money managers, and others in the financial security industry

MONEY MANAGER: expert who manages your financial affairs; someone to whom you pay a large fee so you'll have less money to manage

CONSERVATIVE MONEY MANAGER: the money manager who charges the most for his or her services

PAPER PROFIT: unrealized gains; the kind of profit you'll occasionally make, spent several times over before it disappears

HOT STOCK: stock everybody is buying; what your brokerage firm calls any stock it wants to sell

MONEY SUPPLY M-I: a popular measure of the amount of money in circulation; number invented by the Federal Reserve system to be ignored

INFLATIONARY PERIOD: period when things are worth more than money, and you have more of the latter

DEFLATIONARY PERIOD: period when things are worth less than money, and you have more of the former

FORECASTER: expert who predicts the direction of the economy, interest rates, etc., that will affect the markets; paid guesser

FULLY-INFORMED INVESTMENT DECISION: wild guess

BREAKING EVEN: a loss as explained to family, friends, and neighbors

CALL OPTION: the right to buy a stock later at a price agreed upon today (buyer hopes stock will go up); the chance to buy something later for much more than it will be worth

PUT OPTION: the right to sell a stock later at a price agreed upon today (buyer hopes stock will go down); the chance to sell something later for much less than it will be worth

BULL SPREAD, BEAR SPREAD, STRADDLE, ETC.: buying puts and calls, or options and futures, in various combinations to reduce risk or enhance potential gain; throwing good money after bad

HEDGER: person who uses futures and options to reduce risk of doing business; unknown individual, imaginary character

ARBITRAGEUR: person who buys and sells the same thing simultaneously, but at different prices, thereby securing a risk-free profit; person who ends up with all your money

RISK ARBITRAGE: investing in obvious takeover situations for maximum gain with minimum risk; taking a chance on the latest rumors

TECHNICAL ANALYST: person who thinks market action itself can predict future course of markets; deluded individual

CHARTIST: kind of technical analyst who reads charts; wiggle watcher, solopcist, totem worshiper

FUNDAMENTALIST: person who thinks that earnings, condition of companies, etc., will determine future stock prices; deluded individual

IRRATIONAL MARKET: a market that isn't doing what you want it to; every market

FOR THE BEST IN PAPERBACKS, LOOK FOR THE

In every corner of the world, on every subject under the sun, Penguin represents quality and variety—the very best in publishing today.

For complete information about books available from Penguin—including Pelicans, Puffins, Peregrines, and Penguin Classics—and how to order them, write to us at the appropriate address below. Please note that for copyright reasons the selection of books varies from country to country.

In the United Kingdom: For a complete list of books available from Penguin in the U.K., please write to *Dept E.P., Penguin Books Ltd, Harmondsworth, Middlesex, UB7 0DA.*

In the United States: For a complete list of books available from Penguin in the U.S., please write to *Dept BA, Penguin*, Box 999, Bergenfield, New Jersey 07621-0999.

In Canada: For a complete list of books available from Penguin in Canada, please write to *Penguin Books Canada Ltd, 2801 John Street, Markham, Ontario L3R 1B4.*

In Australia: For a complete list of books available from Penguin in Australia, please write to the *Marketing Department, Penguin Books Australia Ltd, P.O. Box 257, Ringwood, Victoria 3134.*

In New Zealand: For a complete list of books available from Penguin in New Zealand, please write to the *Marketing Department, Penguin Books (NZ) Ltd, Private Bag, Takapuna, Auckland 9.*

In India: For a complete list of books available from Penguin, please write to *Penguin Overseas Ltd, 706 Eros Apartments, 56 Nehru Place, New Delhi, 110019.*

In Holland: For a complete list of books available from Penguin in Holland, please write to *Penguin Books Nederland B.V., Postbus 195, NL–1380AD Weesp, Netherlands.*

In Germany: For a complete list of books available from Penguin, please write to *Penguin Books Ltd, Friedrichstrasse 10–12, D–6000 Frankfurt Main 1, Federal Republic of Germany.*

In Spain: For a complete list of books available from Penguin in Spain, please write to *Longman Penguin España, Calle San Nicolas 15, E–28013 Madrid, Spain.*

In Japan: For a complete list of books available from Penguin in Japan, please write to *Longman Penguin Japan Co Ltd, Yamaguchi Building, 2-12-9 Kanda Jimbocho, Chiyoda-Ku, Tokyo 101, Japan.*

FOR THE BEST IN PAPERBACKS, LOOK FOR THE

☐ **THE TAO JONES AVERAGES**
   A Guide to Whole-Brained Investing
   Bennett W. Goodspeed

Mixing the wisdom of the Taoist sages with the Wall Street savvy of seasoned investors, Bennett W. Goodspeed shows how to use both hemispheres of your brain to anticipate market fluctuations and achieve greater financial returns.

"Illuminating and refreshing"—*Barron's*
156 pages   *ISBN: 0-14-007368-X*   **$6.95**

☐ **ALL AMERICA'S REAL ESTATE BOOK**
   Everyone's Guide to Buying, Selling, Renting, and Investing
   Carolyn Janik and Ruth Rejnis

Covering every aspect of the real estate marketplace, this extraordinary guide contains the up-to-date facts and down-to-earth advice needed to buy, sell, or lease property.

"Exhaustively handles the many aspects of real estate in a calm but interesting way."—*Christian Science Monitor*
852 pages   *ISBN: 0-14-009416-4*   **$14.95**

☐ **GETTING YOURS**
   The Complete Guide to Government Money
   Matthew Lesko

This national best-seller from the author of *Information U.S.A.* is the key to financing any endeavor, from a farm to a college education, with the help of federal and state government funds.

"Lesko gives you hundreds of ways to get dollars and other favors from the federal government."—*USA Today*
368 pages   *ISBN: 0-14-046760-2*   **$8.95**

☐ **DON'T SELL STOCKS ON MONDAY**
   Yale Hirsch

Basing his advice on a detailed analysis of stock market history and trends, a professional market-watcher reveals the patterns and cycles that help you invest shrewdly—by the clock and by the calendar.

"A rich trove of stock market lore"—*Business Week*
232 pages   *ISBN: 0-14-010375-9*   **$8.95**

☐ **SELLING MONEY**
   S.C. Gwynne

A young banker's account of the great international lending boom, *Selling Money* elucidates the workings of the world of international finance and the startling history of the great debt crisis.

"Bids fair to do for international lending what *Funny Money* did for the collapse of the Penn Square Bank."—*The New York Times Book Review*
182 pages   *ISBN: 0-14-010282-5*   **$7.95**